Epistemics of
Development Economics

Recent Titles in
Contributions in Economics and Economic History

The Chinese Financial System
Cecil R. Dipchand, Zhang Yichun, and Ma Mingjia

The Sports Stadium as a Municipal Investment
Dean V. Baim

Food and Agrarian Orders in the World-Economy
Philip McMichael

Economic Structures of Antiquity
Morris Silver

Philanthropy and Economic Development
Richard F. America, editor

Public Policy and the Quality of Life: Market Incentives versus
Government Planning
Randall G. Holcombe

Studies in Accounting History: Tradition and Innovation for the
Twenty-first Century
Atsuo Tsuji and Paul Garner

A New World Order?: Global Transformations in the Late Twentieth
Century
David A. Smith and Jozef Borocz, editors

Transforming Russian Enterprises: From State Control to Employee
Ownership
John Logue, Sergey Plekhanov, and John Simmons, editors

The Development of Local Public Services, 1650–1860: Lessons from
Middletown, Connecticut
Hannah J. McKinney

Rural Development Research: A Foundation for Policy
*Thomas D. Rowley, David W. Sears, Glenn L. Nelson,
J. Norman Reid, and Marvin J. Yetley, editors*

EPISTEMICS OF DEVELOPMENT ECONOMICS

Toward a Methodological Critique and Unity

Kofi Kissi Dompere
and
Manzur Ejaz

Foreword by Mark Perlman

Contributions in Economics and Economic History, Number 165

Greenwood Press
Westport, Connecticut • London

HD
75
D664
1995

Library of Congress Cataloging-in-Publication Data

Dompere, K. K.
    Epistemics of development economics : toward a methodological
critique and unity / Kofi Kissi Dompere and Manzur Ejaz ;
foreword by Mark Perlman.
        p.   cm. — (Contributions in economics and economic history,
    ISSN 0084–9235 ; no. 165)
    Includes bibliographical references and index.
    ISBN 0–313–29513–1 (alk. paper)
    1. Development economics. I. Ejaz, Manzur. II. Title.
III. Series.
HD75.D664   1995
338.9—dc20   94–47438

British Library Cataloguing in Publication Data is available.

Library of Congress Catalog Card Number: 94–47438
ISBN: 0–313–29513–1
ISSN: 0084–9235

First published in 1995

Greenwood Press, 88 Post Road West, Westport, CT 06881
An imprint of Greenwood Publishing Group, Inc.

Printed in the United States of America

The paper used in this book complies with the
Permanent Paper Standard issued by the National
Information Standards Organization (Z39.48–1984).

10 9 8 7 6 5 4 3 2 1

To all that seek social progress for all,
To all practitioners who seek counsel
from theories of economic development,
To all epistemologists, and
To all my students and teachers alike.

Contents

Foreword

FOR NEWCOMERS TO THE PHILOSOPHICAL SUB-FIELD, METHODOLOGY

Contrary to popular usage, methodology is not a cookbook study of how results are obtained; rather, it is a branch of philosophy that identifies the method of solid persuasion chosen by those arguing a case. Does he or she use revelation, logic, empirically derived evidence, plausibility, or some combination of these or other persuasive benchmarks?

Some naive scientists, persuaded that the scientific method involving the statement of a hypothesis, testing it against empirically derived evidence, and eventually refining it to pass those tests, believe that they have discovered the only path to real truth. *Sancta simplicimus*, the world is more complicated than that. At best, for only some ideas is the scientific test immediately well-suited. For many others, thoughts within a cultural context, the scientific test runs into myriad but necessarily insuperable difficulties.

One additional set of complications involves epistemic compared to ontological perceptions. Epistemic perceptions are essentially subjective — although we try to explain them by reference to analogs or parables the fact is that the perception itself is securely grounded only in the mind of the one who perceives it. Obvious examples of epistemic perceptions deal with aesthetics — Maynard Keynes's "which girl will an unknown panel of judges decide is the prettiest" is exemplar of this species of perceptions.

The comparative type, ontological perceptions, are seemingly objective. What is the temperature, what time does the sun set, and so forth. These perceptions are readily handled. The question is how can epistemic perceptions be differentiated from ontological ones, or, even better, how much of any epistemic perception can be delineated and incorporated into the ontological group.

Put briefly, methodology explains how we reach conclusions, what tests satisfy us, and so forth. What the authors of this fascinating study set out to do was to use the spectrum of theories of economic development, as applied against a background of African development experience, to develop what they sought — a logical method of understanding the economic development experience or, to use their phrase, "to advance a metatheory on the analysis of economic development" (p. 5).

THE BOOK'S CONTRIBUTIONS

The authors' line of thought first leads the reader from a review of the current discussion of the nature of science to the presenting of generalizations about differing schools on that subject. Although it is useful to know about that spectrum, the authors bring us to a relevant cognitive reality by referring to specific general criticisms levied by such acknowledged experts as Simon Kuznets (or as Hamlet would have it, "there is more to all the world than your philosophizing" [*Hamlet*, v, 166]) as well as to concrete and intellectually messy economic development situations themselves. Although there is little that is novel in the initial part of their views (including a rehash of the conflict between Kuznets and his strong admirer, Walt Rostow) there are added to intriguing almost extensive detours, first, a useful excursion into Marx's methodology and, second, one summarizing with a wealth of detail Joseph Schumpeter's analytical method. These, alone, are unusual contributions, particularly since they set Schumpeter against Marx, something that is done unusually well. For this reader, this effort gives a contemporary pertinence to the older Marxian analysis.

The line of argument then moves to factor-based theories of economic development. This is economists' meat and drink; putting effects as the result of objective causes gives us the scientists' customary handle. Compare this objective cause-effect relationship to Kipling's epistemic "God of our fathers, known of old / Under whose Awful Hand we hold / Dominion over palm and pine. . . . Be with us yet, Be with us yet" (*The Recessional*) or the admonition in Deuteronomy 28 to "do these things, and all blessings will come to you"; do not do these things and He will destroy you. Instead, the authors endorse the Marxian (and derivatively the Schumpeterian) views of the necessary conditions for economic development, but they wisely divide the interpretations into those consistent with Marxian class analysis and those that differ.

At this point the authors move from strict scientific analysis to prescriptive treatments, that is, to writers who derive from the scientific studies of past experiments the bases for new ones. Of course, development economists do not work in laboratories; they cannot even pretend to control the environment. Nonetheless, they can outline limited efforts that seemingly either abstract from the environment or permit the observer to separate theoretical from environmental influences as seen in the results. Starting with Arthur Lewis's and then Lloyd Reynolds's ideas and moving to such later ones as privatization, the authors fashion a set of conclusions that seem plausible. Obviously, they have had to go beyond the methodology of immanent criticism, that is, pure logic, because of the complexity of the cultural inputs and the various types of interactions.

In the end, the authors reassert their faith in the existence (possibly not yet found) of a scientific theory of economic development, basing their hope on using Schumpeterian-Marxian foundations for the new structure.

Theirs is an interesting exercise — one that excites the imagination even if it admittedly does not clearly convince.

Preface

PHILOSOPHY, in understanding human society, calls for an analysis of facts and events, and an attempt to see how they fit into human life, and so how they make up human experience. In this way, philosophy, like history, can come to enrich, indeed to define, the experience of man.

The critical study of the philosophies of the past should lead to the study of modern theories, for these latter, born of the fire of contemporary struggles, are militant and alive.

— Kwame Nkrumah

The theory of economics does not furnish a body of settled conclusions immediately applicable to policy. It is a method rather than a doctrine, an apparatus of the mind, a technique of thinking, which helps its possessor to draw correct conclusions.

— John Maynard Keynes

Knowledge is a process composed of cognitive forces under tension. Its growth reflects additions of newly accepted ideas. These new ideas are born out of tension. They are nothing but children of cognitive tension. They are always conceived in the womb of old ideas. When they are conceived, they undergo long periods of gestation and are born with great cognitive pain and intellectual resistance. When they emerge, they are viewed as rebels, because they are not only threats to the existing system of ideas but are also contestants of emerging ones. Their acceptance, survival, and longevity depend on cognitive tolerance, congruence with reality, and the degree to which they square with social perceptions and interpretive experiences. When they are accorded acceptance in the system of social thought, they become part of the tradition and their future development is at the mercy of existing intellectual order and restricted or promoted by the basic epistemological ignorance and fears of the unknown. Development economics is not an exception.

Development economics, however, has special epistemic problems. These epistemic problems and theoretical difficulties that they present in the analysis of the phenomenon of economic development are those that command my interest and worries. It was at the graduate school of Temple University in Philadelphia that I first encountered the formal corpus of theories of economic development. It was here that my worries began after taking four courses in development economics. My interest, however, began in my place of birth, Africa. From my mathematical training at the undergraduate school in the same university, I entered the graduate program with an orientation of looking for structures and well-posed problems in all theoretical constructs from theoretical physics to theoretical economics.

In view of this, I sought some scientific clarity in theories of development economics. I found very little, if any. I searched for logical rigor and consistency. I did not get them. I looked for "well-posedness" of the core theoretical problems and questions that are of concern to the theories in economic development. Here, I was most disappointed and confused. I sought out intellectual counsel from my teachers. I ended up with a constant debate with my professors as I pressed them for logical clarity, neat problem specification, exact subject content of theories of development economics, and preoccupation of the basic enterprise of economics of development. Sometimes, my insistence on finding comfort on my worries from intellectual discourse became less and less appreciated by my student colleagues and found less support from my professors. Perhaps they were not aware of my cognitive torments in this branch of economics.

All things considered, I was of an opinion, as I am now and more convinced than then, that development economics as a branch of economics was and is in serious epistemic trouble. I was searching for answers to questions and precepts that I thought defined the foundations of the subject area. As I understood then, so I understand now, that there is no clear image of the content of development economics. It is amorphous. This lack of clear content image has spilled over to the construction of theories of economic development, where it is neither understood nor appreciated that development economics is, perhaps, the most difficult area of economics. It has to deal with time, quantity, quality, change, mechanism of quantity-quality transformation, and complex relations that they engender.

As I reflected then, so I do now, that development is a child of tension, and this tension is produced by socioeconomic agents that must resolve individual and collective conflicts in the socioeconomic decision space. The resolution takes place through the existing institutions that constitute the arteries through which the lifeblood of the social organism flows. Thus, the essential relationships among the mechanism of change, cultural environment for decisions, existing institutions, and their growth must be part of the content of the subject of development. I understand that economic development is not a gift of simple passage of time. It is a victory that emerges out of people's conflicting alternative actions, hard work, strifes, toil, and overcoming of adversities. They all take place through institutions that are, themselves, the creative works of the people. It is through this understanding that I thought that a meaningful theory of economic development must be conceived and crafted. However, as the eminent economist Joan Robinson has stated: "the moralizing doctrine which still underlies orthodox Western teaching fails to provide the basis for a theory of economic development because of confusion in its approach" (178, p. 10).

I came to think then, as I now do, that the main corpus of modern theories of economic development is plagued with logical ills, misleading notions, outright ideological deceptions, and weak theoretical structure that made its scientific character wanting. This is pointed out again by Joan Robinson that "there is a certain complacency in mainstream economic teaching which is misleading even in its homeland and cruelly deceptive when transferred to the Third World" (178, p. ix). It is perhaps these problems that drove some of the finest economic theorists away from the area of economic development. The neoclassical static analysis with its mathematical rigor was a blindfold, and its extension to dynamic analysis was simplistic and less helpful. The main assumptions about institutions in which decisions are made and the value systems that motivate social action and inaction prevent any critical analysis and understanding of how the socioeconomic system goes through quantitative and qualitative transformations where institutions are created and destroyed.

There seems to be a complete crisis in the subject area of theories of economic development. The foundation of the subject itself has become problematic. It is completely infested with methodological ills whose cure must find instructions from theory of knowledge. One is left in limbo as to whether the theories are of an explanatory nature, prescriptive nature, or descriptive nature. This unsureness is compounded by the fact that every expository position presented in the literature can never be proven wrong, because of circularity of reasoning where theoretical propositions are true by definition in their own terms. Here, it became clear to me that to make theoretical headway in this branch of eco-nomics, I should seek counsel outside the subject of economics itself. The advice of Albert Einstein became handy, and I took it seriously that when the subject area of science and its foundation have become problematic, as the study of economic development has become, and "when experience forces us to seek a newer and more solid foundation, the [economists] cannot simply surrender to the philosopher the critical contemplation of the theoretical foundations; for, he himself knows best and feels more surely where the shoe pinches" (22, p. 1).

I was logically convinced that economic development is quantity-quality transformation that involves conversion of categories of levels of development properly defined. In view of this, I accepted the counsel of Nkrumah that:

Philosophy can demonstrate the possibility of the conversion in one or other of two ways: either by means of a conceptual analysis or by pointing at a model. As it happens, philosophy is in a position to do both. Philosophy prepares itself for the accommodation of the hard facts by asserting not the crude sole reality of matter [economic development], but its primary reality. Other categories [levels and stages of development] must then be shown to be able to arise from matter [economic development] through process. It is at this point that philosophical materialism becomes dialectical. (161, pp. 20–21)

With these counsels in mind, I set up a project to examine the methodological foundation of theories of economic development. It was during this period of my graduate education that the ideas about this book were contemplated as I continued to seek an epistemic clarity. I have learned from the methodological insights of Keynes that "the theory of economics does not furnish a body of settled conclusions immediately applicable to policy. It is a method rather than a doctrine, an apparatus of the mind, a technique of thinking, which helps its possessor to draw correct conclusions" (97). In all these, I have been instructed by contending philosophies that social theories are reflections of social currents. They arise from consciousness of social exigencies in an attempt either to explain social circumstances or to charter a new path of social conduct so as to alter unwanted situations. These require critical contemplation.

The work of critical contemplation for epistemic clarity of development economics did not start until I entered Howard University as an assistant professor. It was in my class of doctoral graduate macroeconomic theory that I met Manzur Ejaz, who was then a graduate student. In 1982, I put on the notice board a list of about 30 dissertation topics on certain theoretical problems of interest, including "methodology of development economics," which Ejaz worked on with me as his advisor (82b). I suggested to him that after the completion of the dissertation, we would jointly revise it for a publication. For a number of reasons, Ejaz was unable to contribute to the revision.

My attempt to revise the dissertation has produced a completely different treatise that reflects mostly my intellectual positions and leanings regarding the enterprise of science and its methodology as they relate to the subject areas of development economics. As such, I have entitled the work as I originally conceived it: *The Epistemics of Development Economics: Toward a Methodological Critique and Unity.* I express great appreciation to Ejaz for some of the groundwork. I have rewritten, restructured, and expanded every chapter to provide logical continuity, linguistic connectedness, and epistemic clarity. The end product is a metatheory on theories of economic development. I accept all criticisms for philosophical emphasis on dialectics and approval of methodology of Marx and Schumpeter.

The power of the metatheory advanced here lies in a projection of a thesis that a substantial portion of the literature on economic development theories may be conceived primarily as rhetoric and subjectively descriptive notions rather than rational constructs. When theories of economic development take this form, they mainly project speculativeness and ideology rather than scientific understanding. As such, they fail to illuminate the central problems requiring human understanding and even gravely distort the path to rational insights.

This brings us to the question of whether forms of explanation found in theories of economic development can conform to those found in natural sciences or theoretical economics in their static setting. A follow-up question is what set of principles, if any, must be developed to guide us in selecting a theory in development economics for use and practice. Additionally, one may question whether there are forms of explanation in development economics that must acquire an exemption from the rigor of the discipline of science. Furthermore, a question arises as to whether an illuminating theory of economic development can be constructed by detaching the economic decision actions of human social existence from its political, cultural, legal, and institutional setting. These questions and interrelated ones constitute the central problems of epistemics of theories of economic development as they relate to the theory of knowledge and understanding of the history of human social development.

The judgment of scientific relevance of any theory of economic development must be based, it is suggested, on rational-historical criteria of a composite nature. It is rational in the sense that the central problem of study in development economics has been clearly stated and the critical mechanism of quantitative-qualitative transformation has been systematically isolated where the role and subprocesses of key aggregate variables have been positioned for understanding. It is historical in that the transient path of socioeconomic system constituting the essential history of choice-decision outcomes of the collective is also the development phenomenon whose analysis is logically being constructed.

In view of the epistemic clarity that we seek, two notions of science are examined in this book. The first one is *explanatory science* with corresponding explanatory theories where the object of the enterprise of science is to explain "what there is." The second one is *prescriptive science* with corresponding prescriptive theories where the basic object of the enterprise of science is to improve "what there is" (reality) by actualizing "what ought to be" (the potential). Together, they constitute the unity of scientific enterprise where explanation, prediction, and prescription are integrated in a unified setting. The epistemic nature of the two concepts of science are examined and related to the subject matter of the theories of development economics.

The major difference is found not in techniques and methods of their constructs but in the manner in which the empirical validity of the main and supporting propositions is subjected to "test." The distinction is very important if we are to avoid a scientific theory of knowledge of the socioeconomic system that equates quantitative changes with qualitative social transformation and growth with development. Every qualitative reality is a surrogate of disposition of a quantitative reality that also defines the qualitative disposition of the object of inquiry. Quantity and quality form a unity of every process. They are dialectically inseparable and together define the state at any specified moment of the process. Thus, if theories of economic development are to conform to social reality, they must be guided by general epistemic principles that always keep this objective alive, a set of epistemic principles that will prevent constructions of theories of economic development as if the critical principle of the mechanism for and laws of social transformation are different and that quantitative changes have nothing to do with qualitative changes.

With these things in mind, the book presents a metatheory on the analysis of economic development. The empirical universe of the metatheory is the set of theories in development economics as a subset of theories in economics. The metatheory is a logical construct that would allow one to evaluate the scientific validity of the theories in development economics. It is a study in scientific methods.

Theories in development economics are examined to see whether they meet the test conditions laid down by the scientific community and somehow agreed upon by methodologists regarding the nature of scientific theories, namely, as logical constructs, are they internally consistent in terms of content, structure and reasoning? As logical systems of thought, are they in conformity with the observed behavior of phenomena of economic development? As logical inquiries, do they add to our knowledge and understanding of economic development process?

Central to the discussions are the concepts of category formation, primary category, conversion of categories, quality and quantity changes, laws of motion and mechanism of transmission, and how they logically relate to one another. In the process of discussion, the concepts of explanation, prediction, and prescription are examined to see how they epistemologically relate to each other and to the phenomenon of socioeconomic transformation. The concept of science is repositioned to include two broad areas of scientific theories of explanatory and prescriptive theories.

The study is organized in six parts after introducing the problem and nature of study in Chapter 1. Chapter 2 presents a survey of scientific methods and the debate on economic methodology relevant to economic development. Chapter 3 is devoted to the examination of the relevant properties, problems, and methods for the construction of criteria for evaluating scientific theories and how such a criterion may be used to analyze the scientific status of theories in development economics and, hence, to judge their contributions to scientific knowledge. The stage-based explanatory theories in development economics are examined in Chapter 4, where a comparative analysis of Marx, Schumpeter, and Rostow is provided. Chapter 5 analyzes the factor-based explanatory theories, and their scientific status and contributions to knowledge are scrutinized; here, we deal with capital-based, human-capital-based, and technology-based explanatory theories. In Chapter 6, we analyze the epistemics of prescriptive theories about the economic development process. The conceptual differences among explanation, predication, prescription, and prescriptive theories are clarified, sharpened, and related to economic development. Chapter 7 presents conclusions and suggestions consequent to the study.

The following are central to the development of ideas in this book:

Science is not only about explanation of "what there is" but also about improvement of "what there is."

Redefinition of the subject of science to include both prescriptive and explanatory sciences, where two types of theories about development phenomena are advanced: explanatory and prescriptive theories.

Concepts of category formation, primary category, and categorial convertibility where time, quantity, quality, and mechanism of change are linked.

Construction of an evaluative criterion called the rational-historical criterion.

Classification of theories about the phenomenon of economic development.

Development of an evaluative process of scientific status of these theories.

These features constitute some of the major reasons for the study. The lack of explicit criteria for judging the scientific content of theories in development economics places a limitation on their effective use in practice. It is precisely this limitation, in addition to general failure of economic development policies of international development agencies as applied to developing countries, that provides an extra rationale for the current study. The resources used in creating this book will be said to be well-spent if the ideas in the book anger some, delight others, or provoke new thinking.

Finally, I express my thanks to the faculty members at Temple University, Department of Economics, who collectively served as my teachers. Special thanks, however, goes to L. W. Holmes, who insisted on the development of mathematical rigor; Karl Niebyl, whose orientation provided me with philosophical and historical insights into economics as well as German historical school; J. S. Mehta and N. Sun, for their moral support and advisement; B. P. Klotz, E. Appelbaum, and E. Bond, who constituted my dissertation committee, with B. P. Klotz as my main advisor. I also express my thanks to the following people at Howard University: S. Gujral for generous suggestions and encouragement, Keisha (Kahlil) Kuykendall for her work as graduate assistant in the last days of finishing the book, Modupe Fadope for editorial suggestions, and Mary McCalop for excellent secretarial assistance. I also express my gratitude to K. O. Nti of Penn State University for generous suggestions. All errors are my responsibility.

Epistemics of
Development Economics

1

Introduction

During the long period of economic-growth modernization of Western Europe and the United States, most parts of Africa and Asia were either colonies or waging wars of resistance against European colonial adventurism or going through critical social obstruction, such as slavery and mass population exodus from Africa. The nature of the wars of resistance and colonial status were such that these parts of Africa and Asia had economic structures that either were in ruins or served as appendages to the economies of the colonizing countries of Western Europe.

By the nature of colonial economic structures, the territories of Africa and Asia and a number of islands around the world had no economic development objective. Some non-Western countries, like those in Central and South America, had political independence but were basically economic satellites of Western Europe and the United States. Politically, these countries were colonies whose decision structure deprived them from having any meaningful national economic development objective. Any kind of economic development that occurred in these political and economic colonies was attained accidentally. During this period, analytical work on economic development practically vanished from the mainstream economic thinking of the Western world.

At the turn of the twentieth century and, particularly, since World War II, there have been adjustments in the structure of world politics and in the order of international relationships. Additionally, as Europe lay in physical and economic ruins from World War II, most of the world's territories that were under colonial domination began to achieve some level of political independence. These politically decolonized territories became part of what is currently categorized as either independent countries, Third World countries, Developing World, or Less-Developed world. The newly constituted governments of these decolonized territories, including those of Central and South America, showed a strong desire for rapid economic growth in order to catch up with the economies of the "Western world" and the "Eastern world." Learning from the experience of the reconstruction of Europe and the Soviet Union (now the Commonwealth of Independent States), the governments of the newly independent countries prepared very ambitious development plans. These plans had a number of goals and objectives that included rapid economic growth, internal social development, and improvement of the material conditions of their citizens.

This general awakening to improve the material status of societies and to sharpen the concept of development programs was inspired by a number of factors such as the success of the socialist economic bloc of the Eastern world and its strong initial rate of economic growth and development, which radically altered the world's socioeconomic conditions. Also, the ideology of the socialist bloc, with its initial high rates of material and technological progress, sparked a strong competition with the Western capitalist economic order that had long held these colonial territories under economic and political subservience. The combined effects of East-West ideological competition and the rapidly changing international situation gave incentive to Western industrialized countries to take interest in the plight of these previously colonized areas of the world and to participate in finding a process by which economic development could be accelerated.

Institutions like the International Bank of Reconstruction and Development, now known as The World Bank, and the International Monetary Fund became, at least on the surface, initial instruments to search and promote development by providing financial resources. Additionally, a number of localized development agencies, such as the Overseas Development Agency and the United States Agency for International Development, were created. The declaration of the development decade by the United Nations affirmed the perceived keen interest of the world community in the economic development of the world's poor countries; it also enriched the decision environment in the search for an appropriate process to expedite the needed development. The reconstruction of Europe and the new interest in raising the material standard of the world's poor nations vitalized mental activities on development economics in the mainstream of economic thought of the West. Similar trends were also taking place in the Eastern bloc.

Given that all these intentions and interests, particularly of the Western nations, were genuine, a number of interrelated questions arise: What are the factors that generate underdevelopment and stagnation, and how does one explain the relationship of these factors to underdevelopment? What are the factors that bring about development, and how does one explain the process? Are the factors that generate underdevelopment related to the factors that bring about development? What are the necessary courses of action that must be prescribed to rapidly eliminate underdevelopment and promote internally sustainable development of the concerned areas?

To answer these questions, there emerged a proliferation of theories of development, especially after the mid-twentieth century. The activities of theorizing were undertaken by economists in institutions of higher learning and research. The objective was to map out an internally consistent logical system of thought that would answer the above questions while providing intellectual grounds by which development policies could be constructed. In the process, the proposed theories advanced logical systems that are complementary in some areas and competitive in others. Policy construction and practices of economic development were based on the proposed theoretical constructs for over a decade in an atmosphere of high expectation and hope.

However, in the 1960s and 1970s, the results of the practice based on the proposed theories were disappointing in many countries. These disappointments led to disillusionments as to the validity of the main propositions of the theories as guides to practice. Not only have these countries remained underdeveloped and poor, but the gap between them and the rich and developed countries actually has widened. Additionally, attempts to speed up the development process have created enormous problems of social adjustments and management. The resulting events and practices of economic development plans and policies have not indicated which of the competing theories of economic development has yielded better results in explaining the development process or in prescribing good policy rules. Some of these theories were contradictory in addition to emphasizing different factors as the basis for their explanations and prescriptions. Therefore, it became very difficult for scholars and policy makers to choose.

To deal with these difficulties, various scholars pointed out the shortcomings of existing development theories. Criticisms ranged from empirical observations to pure speculation about the structures of these theoretical constructs. These criticisms, although useful, made it more difficult to choose among the theories on the basis of which development policy construct must be crafted. These criticisms had an important shortcoming: failure to provide an explicit process for an effective choice among competing theories. The process of choosing the appropriate theory of economic development was further complicated by implicitly held ideological beliefs that became translated as fundamental moral postulates in these theories. For example, the fundamental ethical postulate underlying some of the theories is that development can occur only through the capitalist mode of individualism. Other theories opposed this postulate by contending that development can occur only through the socialist mode of collectivism. Decision agents were, thus, confronted with these two fundamental ethical postulates of individualism and collectivism in choosing an appropriate path for organizing economic development. These two postulates have now been extended to the debate over the relative sizes of private and public sectors.

In all these, one thing stands out: there seems to be no criterion that delineates a framework by which development theories could be scientifically scrutinized and either accepted or rejected. A critical need, therefore, exists for the construction of a criterion of choice to indicate a clear development policy model. The development of a criterion for evaluating the strength, weaknesses, and appropriateness of these theories (no matter how these terms are defined) requires a number of cognitive actions. These actions involve a clear understanding of the methodological and epistemological underpinnings of these theories within the context of the philosophy of science and epistemics of discovering scientific truth; explicit specification of the content and subject matter of development economics (as well as the theory of economic development if they are different); direct identification of methods and analytics of theoretical constructs applicable to the subject matter of development economics; and the specification of the process for verifying the scientific truth embodied in the theories of development. On the basis of these cognitive actions, one can construct an evaluative criterion that outlines the characteristics of scientific theory applicable to development economics.

Constructing a criterion of scientific theory of development is, however, complicated, because no consensus exists within the community of philosophers of science regarding the general characteristics of scientific theory. In recent times, the philosophers of science have been trying to establish a criterion by positing various critiques of the existing theoretical frameworks. For example, Karl Popper (170), Thomas Kuhn (112), and Imre Lakatos (120–22), to name three of the contemporary philosophers of science, have scrutinized the conventionalist, positivist, and other methodological positions along widely different lines. Even in the absence of an overall consensus among the philosophers of science, a criterion has to be abstracted from their works and metaformulations in order to access the scientific status of various development theories.

Alternatively, the gains from the discussions on methodological and epistemological problems of traditional economic theory could be used to construct an evaluative criterion applicable to theories in development economics. The problem in this regard is that there is a general lack of a well-developed intellectual correspondence between the philosophy of science and the methodology of economics. This has also been pointed out by Hutchison, who, referring to Morgenstern, states that "the results of the revolutionary developments in recent decades of the science of logic and logical analysis have scarcely been made use of at all. Since Mill, Jevons, J. N. Keynes, and W. E. Johnson when Economics and Logic were closely associated, there has been a division of scientific labor, and against the gains of increased specialization there may be losses to be set off" (83, p. 6).

The discussions on methodology and epistemology of economic theorizing that have taken place remain in the philosophical confines of positivism and instrumentalism. The major participants in these discussions, like T. Hutchison (84), F. Machlup (126), M. Friedman (52), P. Samuelson (193, 197), Mark Blaug (18), and others, have concentrated merely on the assumptions and abstractions of neoclassical economics. A closer look, however, reveals that there is an overall assumption underlying these approaches (of positivism and instrumentalism) that the capitalist system represents the ultimate economic system. This implicit position has led them, in the process of discussions, to dispense with the historical and social relevance of scientific theorizing about economic phenomena. The overall ahistorical context of these debates does not contribute to the understanding of the nature of the transformation process, either from feudal to industrial societies or from one economic state to another. As such, these debates do not leave much by which to examine the methodology of development economics. However, these debates on methodology of economic science, though lacking in many respects, can inspire one to ask meaningful questions about the scientific status of a number of theories about economic phenomena. These questions on the methodological problems of economic knowledge are particularly crucial for theories about economic development where structural transformations of societies touch all aspects of human life and where a change from one economic state to another affects the welfare and psychology of all members of the society.

Because the debates of methodology on the economic analysis neglect the theories of development, we propose to examine the scientific status of theories of economic development and their epistemological problems. In the process, theories of economic development shall be classified into appropriate categories. We shall then construct composite criteria from existing criteria of scientific theory in order to evaluate the scientific status of the theories on development economics.

The main goal of this study is to advance a metatheory on analysis of economic development. The empirical universe of this metatheory is theories in development economics as a subset of theories in economic science. The aim, therefore, is not to pass any moral judgments about the intentions and motivations of theoreticians of economic development but to advance a logical system of thought that would allow one to evaluate the scientific validity of the theories in development economics. More precisely, this study will examine whether theories in development economics meet the test conditions laid down by the scientific community and somewhat agreed upon by philosophers of science regarding the nature of scientific theories, namely, as logical constructs, are they internally consistent in terms of content and structure and, as logical systems of thought, are they in conformity with the observed behavior of phenomena of economic development. Additionally, we shall deal with questions involving type and structure of the theories and explicit and implicit contents implied in them, as well as the contributions to knowledge that they claim to offer.

The discussions in the rest of the book will proceed by first reviewing the existing literature on philosophy of science relevant to economic methodology in Chapter 2. We shall then focus on the needs, require-ments, and criteria of scientific theories in Chapter 3. The theories of development economics will be categorized accordingly in the same chapter. After categorizing these theories, we shall then take up the analysis of the structure of explanatory theories by examining their methodological and epistemological underpinnings; this is done in chapters 4 and 5. We also shall critically examine the methodologies and epistemology implied by prescriptive theories and how their logical structures may be useful to theorizing in development economics, the subject of Chapter 6. Explanatory or prescriptive theories in develop-ment economics will be made explicit and their policy implications examined within the context of their contribution to knowledge.

In the process, we shall examine the relationship between the concepts of explanation and prescription. Prescriptions that are logically implied by explanatory theories in development economics also will be examined. This will allow us to evaluate the nature and relevance of prescriptions for the practice of development economics. Finally, we shall summarize the key ideas of the study in Chapter 7 and make some suggestions that may be considered by economists involved in constructing theories of economic development. We hope that these suggestions will reveal a new epistemic paradigm for research on the phenomenon of development economics.

2

Survey of Literature

METHODOLOGY OF SCIENCE

In the absence of direct literature on methodology and epistemology of development economics, we shall survey the relevant portion of the literature on philosophy of science and debates on methodology in economics that can indirectly help us to construct a criterion of evaluation and to analyze how it may be applied to examine the scientific status of claimed theories of economic development. The literature survey will be carried on from three angles: the essential requirements of a general scientific theory, the specific requirements of methodology and epistemology in economic analysis, and the applicable methodological and epistemological criticism of development economics. The objective in this chapter is to ascertain the relevant properties of scientific theories and how such properties are used to demarcate science from nonscience and, hence, to select scientific theories from a class of theories.

We shall examine the epistemological conventionalism and the position that the conventionalists hold regarding what constitutes science and, hence, a scientific theory. We shall then examine the hypothetic-deductive model of science and how this constitutes a critique of the epistemological conventionalism. This will lead us to examine the test of scientific theories through the eyes of verificationists and falsificationists. We shall extend the examination to Kuhn's paradigm position and Lakatos' scientific research program position.

Conventionalism

The traditional nineteenth-century scientific criterion was that science uses the inductive method. Scientific explanation, therefore, starts with observing the individual outcomes about a phenomenon and then abstracting the universal laws inherent therein. The universal laws are then used to explain and predict the outcome or behavior of the phenomenon. John Stuart Mill summed up the inductive view of science in his *System of Logic, Ratiocinative and Inductive* (145). This view of science is still popular with the layman. David Hume pointed out a fundamental flaw in inductive reasoning that has since been called "the problem of induction" (18). According to Hume, there is an unjustified leap in the induction process whereby one abstracts universal laws from finite observations. An often-quoted example to illustrate the fundamental flaw is that the statement that "all swans are white" is based on the fact that all observed swans are white and a nonwhite swan has yet to be observed. In fact, nobody can claim that he has observed all swans. The problem is that for a large class of phenomena, it is not possible to exhaust the infinite observations in the universe. In short, it never can be demonstrated that anything is materially true, because of human and physical limitations. The main points of conventionalist scientific theory are as follows: the aim of scientific investigations is to discover the truth, the truth is reached by induction, and once the general laws are discovered through induction, the various aspects of phenomena can be explained by inference.

The Hypothetic-Deductive Model

In the last half of the nineteenth century, the inductive method came under fire in the writings of Ernst Mach, Henri Poincare, and Pierre Duhem (18). The main objection of these philosophers was that the objective of scientific investigation cannot be the discovery of truth, because finality of truth can never be established as implied in the inductivist method. Furthermore, the method of induction was attacked and reversed by the "hypothetic-deductive model of scientific explanation" in the writings of the Vienna Circle (125). It was not until 1948 that the hypothetic-deductive model was presented and held as the only valid explanatory procedure in science. A more-authentic version of this thesis appeared in a famous paper by Carl Hempel (73).

The logical structure of hypothetic-deductive model involves at least one universal law plus a statement of initial or boundary conditions that together constitute the *explanans* or premise from which the explanation is derived by deductive logic only. It was further argued that a "prediction" in science involves the same rules of logical inference as explanation in science. Explanation is the same as prediction written backward. Within the hypothetic-deductive model, universal laws are not derived by inductive method, they are derived by hypotheses. The formal structure of a scientific theory, therefore, is nothing more than calculus, whose validity may be tested by using it to make predictions about particular events.

Though this position has widespread support among the modern positivists, it has been criticized by others because of symmetry between explanation and prediction (18). The criticism may be summed up as follows: Prediction need not imply explanation; prediction involves only a correlation, not causation, whereas explanation requires the establishment of a causal notion. The ordinary least square regression is a prediction of a kind in that it establishes a correlation. It, however, does not constitute an explanatory theory about the phenomenon of interest because it does not establish a causal relationship. Short-term economic forecasting is possible with a rule-of-thumb.

A. Kaplan and R. Harre have criticized the symmetry thesis by quoting Darwin's theory of evolution (91). The theory explains how highly specialized biological forms have emerged by a process of natural selection without predicting precisely what highly specialized forms will emerge and under what set of conditions. Therefore, the hypothetic-deductive model cannot accommodate Darwin's theory.

Finally, it is said that the symmetry thesis is normative (41). It excludes much of what some people have regarded as science. Instead of explaining "what there is," it suggests "what should be." W. Dray, arguing against C. G. Hempel, suggests that instead of stating the logical requirements of a scientific explanation, our time should be served in classifying and characterizing the theories that are actually employed (42).

From the hypothetic-deductive arguments, the main characteristics of a scientific theory are at least a universal law and a set of initial conditions, symmetry of explanation and prediction that can be checked against experience, and verification of theoretical propositions against facts and the degree to which the propositions correspond to reality.

From Verificationism to Falsificationism

The hypothetic-deductive model was presented as a solution to the "problem of induction." The ultimate purpose of the hypothetic-deductive model of science was to reject the proposition that "true scientific theories" can be constructed on the basis of induction. Instead, it establishes that a scientific theory can be validated by strict empirical tests. The concept of empirical test made this epistemological model popular among the positivists, who took a more extreme position on the question of "meaningful" and "meaningless" in science and philosophy.

Karl Popper rejects the concept of verification and positivists' attempt to differentiate the meaningful from meaningless. He alleges that Wittgenstein, Ayer, and other positivists have not been able to define, precisely, what meaningful means. Moreover, the positivists' demand that legitimate and scientific concepts are only those that are "derived from experience" is identical with inductive logic. The criticism is revealed by Popper's statement: "They wish to admit, as scientific or legitimate, only those statements which are reducible to elementary (or atomic) statement of experience. . . . It is clear that the implied criterion of demarcation is identical with the demand of an inductive logic" (170, p. 35).

Reinforcing his argument that the positivists' position is identical with that of the conventionalists, Popper further notes that nothing can be proved to be true by inductive logic because it is impossible to exhaust infinite observations; however, it is possible to demonstrate that something is materially false. Popper's criterion of demarcation between science and nonscience is, thus, based upon an asymmetry between verifiability and falsifiability. To Popper, science is that body of synthetic propositions about the world that, in principle, can be falsified by empirical observation. Science distinguishes itself by its method of formulating and testing propositions but not by its subject matter or by its claim to certainty of knowledge. In contradistinction to the psychology of logic, says Popper, the logic of knowledge "consists solely in investigating the methods employed in systematic tests to which every new idea must be subjected, if it is to be seriously entertained" (170, p. 31). The line drawn between science and nonscience is not absolute. Both falsifiability and testability are a matter of degree, according to Popper. There is a frequent reference by Popper to the symmetry thesis, but this is not to say that, for him, the theory is a prediction generating machine. Though an earlier version of the hypothetic-deductive model appeared in his 1934 book, he also appreciated the theoretician's interest in explanation (170, p. 61).

According to Popper, the scientists seek to explain. From the explanations, they derive the predictions that are inherent in their explanations in order to test their theories. A theory is true if it leads to true predictions, says Popper; however, all true theories are provisionally "true," having so far defied falsification. A theory enters the category of science if it yields valid predictions and contains propositions that can be falsified in accord with accumulated data or experience.

In connection with falsifiability, P. Duhem argues that no individual hypothesis is conclusively falsifiable because we always test the entire explanans, the particular hypothesis in conjunction with auxiliary statements, and, hence, we can never be sure whether we have confirmed or refuted the hypothesis itself (18). Popper concedes to the argument by suggesting that: "Disproof of a theory can never be produced; for it is always possible to say that the experimental rules are not reliable, or that the discrepancies which are asserted to exist between the experimental results and the theory are only apparent and they will disappear" (170, p. 50).

Popper accepts the position that no conclusive disproof of a theory can ever be produced. He, therefore, suggests that we need methodological limits on stratagems that may be adopted by scientists to safeguard their theories against refutation. Methodological limits are essential, says Popper, because falsifiability alone is not enough.

Explanation and falsifiability along with methodological rules constitute the criteria of demarcation between science and nonscience (170, Chap. 7).

Popper argues that scientific explanations cannot be appraised except in terms of the predictions that are implied in them. A scientific theory is put to test when a scientist specifies a set of observable conditions that would falsify the theory. The theory that resists falsification in repeated tests and successfully predicts results that do not follow from competing theories is well-corroborated.

Popper reduces most of the traditional list of criteria — consistency, simplicity, completeness, economy in assumptions, generality of explanation, and practical relevance — to falsificationism. For example, a greater generality of a theory widens the scope of its implications and, hence, makes it easier to be falsified. Popper's treatment of simplicity is more controversial; he argues that the simpler the theory, the stricter is its observable sphere of implications and, hence, the easier its testability. Attempts to define a simple theory have failed. Moreover, Popper's concept of simple theory has been challenged by the argument that modern quantum mechanics and relativity theory are scientifically true but not simple.

The concept of "corroboration of theories" has been criticized on the following accounts.

No theory can ever be falsified decisively.

Scientists may cling tenaciously to a refuted theory in the hope that it can be repaired.

It is possible that two rival theories may explain the same phenomenon satisfactorily. For example, in economics, we have the Ando-Modigliani life-cycle hypothesis, Friedman permanent income hypothesis, and Duesenberry relative income hypothesis on the phenomenon of consumption.

These considerations damage the concept of degree of corroboration. In concession to this pint, Popper admits that the comparison of theories is inherently of a qualitative nature. He responds to his critics by stating that a theory A is preferred to a theory B on the basis of its past performance. Because corroboration is an evaluating report of past performance, it says nothing whatsoever about future performances or the reliability of a theory. Popper's main ideas are summarized as follows:

For the advancement of knowledge, we need a criterion for demarcating science from nonscience.

In constructing the criterion of demarcation, only the logic of science should be considered; the psychological, sociological, or historical analysis of theories is useless in examining their scientific status.

The logic of science dictates that it is impossible to "verify" a theory, but it is possible to falsify it in repeated trials.

A scientific theory should, at least, yield propositions that are falsifiable in principle.

Additional methodological rules are required to detect and combat the tendency of some scientists to use various stratagems to safeguard their theories from falsification.

The explanation of a theory should lead to predictions that can be tested against empirical data. A theory is provisionally true if its predictions are valid and its main propositions are not yet falsified.

All true theories are provisionally true, that is, they have not been falsified yet.

If a theory is not falsified in repeated tests, it is well-corroborated but not necessarily true.

Among well-corroborated theories, those that are simpler and general are preferred.

Historical View of Methodology of Science

Popper constructed a normative criterion by which theories must be examined for their scientific status. In sum, Popper suggests that a scientific theory must explain, predict, contain falsifiable propositions, and be corroborated in the sense of not being falsified in repeated tests by an acceptable falsification process in the world of science. Popper's approach to scientific theories is ahistorical in that the evolution of scientific theories is not seen in the context of historical process. Kuhn's book, *The Structure of Scientific Revolution* (112), is a total break with either the position of conventionalists or that of the hypothetic-deductive model. The works of B. M. Kedrov (91, 93, 95, 96) in the 1960s on the nature of scientific discovery are similar in direction to where discoveries in science are viewed as leaps and historical processes.

In rejecting the analytical approach of the conventionalists and the hypothetic-deductive model, Kuhn places emphasis not on normative prescription like Popper but, rather, on positive description on how scientific truth is found. Implicit in Kuhn's analytic work is some notion of science that is either characteristic of scientific theory or the objective of enterprise of science. For Kuhn, the normal science is a problem-solving activity in the context of the framework of scientific orthodoxy. He compares science with puzzle solving, where one believes that the puzzle has a solution in the end. Given an orthodox framework of science, scientists pick up those problems that they perceive as having possible solutions; the anomalies are usually ignored up to a point. Revolutionary science emerges as a consequence of repeated refutations and mounting anomalies. The revolutions in science are exceptions, but progress in science is due to these revolutions.

Every scientific discipline has passed through a preparadigm stage, where there is no general agreement on its fundamentals. Physics passed through the preparadigm stage before Newton, says Kuhn. Once a paradigm takes hold of a scientific community, the science goes through a long period during which the status quo is preserved and is interrupted only by discontinuous jumps. One paradigm is replaced by another as a result of these jumps, with no conceptual bridge between them for communication.

Kuhn uses the term "paradigm" in a dictionary sense, but he also employs the term to denote the choice of problems and set of techniques, as may be infered from his statement: "These I take to be universally recognized scientific achievements that for a time are model problems and solutions to a community of practitioners" (112, p. 182). Kuhn redefines paradigm in his 1970 edition of the same book with a disciplinary matrix. In spite of the change in language, the focus of the argument remains the same, as "the entire constellation of beliefs, values, techniques, and so on shared by the community" (112, p. 182). Kuhn describes the course of science where the practitioners (of science) from an undeclared college in the sense that they are in agreement on the problems that require solution and on the general form that the solutions should take. The scientific investigations of this undeclared college of practitioners, within the context of an accepted paradigm, is described as the normal course of science.

The normal science is a self-sustaining cumulative process of puzzle-solving activity within the context of a common analytical framework. In-depth studies are made within a given framework. The breakdown comes with a proliferation of theories and an appearance of methodological controversies. This stage resembles the preparadigm period. A new framework that offers solutions to the neglected puzzles and anomalies emerges from the controversies as a resolution. The new framework is corroborated by conquering the old one. Then, there is a kind of gestalt switch in the sense of total transformation.

The concept of gestalt switch has been criticized. It is said that scientific resolutions as we know them took several generations for their completion and that a state of dramatic conversion or gestalt switch did not take place. Kuhn asserts that his concept of scientific revolution is not only referring to the major revolutions like Copernican, Newtonian, Darwinian, or Einsteinian but also directed at minor changes within particular scientific fields.

Kuhn's method of analysis of methodology is more historical and descriptive. Through a dialectical process, he shows how old theories disappear and new theories emerge because of a problem-solving mechanism. At the same time, he recognizes the importance of normative judgment of scientific revolutions. "A very different approach to this whole network of problems has been developed by Karl R. Popper who denies the existence of any verification procedures at all. Instead, he emphasizes the importance of falsification, . . . the role thus attributed to falsification is much like the one this essay assigns to anomalous experience" (112, p. 146).

Contrary to Popper, Kuhn is suspicious of cognitive factors like epistemological rationality. He seems to suggest that sociological factors like hierarchy, authority, and reference group are more important to the scientific community in determining scientific behavior. He argues that: "Nevertheless anomalous experience may not be identical with falsifying one. Instead I doubt that the latter exists" (112, p. 146).

We can summarize Kuhn's ideas as follows:

Theories should be evaluated in their historical perspective rather than on the basis of cognitive rationality.

Every science has passed through a period when there was no agreement on fundamentals among scientists. Kuhn calls it a "preparadigm" stage.

All sciences reach a point of development where the participants agree on fundamentals. They agree on the problems to be solved and the general direction that the solutions should take. Kuhn categorizes this shared world outlook of a scientific community as a paradigm.

Within an established paradigm, the scientific community follows the normal course of science. The problems and their solutions are standardized, and certain anomalies are ignored. At this stage, in-depth studies are done without questioning the status quo of the paradigms.

When the number and significance of anomalies increase, some scientists start questioning the existing paradigm. They try to develop a new framework in which the anomalies can be resolved. A conflict, therefore, arises between the old paradigm and an emerging one, generating a scientific conflict. The resolution of this conflict leads to a revolution in science.

When the anomalies can be solved within the framework of the new paradigm, a debate ensues among the scientists. This stage of science has similar properties to the preparadigm stage, during which, according to Kuhn, there is no communication between the proponents of the old and the new paradigms.

With the passage of time, the new paradigm conquers the old paradigm, and there is a conversion of scientists to the new paradigm. This is like a "Gestalt switch," says Kuhn.

A critical examination of Kuhn's system of thought reveals an implicitly held idea as to how science and nonscience may be demarcated. The concept of paradigm seems to be anchored on Kuhn's implicit position of what constitutes a good scientific practice. Given that the scientific enterprise is about problem solving and that such problem solving takes place in a paradigmatic framework, how do the practitioners of science know that a particular theory or edifice constitutes a solution to a problem? Within any ruling paradigm, therefore, there is a criterion for examining the scientific correctness of the solution. Although Kuhn discusses the criteria of normal science, he leaves unanswered the question as to how the work of a scientist is accepted to be a solution to a problem in a ruling paradigm.

Anomalous experiences constitute a test of changes of paradigms; they say nothing, however, about whether the accepted solutions are incorrect relative to a defined problem but wrongly accepted in a given paradigm. There is no way of knowing this in Kuhn's system. Kuhn rejects Popper's falsificationism but does not explicitly acknowledge the acceptance of verificationism. Thus, one is left with an important dilemma as to how two different works that claim to provide different solutions to a problem in a ruling paradigm may be assessed as to their relative accuracy to the "puzzles that characterize normal science" where data-theory fits are plagued by incompleteness and imperfection.

Is the process of scientific discovery different from the process of assessing the "truth" of the scientific discovery, or does the former include the latter? These questions and their answers are important if one conceives the establishment of scientific truth or solutions of scientific problems of interest, along with interparadigm and intrapara-digm chances as processes that proceed from living contemplations to cognitive abstractions and from cognitive abstractions to human practices, and that:

At the level of direct observation and empirical cognition, a scientific discovery presents itself as the establishment of a new fact. At the level of abstract theoretical thought, it presents itself as a theoretical generalization and explanation of facts already known and the prediction of new ones; as the discovery of a new law, the creation of a new theory, the propounding of a new hypothesis. At the level of practical verification and utilization of scientific knowledge, it presents itself as technical invention. (96, p. 16)

Scientific discovery, conceived as such, allows us to relate the role of Kuhn's concept of paradigm to Kedrov's concept of "barrier" and how they relate to generate the dialectic of discovery. Scientific discovery is a victory for increased human ability to understand, control, and manage the social and natural environment with a respectable degree of success. The road toward this victory is rough, slippery, turbulent, and uncertain. The characteristics of this road are very well captured by Kedrov's statement: "On the road to truth there arises, in the minds of men, a definite 'barrier' preventing them from elevating themselves to a higher level, even if the attainment of this level has become not only possible but necessary from the standpoint of the general development of science. The system of views on the object under investigation that has taken shape and become traditional in science comprises this cognitive 'barrier'" (196, p. 23).

This barrier is the paradigm that Kuhn references when speaking about the members of a particular college of science. The destructions of the barriers that stand in the way of scientific discoveries are equivalent to Kuhn's interparadigm changes. Scientific discovery, therefore, is nothing more than a breakthrough of cognitive barriers on the road to scientific truth. A question still remains as to how and when do we know that a scientific truth has been found and that the goal of the scientific enterprise is the discovery of truth. The growth of scientific knowledge in accord with the hypothesis of Kuhn's scientific revolution has been subjected to an empirical test by J. D. Sterman (220). Let us turn our attention to Lakatos and his Scientific Research Program (SRP).

Scientific Research Program

Imre Lakatos' SRP purports that clusters of more or less interconnected theories should be appraised (120). Individual theories are not the appropriate units to be appraised. As a particular research strategy, or SRP, encounters falsification, it undergoes changes in its auxiliary assumptions that may be content increasing or content decreasing. If "excess empirical content" is contained in successive formulations over its predecessors, it is said to be theoretically progressive. On the other hand, if endless ad hoc adjustments are added to accommodate new facts, it is degenerating. The distinctions are not absolute but are, rather, relative. They are applicable over a period of time, instead of at a particular point in time.

According to Lakatos, the theories have two layers: "hard core" and "protective belt." The hard core is treated as irrefutable by the methodological decision of its supporters. It contains, besides purely metaphysical beliefs, a positive heuristic and a negative heuristic; a list of "dos" and "don'ts." The protective belt is the flexible part of an SRP, and it is here that the hard core is combined with auxiliary assumptions to form the specific testable theories with which an SRP earns a scientific reputation. Lakatos asserts that the metaphysics in science is kept out of sight. He sums up his thesis as follows: "The history of science is the history of research programs rather than of theories. All research programs may be characterized by their "hard core" surrounded by a protective belt of auxiliary hypotheses which has to bear the brunt of tests" (120, p. 49).

Lakatos, arguing along Popper's lines, stresses that an acceptable theory should yield better predictions than its rival theory. It means that when two rival theories are under scrutiny, the choice principle is the predictive power. In the Popperian system, one needs two theories for comparison and acceptability. From the two theories, one is chosen on the basis of rationally constructed scientific criteria. In other words, scientists choose one theory over another on the basis of normative rationality. Lakatos applies the same concept by suggesting that two SRPs are needed for comparison and rational choice. He cites the example of Newtonians who moved to Einsteinians' SRP around 1905. He interprets the movement as if scientists had acted after comparing the methodologies of both SRPs. He furthers his claim by stating that all history of science can be similarly described as the rational preference of scientists.

The following is the summary of Lakatos' standpoint on the evaluation of scientific theories.

Every scientific field has research programs that contain clusters of theories. Research programs, instead of individual theories, should be evaluated.

"Hard core" and "protective belts" are two layers of scientific theories. The hard core contains the fundamental metaphysical ideas that cannot be questioned. The protective belt is composed of the operational part of the theory.

A theory is better than its rival if it yields better predictions and ever-increasing empirical content.

Internal history of science has a priority over the external history. Scientists choose one theory over another on a rational basis.

A research program is judged to be progressive in comparison to its competitor if it has "excess empirical content."

A research program is considered degenerating if new facts must be accommodated by making endless ad hoc adjustments.

A theory or a scientific research program is rejected if it is degenerating.

Skepticism and Anarchism

N. R. Hanson, M. Polanyi, and S. Toulmin have softened the strict Popperian normative standards (18). P. K. Feyerabend has carried it further to the point of anarchism (50). They all agree that logical and empirical justification of theories cannot be reduced to its historical origins. They also refute ex post appraisal of validity from the genesis of theories. They join Kuhn and Lakatos in rejecting the ahistorical Popperian approach and stress the public and cooperative character of scientific knowledge. Scientific theories must be appraised in terms of observations that are, at least in principle, available to all observers (169).

Another major point stressed by these writers is that all observations are theory-laden. They argue that the acts of perception such as seeing, touching, or hearing are selective and conditioned by prior conceptualization. If we take facts as theory-laden and couple these with Kuhn's notion of content losses in successive theories and paradigms, then the competing theoretical systems become difficult to compare. In fact, we reach a point where the choice of a particular theory becomes an irrational act (52, p. 179). This kind of anarchist perspective has been further broadened by Feyerabend in his book,

Against Method (50). Feyerabend's main arguments may be summarized as follows:

There are no canons of scientific methodology that have not been violated at some time in history.

The thesis that science grows by incorporating new theories is a myth. Overlapping between rival theories is very rare.

Scientific progress occurs because the scientists have no philosophy of science, and the only principle that does not inhibit the progress is that "anything goes."

The epistemological position of the anarchists is logically disturbing. The anarchists' position denies any rational path to knowing and good decision making. By this position, science and nonscience are indistinguishable and, hence, the same, as implied by Feyerabend's statement that "anything goes." In other words, the anarchists accept no limitation on admissible space of scientific and nonscientific knowledge.

In this book, a criticism of the accuracy of models of methodology of science as a rational process is welcome, acceptable, and encouraged. The denial of the existence of a rational process of inquiry for which an epistemological search is required renders the subject matter of philosophy of science empty. If the position of the anarchists holds, that "anything goes" is a principle that does not inhibit progress, then they should have no criticism for either Popperian or Lakatonian or Kuhnian or any other position, including that of the anarchists.

It may be pointed out to the anarchists and those involved in the study of methods that the objective of discovering rationality in scientific inquiry and research is to ascertain the consistency that may be observed in any satisfactory scientific research process and, thus, deduce from the observed regularities certain rules that may be followed if the objective of the scientist is to be realized. These deduced rules of successful scientific research (as measured against objectives) are then used to prescribe guidelines for good scientific research and practice — in other words, to make the rules of the game in the theater of science explicit.

The systematic explanation or the abstraction of regular patterns associated with successful scientific research and the conversion of these abstracted regularities into prescriptive rules of "good" scientific practice constitute what we would like to view as the subject matter of philosophy of science. It is a theory on theories, a metatheory. Its scope of interest is viewed as the critical investigation into the morphology of rules of good scientific research and the development of metaalgorithms to realize these rules. For the metatheory to be useful, the abstracted rules must be systematized into a calculus for discriminating among alternative paths of scientific research on the basis of which a good scientific practice is followed. The set of these rules for good scientific practice is the *human intelligence* in the practice of science. Practices of science are said to be rational, and human inquiries into nature and society are said to be scientific if they follow this human intelligence. The criterion for demarcation between science and nonscience is a decision-choice construct that is also subject to critical analysis. A similar argument on epistemology and decision-choice rationality has been offered by K. K. Dompere (41).

All discussions on philosophy of science that directly or indirectly center around criteria for validating the scientific character of human inquiry, implicitly or explicitly, assume that there is a rational path or human intelligence to good scientific practice and that this human intelligence of good scientific practice can be and must be found. The search of validation is to limit subjective disagreements and improve consensus. The search for a rational path of good scientific practice is to minimize cost and maximize the probability of discovery of scientific truth. The position of the anarchistic methodologists is chaotic and cannot help to explain the setup of referring systems in publications, scientific research, and awards of research grants.

All philosophical systems on every aspect of methods of science are attempts to give rational accounts of scientific practice, not of the fact that we have human inquiry about things, processes, and phenomena, but on what code of conduct must good scientific practice be based, and not only that reality exists, but also how we consent to a scientific discovery of aspects of the real world of things, processes, and phenomena. The conviction, here, is that philosophy of science is a general theory about science and scientific practices, and cognitive practices in different areas of human endeavors are mere specificities that give content to the test of the implied hypothesis of metatheories on science and scientific practice. Fundamentally, the psychology of scientific research and discovery remains invariant in time and place. This invariance principle calls on philosophy of science, as a meta-theory, to examine stable relationships among key variables that affect the quality and outcomes of scientific practice.

It may be noted that, without a metatheory on scientific practice, scientific knowledge inevitably will remain confused and accumulation of scientific ideas will remain as a cognitive map of incomprehensible collection of opinions where "everything goes" and every opinion counts without any logical guidance. Scientific practice without metatheory is mere confusion, and a metatheory without the practice of science is empty and unworthy of social effort. This entails that in understanding scientific practice, philosophy of science calls for analysis of facts and events of human search for knowledge and then attempts to see how these facts and events fit into the practice of science and, hence, constitute the experiences of scientific discovery. In this respect, philosophy of science, like the history of science, may enrich the human

TABLE 2.1
Summary of the Main Ideas on Criteria of Science: Major Schools

Conventionalism
>The aim of scientific investigations is to discover the truth.
>The truth is reached by induction.
>Once the general laws are discovered through induction, the various aspects of phenomena can be explained by inference.

The Hypothetic-Deductive Model of Scientific Explanation
>A theory must contain at least a universal law and a set of initial conditions for explanation.
>Symmetry of explanation and prediction that can be verified against experience is part of a theory.
>The truth in the universal law can be verified against experience.
>A theory is scientific if it explains and predicts.
>The objective of scientific theory is explanation and prediction; hence, the criterion of acceptance is the degree of explanation and prediction that is contained in the theory.

Falsificationism — Popper
>A criterion for demarcating science from nonscience is needed for the advancement of science.
>The construction of the criterion should consider the logic of science only. The psychological, sociological, and historical conditions and factors must be excluded.
>A scientific theory should at least yield propositions that can, in principle, be falsified.
>A scientific theory must contain explanations and predictions (i.e., empirical content) relative to empirical data.
>A scientific theory must be internally consistent in its logical construct.
>A theory is rejected to be unscientific if (three to five) conditions are not met. A scientific theory is rejected if it is not corroborated (i.e., falsified). Simpler, general, and corroborated theories must be preferred and, hence, selected.

Historical School — Kuhn's Paradigm
>A scientific theory must belong to a paradigmatic system.
>A paradigm consists of a set of problems, solutions to conquered ones, acceptable structure and form of solutions, constellation of beliefs, values, methods, and techniques acceptable to a community of a particular science in the course of normal science.
>The objective of normal science is problem solving defined in the context of scientific orthodoxy.
>A theory is considered to be scientific if it satisfies all the conditions of problem specification, morphology of solutions, and the nature of analytical construct as agreed to by the practitioners in the ruling paradigmatical system.
>A scientific theory is accepted as valid within a given paradigm if it contributes to the problem specification, solution, technique and method, or analytical construct as accepted by paradigm's practitioners. Thus, the degree to which a theory contributes to the problem-solving activities constitutes the criterion of validity and acceptance in paradigm.
>Paradigms are accepted or rejected in whole but not in part.

20

Table 2.1, continued

Historical School — Kuhn's Paradigm, continued

    An existing paradigm is either retained or abandoned by means of a criterion of the number and significance of accumulated anomalies.

    A new paradigm is accepted in place of an existing paradigm by the means of a test criterion of the degree of success in solving the accumulated anomalies in the existing paradigm, in addition to providing solutions to already solved problems.

Scientific Research Programs — Lakatos

    Every area of science has research programs.

    A research program consists of a cluster of interconnected theories (subtheories) that are testable, as well as a set of problems and anomalies.

    A theory consists of a main hypothesis (laws), hard core-auxiliary hypothesis (assumptions-protective belt), empirical content, and a problem-solving mechanism.

    A criterion for accepting a theory into a research program is that it satisfies the previous idea in addition to the requirements of scientific orthodoxy (explanation, logical consistency, and prediction) as well as dealing with a solution to one of the problems in the set.

    A criterion for accepting an SRP over others is the degree to which it accounts for all the facts in others, the degree to which it provides extra empirically confirmed predictions, and the degree to which it adds to its accumulated empirical content.

    The objective of science is prediction and problem solving.

Skeptics and Anarchists

    All canons of methodology of science have been violated at some point in history.

    The thesis that the growth of science proceeds by incorporation of new theories is a myth.

    Overlapping between rival theories is very rare.

    Progress in science takes place because scientists neither have philosophy of science nor act rationally.

    The "anything goes" principle is one that does not inhibit scientific discovery and progress.

    Science and nonscience cannot be separated.

---

quest for knowledge and help to define the path of progress of science and general cognition. Here lies the social utility of human effort in philosophy of science. A similar position on philosophy and society has been expressed by Nkrumah (161). The main ideas and implied criteria on various positions are provided in Table 2.1.

METHODOLOGY AS APPLIED IN ECONOMICS

Methodology of Classical Economics

The Scottish historical school never formulated its methodology explicitly. It appears that it had a firm belief in the stage theory of history that rests on the interaction among different modes of production along with certain eternal human nature. It seems to suggest that theories should be simple and elegant. A theory having these characteristics is adequate for explanation in both physical and social sciences. Adam Smith's article *The Principles which Lead and Direct Philosophical Inquiries, Illustrated by the History of Anatomy* was an erudite contribution in this regard (218, 219b).

Adam Smith was very impressed with Newton's theory of gravity, which could explain the movements of diverse bodies with a single principle. He stressed the advantage of being able to explain different phenomena by a single familiar principle more than predictions. Smith, therefore, seemed to favor the principle of explanation over the principle of prediction.

By accepting the definition of scientific theory of the hypothetic-deductive school, Adam Smith tried to explain economic phenomena on the basis of historical, institutional, and factual aspects of methodological deductivism in a more or less informal way. On the other hand, Ricardo adopted what we now call "the hypothetic-deductive model of scientific explanation" to vigorously deny that facts can ever speak for themselves. It is very difficult to determine whether Ricardo regarded the predictions of his system as purely conditional tendencies or as unconditional historical facts.

Malthus inexplicitly had a strong objection to Ricardo's concept of long-run equilibrium. He always held that Ricardo had abandoned the inductive method of Smith. Nevertheless, Malthus' style of reasoning was identical to Ricardo's. Both followed Adam Smith. They believed in the natural law of economics as presented by Adam Smith. They also agreed on the natural order inherent in capitalist economic processes and sought to explain them. The emphasis was on explanation and prediction as is revealed by the law of population and war.

Senior and John Stuart Mill formulated the methodology of political economy. Senior was the first one to make a distinction between positive science and art of economics. He gave the first explicit formulation of the general propositions that are essential to economics (18), such as the desire to maximize wealth with least sacrifice, the means of subsistence increasing slower than the population, that labor produces net positive product with machine, and that agriculture experiences diminishing returns.

Mill kept Senior's distinction of positive and normative science. He defined economics as "mental science" that basically is concerned with human motives and modes of conduct in economic life. Methodologically, therefore, Mill accepted the position of positivist description of science in addition to subjective judgments. Mill says that "economic man" is not the whole man, so, we should only try to predict his behavior in economic affairs. Mill's fictional man was adopted by Alfred Marshal and almost by all the modern economists. Mill's fictional economic man led him to characterize political economy as essentially an abstract science that employs "method a priori." He used the term "a priori" in the sense of reasoning from an assumed hypothesis that is based on introspection, as opposed to "a posteriori," which refers to a specific experience, that is, facts. A hypothesis, therefore, may be assumed or derived from a logical system without being based directly on facts. In this respect, he states that "the conclusion of political economy consequently, like those of geometry, are only true . . . in the abstract" (145, p. 325). Scientific truth in economic theory is a logical one.

Accordingly, Mill considered political economy as composed of deductive analysis that is based on assumed psychological premises that are abstracted from all noneconomic aspects of human behavior. To apply the principles of political economy, all relevant circumstances that are disturbing causes have to be taken into account. In this way, Mill introduced induction combined with deduction. The mixed deductive-inductive method of a priori is the only appropriate method, because controlled experimentations on human conduct are not possible. The statement that, in the study of principles of political economy, all circumstances have to be taken into account is very close to the position of verificationism. The need to verify led him to the discussion of "tendency laws." Mill clarified the issue by suggesting that a tendency may be regarded as a power acting with a certain intensity in a direction. This tendency will produce expected results, given the state of "disturbances," which now are called "ceteris paribus" in economics.

Mill's system of logic was an attempt to demolish Kant's a priori propositions. He devoted a whole book to the defense of the inductive method, but when he turned to "moral science" in the closing section, he declared that inductive methods are not appropriate. Furthermore, he is remembered among the methodologists for his treatment of four steps of methods of induction — the methods of agreement, difference residues, concomitant variation, and his analysis of causation. It is, thus, surprising for him to admit that these canons are not fit for the social sciences. In the last section of his logic, he asserts a methodological monism and insists that positive analysis is the key to science in the social sciences, but again, he did not state his methodology in his *Principles*.

Mill's *Principles* retained the Ricardian system. To Mill, the test of a theory in social science is not its ex ante predictive accuracy but its ex post explanatory power. Scientific theory, therefore, must seek to explain "what there is." If a theory fails to predict accurately, a search should be made for supplementary causes, because the theory is correct only as far as it goes by the nature of its assumptions.

John Eliot Cairnes gave a finishing touch to the "classical methodology" in his *Character and Logical Method of Political Economy* (25). Cairnes was more dogmatic in denying that economic theories can ever be refuted by facts. In other words, verification and falsification of truth are not possible in economic science. For him, political economy is hypothetic-deductive science that will "correspond with facts only in the absence of disturbing causes — in other words, they represent, not positive but hypothetic truths" (25, p. 64).

There is nothing hypothetical about the premises of political economy, because they are based on indubitable facts of human nature. Political economy, therefore, is a hypothetical science in the sense that it makes conditional predictions about events that are subject to a "ceteris paribus" clause. Cairnes concludes that economic laws "can be refuted by showing either that the principle and conditions assumed do not exist, or that the tendency which the law affirms does not follow as a necessary consequence from its assumptions" (25, p. 110). In short, scientific theories in economics, according to Cairnes, are refuted by either proving that the assumptions are unrealistic or demonstrating a presence of a logical inconsistency. A theory, therefore, should not be abandoned because of refuted prediction. A theory in economics is judged to be scientific if the assumptions are realistic and the argument is logically consistent. A test of the scientific validity of a theory in economics is based on the realism of its assumptions and the consistency of its logical construct.

Neville Keynes admired Adam Smith as an ideal economist because Smith combined methods of historical inductivism with abstract deductivism; he emphasizes that even the a priori logical method of the "classicals" begins and ends with empirical observations. Thus, facts and logic are the conceptual tools of scientific inquiry. He summarizes the tradition of Senior-Mill-Cairnes in five points (97, pp. 12–20).

There is a distinction between positive science and normative political economy.

To some extent, economic aspects can be isolated from the social phenomena.

Method a posteriori is not appropriate for economics.

A priori is the right method, starting from indubitable facts of human nature.

Economic man is an abstraction and political economy is a science of tendencies only, not of matter of facts.

Lionel Robbins restated the classical methodology amid the rising tide of institutionalists and inductivists. He argued in his essay, *An Essay on the Nature and Significance of Economic Science* (175), that economics is neutral with respect to economic policy. His definition of economics "as science which studies human behavior as a relationship between ends and scarce means which have alternative uses" (175, p. 16) purposely captures an aspect rather than the total human behavior.

To Robbins, the basic postulates of economics are a priori analytical truths. He suggests that : "In economics, as we have seen, the ultimate constituents of our fundamental generalizations are known to us by immediate acquaintance. In natural science they are known inferentially" (175, p. 105).

Robbins claims that economic effects never can be predicted in quantitative terms. Economists use qualitative calculus, which may not apply in particular cases. He rejects the historical school's stress on relativity and historicity of facts and shows deep contempt for institutionalists. Remaining loyal to the classical tradition, he argues that "the validity of a particular theory is a matter of its logical derivation from the general assumptions which it makes. But its applicability to a given situation depends upon the extent to which its concepts actually reflect the forces operating in that situation" (32, p. 120). Thus, given the basic assumptions, the validity of a theory in economics is judged by its logical consistency and the realism of its assumptions.

The main points of the methodology of classical economists may be summed up as follows:

Assumptions are the most important part of economic theory.

Assumptions are indubitable facts of life. They are taken as a priori truths that establish the environment and boundaries of validity of a theory as well as area of applicability.

Given the factual correctness of the assumptions, the construct of a scientific theory in economics is a matter of logical syllogism.

From simplified assumptions like economic man or diminishing returns, one can arrive at simplified predictions.

Criteria for accepting the scientific character of an economic theory are realism of assumptions and logical consistency.

Theories cannot be refuted on the basis of invalid predictions. The predictions may be wrong because all the relevant circumstances of the theory have not been taken into account in the empirical work.

The demands of a theory in social sciences should be different from natural science.

As it stands, the main methodological structure of the classical economists allows us to test the factual correctness of the assumed conditions of the theory. The validity of the theory cannot be subjected to empirical test by either verificationism or falsificationism. The main body of the theory is tested on its logical consistency. The theory cannot be faulted by facts when the assumptions are accepted. In this sense, a degenerating theory, in the sense of Popper, can always stand the test if the assumptions are accepted as satisfying the conditions of realism.

The Historical School

The historical school adopts the position that the so-called laws discovered by classical economists are neither absolutely valid nor perpetually applicable. According to the members of the historical school, the laws of economics necessarily exist relative to time and space. Because economic laws operate within the framework of constantly changing environment, the historists argue that it is necessary to replace the classical method of deduction by induction to discover the nature of the environment. In the view of the historical school, the study of political economy should proceed by collection of a mass of historical data from which generalizations will be eventually drawn. In other word, we must proceed from the specific to the general.

Scholars such as Wilhelm Roscher of the older school and Karl Knies and Gustav Schmoller from the younger generation took the position that nothing can be learned by using the deductive method of reasoning. The following are the main points of the historical school:

Deductive method used by classical economists is not valid because it generalizes on the basis of a priori notions.

Inductive method should be applied to abstract the generalizations.

Human behavior can be understood only by collecting historical data and not by theoretical construct based on sometimes unfounded assumptions.

The Austrian School

Under the leadership of Ludwig von Mises and Friedrick Hayek, the modern Austrian school attacked methodological monism in favor of a methodological individualism. Von Mises' attack on the monist view of methodology of science is based on his distinction and insistence on dualism in science where different cognitive paths to knowing are required in search of truth in social and physical sciences. In some of his works, which are represented in *Human Action: A Treatise on Economics* (146) and *The Ultimate Foundation of Economic Science* (147), von Mises presents an argument that the assumption of a purposeful individual action is an absolute prerequisite for explaining all behavior, including economic behavior, which constitutes a synthetic a priori principle that speaks for itself.

He states that "in studying the actions of individuals, we learn also everything about the collectives and society. For the collective has no existence and reality but in the actions of individuals. . . . The only way to a cognition of collectives is the analysis of the conduct of its members" (147, p. 81). Accordingly, von Mises concludes that "the ultimate yardstick of an economic theorem's correctness or incorrectness is solely reason unaided by experience" (146, p. 858). Blaug has countered von Mises's point by suggesting that : "Although all this is said to be a continuation of Senior, Mill, and Cairnes, the notion that even the verification of assumptions is unnecessary in economics is, as we have seen, a travesty and not a restatement of classical methodology" (18, p. 92). The position of the New Austrian School reduces to a methodological inductionism without empirical test either on assumptions or on the derived propositions.

The methodology of Austrians can be summarized in the following points:

Methodological individualism as an a priori heuristic axiom, derived from the fundamental postulate of existence of individual consciousness.

Suspicion for general-to-particular analysis and, hence, derived results from macroeconomic-theoretic constructs.

The laws of human action are qualitative where free will precludes quantitative laws.

Categorical rejection of mathematical economics, econometrics, and testing of qualitative predictions of economic phenomena.

More stress on convergence of market equilibrium rather than analyzing the properties of state of final equilibrium.

Economic theory and a priori propositions not subject to empirical test.

Methodology of Modern Economics

The debate on methodology in economic science is just as intense as that of the subject matter and its position as science. The debate includes positivists, instrumentalists, and many more. We shall now examine the main ideas of the various positions.

Positivists

Popper had already published his book on logic in 1934 (170), but it was Ayer's *Language, Truth and Logic* (7a) that carried the day. Torrence Hutchison then tried to apply the principles of logical positivism, which were formulated by Ayer and other logical positivists, to economics (83). Like the positivists' differentiation between "analytical" and "synthetic" propositions, the heart of Hutchison's argument is an exhaustive classification of economic propositions into tautological and empirical components (83, p. 13). Hutchison rejects those economic propositions that have unspecified ceteris paribus clauses as tautologies. He claims that tautological statements do not forbid any conceivable occurrence of the state of the world, but empirical propositions do forbid at least some conceivable occurrences of these states.

The core of Hutchison's methodology is that economic theory should limit itself to empirically testable propositions. There is some degree of vagueness in Hutchison's position regarding the prescription of criteria of testability of assumptions or the prediction of the theory or both for judging the scientific validity of a theory in economics. Machlup alleges that Hutchison is an example of an ultraempiricist who "insists on independent verification of all assumptions by objective data obtained through sense observation, . . . a program that begins with facts rather than assumption" (126, pp. 143–44).

Hutchison clarifies his position by suggesting that it is the "finished propositions" of economics that should be testable, not the assumptions. The overall impression created by his argument is that empirical work in economics should be applied to the assumptions as well as to the predictions of the theory. In this respect, Machlup suggests that the fundamental assumption of rationality is not empirically testable (126, p. 147).

Frank Knight expressed irritation with Hutchison's work and termed it "positivist" (105, pp. 75–53). Knight attempts to revive the a priorism by claiming that truth in economics means the same thing as truth in natural sciences. He asserts that verification of economic behavior by any "empirical procedure" is not possible, because of its being goal directed. Moreover, verification of economic behavior depends on intuitive knowledge for its meaning. The main points of the positivist methodology as applied to economic reasoning are as follows:

Scientists should concern themselves only with the empirical world, which should constitute the environment of theoretical construct.

Differentiation should be made between meaningful and meaningless statements on empirical grounds.

Only those statements that can be verified by empirical data should be considered as scientifically meaningful.

All propositions of a theory, including the assumptions, should be tested for their factual correctness and empirical validity.

Operationalist

Percy Bridgman constructed a refined form of methodology of operationalism in his book, *The Nature of Physical Theory* (23b). His basic objective is to provide a methodological unity between abstract theoretical concepts and measurements in physical experiments within the field of science.

Paul Samuelson also tried to further the operationalist tradition in his book (190). He adopts a methodological operationalism by presenting a theoretical construct that seeks a correspondence between the empirical world and theoretical propositions where such propositions are supported by operationally meaningful theorems. The main propositions and operationally meaningful theorems may then be subjected to empirical and logical consistency tests. As such, Samuelson suggests that "our theory is meaningless in the operational sense unless it does imply some restrictions upon observable quantities by which it could conceivably be refuted" (190, p. 7). (He explicitly argues the operationalist position in [193] and [194].)

Machlup has strongly objected to methodological operationalism on the grounds that a theoretical construct composed only of operational concepts that are measurable in terms of physical quantities would constitute a lower-level cognitive generalization about the physical world. Given other criticisms in addition to those of Machlup, Gordon (62) attempts to tighten the main ideas of methodological operationalism as it may be applied to theoretical constructs in analytical economics. He suggests that operational propositions should be defined as ones that state or imply operations that, when performed, will in principle result as tests for the propositions.

The major points of methodological operationalism are:

Theories should yield propositions that are operational in the sense that concrete scientific functions can be performed through them.

Scientific theories must relate to the real world through operational propositions that establish correspondence with the empirical world.

The operational propositions should be able to indicate at last the direction of the qualitative change.

The set of operational propositions about quality and quantity must satisfy empirical conditions and conditions of logical consistency.

It may be pointed out that the epistemological meaning of the concept of operational proposition depends on how one sees the subject matter of science and the objective of enterprise of science. If one considers the primary objective of scientific enterprise to be the explanation of reality, one ends up with a specific conceptual interpretation of operational proposition. A different conceptual interpretation ensues when one views the primary objective of the enterprise of science as the improvement of reality relative to human existence. In this case, operational propositions are viewed in terms of problem solving, which then leads us to examine the epistemic positions of Kedrov (93, 95, 96) and Kuhn (112).

Instrumentalist

Methodological instrumentalism has been activated in economic scholarship over two decades. The basic tenets in their contemporary form are advanced by M. Friedman in his 1953 essay (52). Instrumentalism is derived from conventionalism, which is anchored on the idea that false assumptions may lead to valid consequences. As such, theories constructed on false assumptions may have great predictive power. The methodological instrumentalists carry this epistemological position further. They abandon the concept of validity of theories based on explanation. They contend that theories are neither true nor false but merely instruments for predicting outcomes. Here, the object of scientific theory is conceived not in terms of how well it explains but how well it predicts, even when the initial assumptions do not satisfy the conditions of factual correctness.

Although accepting methodological unity in scientific works, Friedman makes an important distinction between normative science and positive science. Stressing the unity of science, Friedman, like the preceding instrumentalists, emphasizes the degree of predictive power. He states: "Viewed as a body of substantive hypothesis, theory is to be judged by its predictive power for the class of phenomena which it is intended to 'explain.' Only factual evidence can show whether it is 'right' or 'wrong' or better, tentatively 'accepted' as valid or 'rejected.' ... The only relevant test of the validity of a hypothesis is comparison of its predictions with experience. The hypothesis is rejected if its predictions are contradicted" (52, pp. 8–9). As it stands, the instrumentalist position is not different from the hypothetic-deductive model of science. In fact, in this context, prediction and explanation are different sides of the same coin.

Stating the fundamental requirements of a theory, Friedman suggests that if a theory predicts well, its assumptions do not have to be realistic. He declares that, as a matter of fact, the assumptions are better if they are not realistic.

This methodological position of Friedman generated an intense debate about relevance, realism, and the role of assumptions in theoretical constructs about economic phenomena. It may, however, be pointed out that Friedman's irrelevance-of-assumption thesis, as it came to be known, is a degenerating methodological version of conventionalism that rests on the basic acknowledgment that false assumptions may have correspondence with outcomes (18, 132, 195, 197). The irrelevance-of-assumption thesis is against the classical methodologists, particularly the position of Cairnes (25). Because a test of consistency is not emphasized, Friedman's position is also against the logical consistency thesis (73). From this conventionalist position, Friedman advanced his irrelevance-of-assumption thesis. A problem generally arises with such an extreme position as Friedman's regarding the conceptual interpretation of unrealistic assumptions.

In respect of this, Mark Blaug has tried to discern the multiplicity of interpretations that may be attached to the term "unrealistic" as used by Friedman (52, pp. 105–7).

An assumption of economic theory may be termed "unrealistic" in the sense of its being abstract. This is one of the meanings Friedman attaches to it. To Friedman, realism in assumptions means descriptively accurate in the sense that they account for all the relevant background facts and nothing is left out.

Friedman interprets the "realistic assumptions" in the sense that when we attach certain motives to the economic agent, they should be comprehensible to other human beings. For example, the assumption of utility maximization or profit maximization would be considered realistic if the individual household or a business entrepreneur is aware and conscious about the conditions of maximization.

Unrealistic assumptions may mean that they are either false or highly improbable in the light of directly observed or perceived behavior of an economic agent. Mark Blaug thinks that Friedman's critics have the third interpretation in mind (18, p. 105).

Methodologically, Friedman argues that assumptions can be used to specify the range in which a theory will be applicable; thus, "the entirely valid use of 'assumptions' in specifying the circumstances for which a theory holds is frequently, and erroneously, interpreted to mean that the assumptions can be used to determine the circumstances for which a theory holds" (52, p. 19). If one considers Friedman's instrumentalist position as part of degenerated conventionalism, then one would assign to Friedman's concept of irrelevance-of-assumption thesis the meaning that the assumptions are false in the sense that they fail to meet the conditions of factual correctness.

Friedman's methodological position has led Blaug to point out that Friedman leans heavily on G. C. Archibald's thesis: the notion that all motivational assumptions in microeconomics may be constructed as "as if" statements (4). In a way, Friedman is repudiating the methodological individualism of the neoclassical approach to economic questions by relying on a new kind of causal mechanism, namely, a dynamic selection process that rewards those businessmen who, for various reasons, act as if they were rational maximizers while penalizing with bankruptcy those who act otherwise.

The main points of the instrumentalist methodology on economic science may be summarized as follows:

All sciences have a methodological unity.

Scientific theories are instruments by which scientists perform the task of explanation and prediction.

The questions of truthfulness of the assumptions in a scientific theory are irrelevant, because successful scientific theories are based on unrealistic assumptions in the sense that they are idealized abstractions of the environment of the theory. In social science, the assumptions may not be empirically verifiable and, hence, may be irrelevant to the usefulness of theory in predicting the future behavior of the phenomenon of interest.

A scientific theory is judged to be valid and acceptable if it successfully accomplishes its intended job, the job of prediction.

A Short Reflection on Some Aspects of Methodology of Economics

The core of all these debates encapsuled in the metatheory on science is, simply, what criterion must be used in accepting a theory as scientific, in ranking scientific theories about the same phenomenon, and in validating the practice of science in different areas of human endeavor. The needed criterion for imposing scientific discipline has been at the center of the controversy and intense philosophical debate with many different cognitive eyes. The debate acquires an interesting ideological component when the subject matter of economics is placed in the topological space of science.

There are writers like S. Schoeffler (202) and A. G. Papandreou (166) who deny economics the status of science. Schoeffler seems to suggest that, unlike physical sciences, the derivation of universal laws is not possible in economics and that scientific prediction also is not possible. Papandreou offers a similar position with a different argument anchored on a distinction between models and theories, where he suggests that theories in seconomic cannot be refuted, because the relationship between theories and empirical content about economic phenomena cannot be completely verified. Joan Robinson places the study of economics on the two footings of science and propagation of ideology (176). In this respect, theories about economic phenomena are value driven, and the interpretations of scientific results get entangled in ideological slogans. Hollis and Nell have raised objections against the epistemology of neoclassical economics (81).

All the intense discussions and debates on methodology of science are shaped by what one considers to be science and the goals and objectives of the enterprise of science. Most of the discussions accept the classical concept of science as well as the objective of enterprise of science. Given the classical concept of science, differences arise among methodologists on a number of grounds where the differences show themselves as conflicts in the metatheory. One conflict involves whether a distinction between explanation and prediction is necessary and logically material. If such a distinction is of cognitive necessity, where, then, should the emphasis be placed in applying the test of scientific validity of a theory?

Another conflict arises between those who accept the classical definition of science where the objective of science is to explain and predict and those who conceive the objective of enterprise of science as improvements of reality or problem solving. Within this particular conflict, two parts of science emerge: the *explanatory science* of classical type and the *prescriptive science* of nonclassical type. Along these lines come two theory types of explanation and prescription; the methodology of their constructs and the validation of their scientific status have intensified the conflicts over many of the contested grounds of disagreement.

These conflicts bring into focus some important questions surrounding the subject matter of philosophy of science as well as the goals and objectives of metatheory. On these questions, two positions are at contest. One position views metatheory as an explanation of what the scientists do and how discoveries occur in science; this entails the construct of explanation of the process of *scientific discovery*. The other view does not have explanation as its focus; rather, it focuses on abstraction from experience, rules of good scientific practices, and successful processes to discoveries in science. These rules are then logically arranged into an *intelligent system* (rationality) for good scientific practice with the hope of improving the chances of discoveries in science by the practitioners when such an intelligent system is used. (For detailed discussions on decision-choice rationality, see Dompere [41].)

In this respect, a metatheory is viewed as a framework, a cognitive apparatus, and a thinking system that aids the user to improve the probability of scientific discovery. In other words, the metatheory is to improve reality of practices in science. A metatheory does not provide already-made rules that are immediately applicable to either the successful practice of science or the discovery of a scientific truth. It is merely a thinking system that empowers its possessor to find an efficient path of successful scientific practice, as well as the cost-effective road to the discovery of scientific truth. It is not a doctrine but a method and an organized cognitive environment of scientific activities.

Selected Reflections on Theories of Development Economics

Given the framework of methodology of science and the practices of theoretical constructs in economics, some economists have reflected on theories about the phenomenon of economic development.

Stephen Enke reviewed the development theories of the 1950s and 1960s (47). He suggests that economic development is not an academically structured branch of knowledge. His view is that economic development has attracted only those scholars who are interested in institutional and social problems, rather than quantitatively and theoretically inclined economists. The more prominent names in economics lose interest after giving very brief attention to theories of economic development.

According to Enke, economics in developed areas is characterized by abstract and deductive theorizing. This kind of methodology is not possible in development economies because there are enormous cultural variations among different countries. Monopolistic model, Keynesian theory of liquidity preference, and growth models are the latest in economic theory, but they are applied obliquely to the economies of the most underdeveloped countries. He declares that "no integrated, explicit and unique theory of development exists as of today" (47, p. 112).

Dudly Seers argues that the present economic theory is a special case that deals with the materially advanced capitalist countries (212). Economic theoreticians are familiar only with industrialized economies, and they have failed to explain why different economies grow at different rates. The construction of a "general theory" from the examples of a few Western countries is inherently improbable. The Western economies are organized in different sectors in a certain way, and economists assume this type of society everywhere. Seers says, "What is assumed is an autonomous and flexible socio-economic structure in which each human being responds individually to material incentives offered and which is subject to no formidable exogenous strains" (212, p. 55). Seers points out some other methodological limitations of economists dealings with development problems:

Static analysis is inappropriate where there is a need for social and economic changes to take place simultaneously.

The economists have a "fashionably uncommitted attitude to growth, intellectually cloaked in positivism" (166, p. 56).

Insufficient attention is paid to the social structure.

Economists are ill equipped to deal with the nonindustrialized economies in the context of world economies.

These limitations seem to curtail the ability of economists to develop a scientific theory of economic development. N. Georgescu-Roegen defined the theory as "a logical file of our factual knowledge pertaining to a certain phenomenological domain. . . . To each theory, therefore, there must correspond a specific domain of reality" (56, p. 59). Given this definition, Marxist and traditional theories do not correspond to the reality of feudal-agricultural societies because they are based on traits of the capitalist economic system. Moreover, different economies are characterized by their institutions, not by the technology they use. If this point is granted, the derived conclusion is that Marxist and traditional theories are not valid for analyzing the noncapitalist economies because important parts of capitalist institutions are absent.

P. T. Bauer has defended the use of traditional theory to solve the development problems (12). Economics, Bauer argues, is a science, which provides the tools for efficient use of economic resources, as well as determining costs, prices, and returns on different projects. There is no reasonable substitution for traditional theories to address these problems. According to Bauer, the traditional theory has not failed — it only has not been properly applied. He further contends that there has been a gross neglect of basic economic considerations and a disregard of the implications of the institutional background in the process of applying the standard theory.

Hla Myint has also argued in favor of the traditional theory by suggesting that criticism against the use of standard economic theory in development problems is unfounded. He suggests that economic theory is "ethically neutral" (153). Economic theory, Myint contends, does not look realistic when applied to development problems because inappropriate theoretical models are chosen. The problems posed by noncapitalist economies are just distortions and can be taken care of within the framework of existing theory. Myint further argues that if the standard theory has limited applications, the popular development theories of the 1950s and 1960s had also limited application to few countries like India and Pakistan. The traditional theory is relevant because no alternative economic dynamics have been discovered. He even tries to explain that the analysis of a social revolution, instead of the use of development planning, can be accommodated by traditional theory within Schumpeterian framework.

Simon Kuznets takes the opposite position by stating that the present theory and methods of analysis are not capable of analyzing the growth problem, even in industrialized countries (115). Epistemologically, the present theory and method of analysis are deficient because they do not uncover all the costs and returns when a new innovation is introduced into society, they do not conceive the growing capacity of an economy as an interplay of advancing technology and institutional and ideological adjustments, and the analysis of developing countries is complicated further because the stack of data and of economic analysis is far poorer for these countries (less developed) than for the developed countries.

Our main concern in this book is the metatheory of development economics and implied theoretical constructs. Any relative evaluation calls for a criterion, which may be explicit or implicit. The main ideas of different schools on the construction of the required criterion for assessing the scientific status of economic theories in general are summarized in Table 2.2.

TABLE 2.2
A Summary of the Main Ideas on Criterion of
Science as Applied to Economics: Major Schools

Classical Economists

Assumptions are the most important part of economic theory. They are
indubitable facts of life. They constitute a priori truths that establish the
environment and validity of a theory and its application.

Given the factual correctness of the assumptions, the construct of scientific
theory in economics is a matter of logical syllogism.

On the basis of simplified assumptions, the theory must contain predictions.

The degree of fulfillment of such predictions cannot constitute a criterion to
accept or reject a theory because all relevant circumstances cannot be
accounted for in empirical works.

The criterion for acceptance of a theory in social science must be different from
natural science.

The criterion for accepting a theory is its internal logical consistency, not an
empirical support after assumptions are accepted.

Historical School

Deductive methods used by the classical economists are invalid because the
explanations or predictions and generalization are constructed on the basis of
a prior notions.

Abstract generalizations and analysis in economics must proceed by methods of
induction.

Historical data provide the material to analyze and understand human behavior.

Economic truth is accepted on the basis of historical data.

Austrian School

Methodological individualism is taken as an a priori heuristic postulate.

Quantitative (mathematics and econometric) methods in economic analysis
leading to explanation and prediction are completely rejected.

Empirical verification of economic theory and assumptions (a priori propositions)
is rejected.

The criterion for accepting a theory in economics is based on the degree of
understanding of economic behavior derived on the basis of a priori system of
thought.

Positivist School

Empirical world constitutes the environment of theoretical construct.

Meaningful and meaningless statements in theoretical construct should be
distinguished on empirical grounds.

Scientifically meaningful statements are those that are verifiable by empirical
data.

Assumptions and theoretical propositions in economics should be tested for their
factual correctness and empirical validity.

The main objectives of scientific theory are explanation and prediction, which
should constitute the criterion for acceptance.

Table 2.2, continued

Operationalists

    Theories in economics must be composed of operational propositions that provide concrete scientific functions that can be performed through them.

    Operational propositions must relate theory to the real world by establishing a correspondence between them and the empirical world.

    Operational propositions should, at least, indicate the direction of qualitative change.

    The set of operational propositions about quality and quantity must meet conditions of logical consistency and empirical content.

    The criteria for evaluating scientific theories in economics are logical consistency, empirical content, and the degree of correctness of their operational propositions regarding quantity and quality.

Instrumentalists

    All sciences have a methodological unity.

    Scientific theories are instruments constructed by the scientists to perform tasks of explanation and prediction.

    The factual correctness of the assumptions in scientific theories is irrelevant, because successful scientific theories are based on idealized abstractions of the environment in which the theory is applicable.

    In social sciences, the assumptions may not be empirically verifiable even though the theory may be instrumentally useful for the task of prediction.

    The criterion for acceptance of scientific theory is the predictive power of the theory.

3

On the Criterion for Evaluating Scientific Theories: Problems and Methods

THE NEED FOR AN EXPLICIT EVALUATIVE CRITERION

It was mentioned in the previous chapter that some critics of theories of economic development hold the view that this branch of knowledge is not well-structured and also is not clearly defined in scientific terms. There are others who think that it is as scientific as any social science can be. This dispute is not unique to development eco-nomics. There are similar disagreements on such fundamentals in most of the social sciences. Even the natural sciences have, from time to time, passed through periods when the practitioners of a particular scientific field disagreed on the fundamental notions and content of their respec-tive fields (6, p. 88). Copernicus, complaining about the confusion of the astronomers of his period, said, "(astronomers are so) inconsistent in these investigations that they cannot even explain or observe the constant length of the seasonal year" (34, p. 138).

All these arguments and disagreements stem from the nature of the concept and definition of science to which one subscribes. Additionally, they stem from what is believed to be the major enterprise of scientists. From the concept and definition of science that are explicitly or im-plicitly held and from what is believed to be the enterprise of scientists, certain requirements of scientific theories are advanced. The bound-aries of a set of activities in the enterprise of science imply a definition of science that is generally acceptable. Such definition of science and the requirements of scientific theories were discussed in the previous chapter.

Importantly, the definitions and requirements of scientific theories and the boundaries and legitimate activities of science have been changing by the dynamics of scientific enterprise as the walls of old knowledge collapse under the weight of discoveries of new knowledge. Some recognized sciences and scientific theories of the past are today considered mythology. Serious questions, therefore, arise: What is science and what are scientific theories? Is there a criterion by which one can demarcate science from nonscience and distinguish scientific theories from other theories? Does the process of demarcation either help or retard the advancement of knowledge? How and when does a scientist know that a new knowledge has been discovered through a given theory, and what justification can the scientist give in holding onto the theory as correct? This is the evaluation problem in science leading to acceptability or rejection of theories in science based on some criterion of judgment. The main concern of such a criterion is to prescribe good scientific practice.

However, skeptics, like Feyerabend (50), have dismissed the use of any criterion formulated by philosophers of science as useful. They argue that scientists do not follow any set criterion and even violate all the prescriptions of philosophy when they have to make breakthroughs or establish new theories. On the other hand, Karl Popper (170) advocates strict scrutiny of scientific theories by some normative criterion. Imre Lakatos (121) agrees with the Popperian viewpoint but with certain reservations.

In our view, the skeptics' position is not justified, because it assumes a strict dichotomy between the practices of science and philosophy. It ignores the fact that debates among practitioners of a scientific field proceed always on the basis of explicit or implicit epistemological positions of individual scientists. An acceptable criterion must be used to reject or accept the position of the other side. It is possible that the scientists involved may, perhaps, not be directly conscious of the philosophical assumptions of their respective criteria of what constitutes science and, hence, a scientific theory. Furthermore, the scientists may be generally ill-equipped to express the methodological and epistemological underpinnings of their approaches to scientific knowledge in philosophical jargon. However, this does not suggest the presence of anarchism or an absence of a criterion. The fact, however, remains that there are always conflicts and disagreements among various perspectives in the enterprise of science. Such conflicts and disagreements in science are rooted in the philosophical stands — the philosophical difference of world outlook, as Thomas Kuhn would say (112). This philosophical world outlook provides the torchlight for the search for new knowledge.

If theories are rejected or accepted by scientists regarding their knowledge worthiness, then there is an implied discriminatory process for this very activity of scientists. Whenever alternatives exist for choice, some ranking process is required. Such ranking, in turn, requires the use of an implicit or explicit criterion index. The criterion index derives its meaningfulness from the philosophical underpinnings. Under such conditions of choice, therefore, an understanding of the philosophical underpinnings and formulation of a criterion for evaluating the scientific status of theories will be useful in judging the contributions of competing theories to existing knowledge. An analogy may be helpful to elaborate this point and illustrate the problem of choice in the whole enterprise of science. For example, everybody, irrespective of the society in which one finds himself or herself, uses some kind of understanding and views of economics in day-to-day affairs of life, but this understanding and view may be fictional and ideological rather than scientific. The intuitive insight of the layman cannot be said to compete with the theories of economists in explaining and predicting the behavior of economic phenomena.

Likewise, the practitioners of a field of science may have gained an intuitive understanding of the criterion for judging the scientific status of theories (and, hence, the philosophical outlook) in their field, but this does not mean that explicit understanding and construction of the implied criterion and its philosophical perspective are not needed. As a matter of fact, the theoretical foundations of a particular area of science are questioned on philosophical grounds when it is experiencing a crisis in its normal course or passing through a preparadigm stage. Commenting on the crisis of physics of his time, Albert Einstein said: "At a time like the present, when experience forces us to seek a newer and more solid foundation, the physicist cannot simply surrender to the philosopher the critical contemplation of the theoretical foundations; for he himself knows best, and feels more surely where the shoe pinches" (46, p. 1).

Whether a science is passing from a preparadigm stage or is entrenched in deep epistemological crises, the need for evaluating the scientific status of competing theories and views remains an important and the only logical avenue out of the crises. It is only through scientific evaluation that one can point out which of the competing theories explains "what there is" and predicts "what might be" better than its rival theories. The identification of better theories can result in better utilization of given intellectual and material resources. In the social sciences, the identification of better theories can guide the policy maker in the right direction and reduce costs of social experimentation. This point is extremely important for examination of policies relevant to economic development. As such, from general properties of successful scientific theories, we shall construct an explicit criterion that would allow one to examine the scientific status of views and theories of economic development.

THE NEED FOR AN EPISTEMOLOGICAL CRITERION FOR EXAMINING THEORIES OF ECONOMIC DEVELOPMENT

The explicit understanding of methodological problems, epistemological underpinnings, a constructed evaluative criterion, and the use of such a criterion to assess the knowledge content and scientific status of theories are all the more important in the area of development economics for the following reasons:

Development economics is still at a stage where there is basically no consensus on the fundamental notions and concepts of development economics. Generally, economists differ on the basic concept and analytical structure of development economics. The subject content of this area of economics is muddy. Moreover, the problems to be solved are vague, and the goals and objectives of theories on the phenomena of development are less understood and appreciated. Borrowing Kuhn's terminology, we can safely say development economics is passing through a preparadigm stage. As such, even the subject matter is not agreed upon, and the discussions on the basic concepts are more of a contrast of different philosophical world outlooks. An explicit discussion of these philosophical outlooks in a logically systematic way may help to sort out the fundamental problems in development economics and create conditions for their solutions.

The discussions and views on development economics are ideologically conflicting and loaded. Economists' conflicting ideological positions lead to a state of ineffective communication among themselves, thus, hindering the progress of scientific discoveries in this field.

Many a time, much intellectual energy of the people interested in development economics is devoted to fighting ideological battles instead of producing critical scientific works. The antidote is an appeal to rationality, even though rationality in humans has limitations. Rationality in scientific inquiry is considered a powerful cognitive approach to discover new knowledge. This requires a process of analysis that is based on a logic of inquiry rather than on conflicts of beliefs and preconceptions. In other words, rational discussions and inquiries as the core of scientific enterprise must supersede beliefs. The approach of rational discussions may proceed best by a logical filing of the theories and then subjection of them to tests based on a specified criterion, which must be constructed.

We will, thus, construct a criterion to evaluate development economics by combining the two major approaches advanced in modern philosophy of science. On the one hand, we will accept the Popperian viewpoint that scientific theories should be evaluated from the standpoint of logic. This element of a criterion will be essentially normative. Furthermore, we will also concede to Popper's position that inductivism and verificationism have some serious flaws and that the principle of falsifiability is more appealing and practical. This property will be incorporated in the criterion. On the other hand, every science has historical limits and must absorb rationality within those limits. Kuhn's and Kedrov's main ideas on history of science are, therefore, essential. They must be included in the construction of an evaluative criterion. Here, the properties of history will be captured through the concept of transformation.

Let us assume that economists and practitioners have at their disposal a collection of theories on the phenomena of development economics. These theories may project alternative and/or competing hypotheses. Our two tasks are sequential in nature. The first task involves analyzing the process whereby economists acquire the assemblage of theories of development. The second task involves the construction and analysis of procedure that would allow one to accept these hypotheses as valid in a scientific sense.

THE GENERAL CONDITIONS OF CRITERION
FOR EVALUATING SCIENTIFIC THEORIES

Generally, the criterion of evaluation that is to be constructed must fulfill two broad conditions of historicity and rationality. If the goal of a scientific theory is to explain ex post, then it must place strong emphasis on answering the question "what there is" in addition to "why there is" in the process of rational inquiry. On the other hand, if the goal of a scientific theory is to explain ex ante, then it must place most emphasis on answering the question of "how to change what there is" in addition to answering the question of "what ought to be" in the process of rational inquiry.

In the explanation ex post, the objective of the theoretical construct is to develop a system of logic that allows one to understand how the potential was actualized — in other words, to explain the process that leads to "what there is." In the explanation ex ante, the objective of any theoretical construct is the development of a logical system that allows the understanding of how a particular potential can be actualized by the rules implied in the logic. The explanation ex post is seen here as the classical explanatory theory. The explanation ex ante is seen as prescriptive theory. The criterion of any scientific theory, irrespective of the type, must incorporate elements of historicity and rationality.

The Historical Perspective of the Criterion

Different branches of science have developed at differential paces in history. Natural sciences, which are considered to be more exact sciences than social sciences, have always led the way. The criterion of acceptance applicable to the theories of natural sciences may not prove to be very fruitful when directly applied to the theories of social sciences. Development economics is a social science, and the criterion whereby theories in this area of knowledge have to be scrutinized should take into account the existing limitations of the classical definition of science. The level of scientific know-how in this field should provide the initial conditions that would mold the criterion of evaluation accordingly.

For the purpose of constructing a criterion useful in evaluating the scientific status of theories about the phenomenon of economic development, we need to explore the scientific characteristics of existing theories of development economics. We shall first apply the method of Thomas Kuhn (112). In so doing, a set of questions arises concerning development economics: specifically, how do economists engage in problem-solving activities to accomplish economic development, and how do the problem-solving activities generate the prescriptive or explanatory theories in development economics? Similarly, there are questions concerning acceptable solutions and the existing anomalies in the theories of development economics. In essence, the internal history of this branch of knowledge has to be recognized as the basis of analysis as suggested by Imre Lakatos (120, p. 120).

Rationality as a Basis of Criterion of Evaluation

To select rationality as a basis of a criterion intended to evaluate the scientific status of a theory presupposes the existence of rational inquiry to unravel the veil covering the mysteries of the unknown. In other words, it assumes that there is a rational cognitive path to the discovery of scientific truth. The concept of rationality is a disturbing one in epistemology because of differences in its interpretation and usage even when the same epistemological problem is being considered (41). Traditionally, rationality as applied to the construct of scientific theories has many facets, the most important ones being logical rationality and empirical rationality within the framework of bounded rationality and fuzzy rationality in human decision-choice process.

Logical rationality stresses the use of pure rules of objective logic to arrive at scientific truth. These logical rules, as constructed, are taken to be indifferent to space and time. The basic thrust of logical rationality as a criterion, therefore, is to investigate the appropriateness and acceptability of the logic of the process of acquiring social knowledge but not the psychology or sociology of the logical construct. By making the logical construct timeless and spaceless, the criterion of logical rationality lays claim to universality without reference to historicity of evolution of social knowledge. Holistic assessment of validity and acceptability of a scientific theory demands an account of space and time as important reference points of critical inquiry, whether in the explanatory sense or the prescriptive sense. Therefore, a position in the thought process that is offered here is that the set of conditions of logical rationality should be developed in the context of history without meddling with either the psychology or the sociology of knowledge, even though these are pertinent to accumulated knowledge up to the point in history of the logical construct.

Given the internal history of a research program, therefore, it would be helpful to identify those theories, within a group or a research program, that could stand the test of a criterion of evaluation constructed on the basis of logical rationality as revealed in the context of underlying historical process. This criterion as applied to development economics will help to sharpen the focus of the debate among the practitioners as well as the theoreticians of development economics. Further, it would help to clearly identify and bring about some degree of consensus on the theoretical and applicational problems of interest and, hence, lead to finding appropriate solutions.

The methods of historicity and rationality as applied in the context of evolution and accumulation of social knowledge have been considered to be mutually exclusive by Kuhn (112) and Popper (170), and by and large, the combination of the two is incompatible. This should not be the case; hence, we tend to agree with Lakatos that the two approaches are reconcilable (121, 122). It is insisted here that the sociology and history of societal knowledge do not stand in contradiction to the logic of scientific knowledge, because logic as a tool of reasoning and rational inquiry has its own evolution, progressing qualitatively and quantitatively with the passage of time.

Every era of human history reveals accounts of human beings having devised and improved the tools of reasoning in order to evaluate the correctness of its system of reasoning and understanding, as well as the manner in which knowledge is considered socially acceptable. Logic has its own history of evolution, and history has its own logic of understanding. Generally, various aspects of human knowledge and the process of acquiring them are interdependent, interwoven, and evolutionary, with cognitive jumps. As such, a simultaneous investigation of the history and logic of the same branch of knowledge is not only in order, it is also the most powerful way to understand the human struggle to uncover ignorance and discover the hidden secrets of society and nature. The full understanding of how scientific knowledge proceeds in society demands a holistic approach. As such, our criterion of evaluation of scientific theory will be rationalistic but within a given historical context. This criterion properly may be called a *rational-historical criterion*.

SPECIFIC CONDITIONS OF THE EVALUATIVE CRITERION

We now explore the specific requirements and conditions demanded of scientific theory by the rational-historical criterion. It may be suggested, within the structure of this discussion, that modern scientific theories may be grouped under two categories. The first category covers *explanatory theories*, while the second covers *prescriptive theories*. The grouping of theories into these two categories allows us to speak of *explanatory science* and *prescriptive science*. Together, they constitute the unity of science as applied not only to nature and its processes but also to society and its evolution. The implication of these two broad categories of science is that the classical requirements and, hence, definition of science are too limiting to include a number of areas of scientific studies such as artificial intelligence, expert systems, cybernetics, and soon. In Chapter 5, we pick up the discussion of these two broad categories of scientific theories as they relate to the subject area of development economics and a broader definition of science. The specific requirements of scientific theories, as demanded by the rational-historical criterion, must be developed within the framework of a broader definition and unity of science.

Viewed in this context of unity of explanatory and prescriptive science, we may abstract the following as the specific requirements of the rational-historical criterion that will be used to evaluate the scientific status of any theory of development economics. These specific conditions are:

Consistency condition
Problem-specification conditions
    Generality
    Manageability
Explanatory conditions
    Appropriateness of assumptions
    Existence of empirical content
    Congruence with reality
Predictive condition
Conditions of structural propositions
    Whys
    Hows
    Oughts
Prescriptive conditions
    Appropriateness of assumptions
    Existence of empirical content
    Congruence with reality

We shall now turn our attention to elaborate on the character of these specific conditions and how they may be modified to analyze the scientific character of theories in development economics.

Consistency Condition

All theoretical and axiomatic systems in empirical and nonempirical sciences require that the propositions of any theory be internally consistent. This condition of internal consistency of the system of propositions implied by the theory necessitates that minor propositions be inferred from the major proposition or have clear logical links if one of them is the major or minor proposition. In terms of consistent reasoning leading to a derived conclusion, an impossible situation is created if one proposition contradicts another or if any one of the propositions violates any of the assumed conditions in the same theoretical system. This impossible situation is because of the resulting self-contradictory system.

A self-contradictory system would mean that one proposition of a theory affirms a necessary causal relationship between two events, while another proposition of the same theory implies causal independence of the same two events; this is a logical impossibility. For example, suppose that $A = \{a_1, a_2, a_3\}$ is a set of conditions that is necessary and sufficient to derive $B = \{b_1, b_2, b_3\}$. It would, therefore, be a logical impossibility if B is derived without A. Furthermore, the system would be said to be self-contradictory if $C = \{c_1, c_2, c_3\}$ is a necessary and sufficient condition for A not to be derived while C is necessary and sufficient for B and A is necessary and sufficient for B in the same theoretical system. The important point here is clearly stated by Popper, who suggests that "a self-contradictory system is uninformative" (170, p. 92).

A practical example from development economics may illustrate the point of logical impossibility and self-contradiction. Suppose that a universal social law states that all changes in a sociopolitical organization affecting the form and content are caused by internal forces and dynamics. Suppose, also, that this social law is a major proposition of a theory. Let a minor proposition in the theory state that the sociopolitical organization is dominated by a foreign power. Let an inferential proposition be that the foreign power is dominating because it is clever. The inferential proposition in the theory contradicts the social law presented in the major proposition. The major cause of change is internal by the social law but external in the inference. The cause of foreign domination should have a logical link to the major proposition. For example, an inferential proposition that suggests that the domination is explained through the internal institutional weakness of the sociopolitical organization would sustain a logical link. The first inferential proposition is logically impossible. Logical consistency is a general requirement of all theoretical constructs. This requirement provides an element for examining desirability and acceptance of different theoretical systems as applied to the same phenomenon.

Problem Specification Condition

The enterprise of science is directed toward answering questions or solving various problems confronting society. The class of questions and problems defines the character of scientific enterprise and the theories that are developed within it. Theories are developed to answer questions. Theories are developed to solve problems or provide directions toward solutions of questions of interest. The manner in which questions are raised and problems are specified undoubtedly will affect the character of theories advanced. The scientific validity of both explanatory and prescriptive theories is, therefore, contingent on the way questions are raised and problems are specified. The structure of the specification of the questions and problems defines the legitimate boundaries of answers and solutions.

Additionally, the problem's specification defines the domain of acceptable investigation and theoretical possibilities. The objective of every theoretical construct is contingent on the questions raised and the problems at issue. In the act of constructing a theory, a clear indication must be made as to whether the theory is meant to explain a phenomenon or prescribe a future course of a phenomenon. In other words, the aim of the theory must be defined clearly by whether it is directed toward answering the question of why "what there is" is there or toward solving the problem of how to actualize "what ought to be." If the objective of a theory is that of an explanation, then we must answer the question as to whether the theory is designed to explain the whole process of a phenomenon or to explain the effect of a factor on the process. Furthermore, it must be made clear whether an act of data analysis or explanation is the implied objective of the logical construct.

The conditions of appropriateness of the questions and whether the problems are well-posed should be part of any constructed criterion to examine the scientific status of a theory. Two additional subproperties of the problem specification must be examined. To what extent are the problems and questions general and manageable? A more general question with manageable property is preferable to a specific question when a particular phenomenon is under examination, ceteris paribus. The condition of generality of questions and problems permits a wide range of understanding regarding the phenomenon. The condition of manageability, on the other hand, creates the ability to deal with specific questions within the general.

Examples of problem specification can be given from development economics. What types of relevant questions may be raised when the objective is to develop explanatory theories of economic development? An explanatory theory of economic development should answer how and why certain economies have remained relatively underdeveloped, in addition to explaining what has happened. In the process of raising the relevant questions, a clear differentiation must be made between the problems of establishing causal relationship and simple correlation or analysis of accumulated data on economic development.

For example, in examining states in economy, it is possible to observe a simultaneous occurrence of phenomena of underconsumption and underdevelopment. In this situation, the question arises as to whether underconsumption and underdevelopment are causally or correlationally related. Moreover, even if underconsumption is the apparent cause, can we identify it as a primary cause, or has underconsumption itself been produced by another causal factor that, in turn, has caused underdevelopment.

Similarly, one may ask what the relevant questions should be when the objective of a logical construct is to develop a prescriptive theory of economic development that would allow the potential to be actualized. It is suggested that prescriptive theories of economic development should delineate clearly whether they are directed toward investigating the rules of practice by which qualitative and quantitative changes can be brought about to transform underdeveloped economics. In this respect, prescriptive theories of development must address the questions of "what ought to be" and how to actualize "what ought to be." Additionally, the theories must indicate the types of economic goals that are desirable for a social system.

Explanatory Conditions

We shall now examine the explanatory condition of the evaluative criterion. This will be done by exploring the conceptual structure of each property of the explanatory condition and then relating them to the judgmental process of acceptability of a scientific theory.

Existence of Empirical Content

A theory, we have suggested, must consist of a set of internally consistent propositions. The set of propositions within a given theoretical system must correspond to some phenomena of the real world if the theory is to qualify for examination as scientific. This means that the fulfillment of the consistency condition is not sufficient to qualify a theory as scientific. For example, a set of mathematical equations may be internally consistent but structurally empty when viewed against the natural and social order of events and processes. In other words, a logically consistent theoretical system of thought may have nothing to offer in our current understanding of the world of things and processes of nature and society. The explanations and prescriptions of a theory can be tested against the real world of events only if they have some empirical content relating to conceivable natural or social phenomena that currently exist or can be shown to exist in the future by categorial conversion. The principle of verifiability, falsifiability, or any other criterion can be applied to scientific theories only if they have some link directly or indirectly to reality. Every conceived criterion tests the performance of a theory against the empirical phenomena. As such, the presence of an empirical content of the system of propositions of a theory is an imperative requirement in order to establish its scientific status and usefulness. This is logically relevant for both explanatory and prescriptive theories. To discover the empirical content of a theory, one must examine whether the system of propositions has a direct or indirect correspondence to reality as can be ascertained by data.

Congruence with Reality

The presence of empirical content of propositions of a theory is only one aspect of the explanatory condition. For a theory to satisfy the test of scientific status, the empirical content must have congruence with reality. The empirical content of the set of statements constituting the explanation must satisfy some condition of factual correctness. The empirical content must be highly confirmed by all the relevant evidence available at that point in time. Alternatively, the empirical content must be able to withstand all falsification attempts on the basis of current data.

The test of congruence with reality implies that a theory should relate thought experiment to experience, observables, or facts. This relationship must proceed through an acceptable logical construct, and if the empirical content is not directly related to experience and observables, then, at the very least, it should be shown to relate indirectly through a process of reduction and, hence, in congruence with reality.

The discussion on the test of congruence with reality of the empirical content of propositions in a theoretical system reveals an important applicatory and ontological difficulty of the concept of reality in science and philosophy of science. Does reality mean general knowledge or causal observation and representation thereof? The requirements that theoretical propositions contain empirical content that must be assessed against reality and that the empirical content squares with reality before acceptance cannot be imposed if we cannot know what is real and what we mean by reality. The problem of reality is a disturbing one in the physical sciences and even more disturbing in the social sciences.

To deal with the problem, we would begin from the postulate that reality is part of descriptive language of common sense and science and part of reporting language of scientific research and discovery. This postulate is supported by a second postulate that reality exists independently of humans. Reality will exist whether human inquiry about physical and social worlds leads to knowing it or not. The human methods of accessing reality are through direct and indirect observations.

Viewed in this way, two types of theories are constructible where the empirical content of the main propositions may be examined against reality. One is the class of explanatory theories; the other is the class of prescriptive theories. In the former, the empirical content of the main propositions is examined against known reality. In the latter, the propositions of the theories are rules rather than statements of fact for establishing congruence between the empirical content and the reality yet unknown. The propositions are a set of rules for establishing new realities. In both types, reality may be of direct or indirect observation; we also can raise questions of scientific truth and falsity. The process of testing the scientific truth of explanatory and prescriptive theories will be discussed when we examine the main tenents of these theories.

Appropriateness of Assumptions

All scientific theories are constructed on the bases of assumptions. Usually, the assumptions are idealized conditions under which either a causal relation or empirically based propositions may be established. Thus, given the empirical content of a theory, we must examine the assumed environment. This assumed environment constitutes the structure of assumptions. The structure of assumptions always has been controversial among metatheoreticians as to whether the assumptions are a priori truths or based on empirical observations. If the assumptions are required to meet the conditions of empirical reality, then a question arises as to whether the assumptions should be directly verifiable as singular statements or if their validity should be judged indirectly through the test of the theory for which they are put forth. This is the metatheoretical issue of empirical reality of assumptions. In very recent times, the question has been posed in terms of the importance of realism of assumptions in constructing a theory. In the field of economic science, there are some who hold that the set of assumptions that specifies the environment of the theory must be bounded by the conditions of empirical reality (92, 197). Other opinions indicate that it does not matter whether these assumptions are realistic in the empirical sense (52, 147).

It may be argued that the controversy over realism of assumptions depends on the process through which assumptions are derived. Every assumption of any theory is empirically grounded. It is our position that the mind is incapable of making assumptions that have nothing to do with the world around us. All assumptions are directly or indirectly abstracted for our current understanding of the world in which the phenomenon of interest operates. The abstractions are our perceptions of reality that define the boundaries of the theoretical constructs. The question, therefore, is not whether the assumptions have something to do with the world of things and, hence, are empirically grounded. The question is whether the abstracted assumptions are a good and meaningful approximation of the environment in which the phenomenon operates to serve as a reasonable basis to construct either an explanatory or a prescriptive theory of the phenomenon.

In fact, the test of assumptions in any theory must meet conditions of empirical content if such assumptions are to define the environment in which the theory is to be examined for its scientific status. All assumptions must be relevant to the phenomenon for them to serve as a basis for a theory about such a phenomenon. This is the condition of relevance of assumptions. The test of relevance is the degree of empirical content relative to the phenomenon around which the theory is to be constructed. This position can be objected to only on the grounds that the scientific status of a theory is determined solely by its predictive power. Such a position seems to be in accord with the school of positive economics, which seems to hold that a theoretical system must be "judged by the precision, scope and conformity with experience of the predictions it yields" (52, p. 4).

Assumptions are always abstracted or must be abstracted from reality and may be viewed as idealizing the environment for construction of theory. The making of assumptions is an act of abstraction and idealization in the sense that it helps to establish commonality in diversity and simplicity in complexity. The idealized conditions may not be empirically confirmed in any particular element of the phenomenon at any particular time, but they may be generally reflected in the longer span of time. Partially, they may be reflected in the particular but not in the general. Friedman's assertion that the realism of assumptions is irrelevant or (even better) that the assumptions are not real (52, p. 14), must, we think, be taken in this sense of idealized conditions. It must not be taken in the context that the simplicity and empirical content of the set of assumptions are irrelevant to the environment in which the theory is anchored. This would be a travesty of the enterprise of science.

We agree with Friedman that the truthfulness of assumptions is reflected in the empirical test of the theory. If a theory explains and predicts well the class of phenomena for which it is meant, the appropriateness of assumptions is confirmed. The relevance of explanation is just as important as the relevance of prediction. We have previously argued that the relationship between explanation and prediction is not a logical "if and only if" causation. There are representations where predictions may exist without explanation in the sense of scientific theories, and even then, the system may violate an important requirement of logical consistency.

Assumptions define the domain of the theory. For example, there are theories that have been constructed to explain the monetary phenomena of industrialized economies. The question that arises is this: can the said theory explain similar phenomena in nonindustrialized economies as well? If not, can it be used by making adjustments to the theory, or is there a need for another theory based entirely on a different set of assumptions about the environment of the theory? These questions are of fundamental importance for the present discourse.

In a previous section, we discussed some important aspects of reality, its meaning, and how reality may be perceived within the process of construction, validation, and acceptance of a theory. The views expressed in that section concerning the congruence of the empirical content of the main propositions of a theory with reality also hold here for assumptions. The establishment of reality in scientific contexts often involves direct and indirect observations within a framework of the phenomenon under study. This framework is established through a conceptual scheme that cannot be isolated from human experience and perceived reality up to the time point of the inquiry. Assumptions in theoretical constructs are influenced by perceptions and interpretations of reality. Such perceptions and interpretations can run counter to reality because of preconceptions and the subjectivity of the scientist. It is, thus, necessary and perhaps imperative to examine the ontological conditions of factual correctness of the assumptions in a theory.

It is, therefore, an ontological mistake and perhaps analytical deception to hold a position that most fundamental assumptions in economic theory and, for that matter, any social theory involve empirically unobservable variables and that it is meaningless to demand that such variables should conform to reality as it is implied in the "irrelevance-of-assumption" thesis and argument (22, 52). Such a claim neglects channels of observation, which may be direct or indirect. We do not directly observe itching, taste, or pain. Are we, therefore, in a position to deny that they are real? In scientific analysis and study, the model of reality within which discussions take place depends upon the conceptual framework against which one works and the language of description and analysis that is used. The language as a mode of description, analysis, and communication consists of a complete system of concepts that constitute a frame depending on human experience that has been acquired through direct or indirect observations. Every conceptual system that has an empirical content, implied by its propositions or assumptions or both, will always have its candidate for reality. As such, it is meaningful and, in fact, useful to ask how well a set of assumptions approximates reality in a theoretical construct. The realism of assumptions of a theory is, thus, a necessary requirement for the criterion in accepting a theory as scientific and, perhaps, useful. This point is extremely important in social science and, hence, economics where pseudoscience can easily emerge and where the results of a theory can be twisted to support ideological positions and social prejudices that may have grave political and ethical consequences for human social practice.

Predictive Condition

Theories that are cognitive systems of logically ordered propositions should not only explain the phenomenon but should also be able to generate predictions in the case of explanatory theories. Generally, we speak of explanation in theories if we know that a phenomenon has already occurred and, hence, is part of an accumulated experience and that a suitable set of propositions that is empirically grounded is advanced afterward. On the other hand, we speak of prediction from a theory if the empirical content of the set of propositions implied by the theory constitutes the necessary and prior condition for future occurrence of the phenomenon. It may be argued that explanatory theory is not fully adequate unless its propositions can serve as a suitable frame for predicting the phenomenon under consideration when time is accounted for.

We agree in part with Oppenheim and Popper that predictions are implied in the explanation of a theory or that the predictions are explanation written backward (170). However, we hold some reservations when the statement is put as "the predictions are explanations written backward." We have already noted Kaplan and Harre's objection against this view of symmetry in Chapter 2 — that Darwin's theory explains the evolutionary process of species but cannot predict. Although Kaplan and Harre's objection does not establish asymmetry between explanation and prediction, it leads to the argument that whenever there is explanation, there is, directly or indirectly, an implied prediction but not vice versa (91). However, one may argue that Darwin's theory deals with exceptional phenomena and may not be able to generate immediate predictions directly. This exceptionality hypothesis is not credible in a metatheoretic construct about science.

The law of natural selection as advanced by Darwin has been used to explain historical and social phenomena that lead to verifiable predictions. An example may be found in economics, where the survival of the fittest applies in the perfectly competitive market. It is no surprising that Darwin was an advocate of the hypothetic-deductive model of scientific explanation, which holds that there should be a symmetry between explanation and prediction (4, p. 31). The metatheoretic problem with which the hypothetic-deductive position must deal is to show that whenever there is a prediction, we should find the counterpart of explanation. As it stands, such a symmetry does not seem to hold logically. It is, perhaps, the recognition of this logically inconclusive symmetry and asymmetry between explanation and prediction that led instrumentalists like Friedman to deemphasize explanation in favor of prediction. It may be argued that a large number of contemporary economic models, such as forecasting, follow this direction. Given the various positions on the symmetry and asymmetry of explanation and prediction, we can firmly hold the view that an explanatory theory must have some degree of predictive power.

The degree of predictive power of any explanatory theory is latent in the set of logically ordered predictive statements that are implied by the logically ordered main propositions of the explanatory theory, even though some may argue that a theory must be quantitatively anchored in order to yield predictive propositions. This is not the position taken here. Such a position will immediately exclude important aspects of qualitative phenomena. We mainly require that a theory must be empirically anchored.

The appropriate position to hold, we think, is that the concept of empirical content must be broadened to encompass qualitative and quantitative experiences. The only difficulty of predictive propositions implied by an explanatory theory of qualitative phenomena is testability. The ability to overcome this difficulty is part of the art and science of both verification and falsification that must test the congruence of the empirical content with reality.

The empirical test of theories of development economics, like other theories in social sciences, cannot be quantitatively pure. As a matter of fact, one may argue that most of the social sciences have not reached the level where the predictions of their theories can be compared with the quantitative accuracy achieved in natural sciences. The problems of quantitative accuracy are further complicated in development economics because data are not available on many aspects of societies of developing countries. In addition, the available quantitative and qualitative data are not very dependable. Comparatively, the data about industrialized societies are more accurate. The discrepancy between these two sets of data hinders the formulations of universally empirical economic laws and testing on the same scale as theories about physical systems.

The test of predictive power of an explanatory theory will be different for both data accuracy condition and data type condition. If the theory is quantitatively grounded, then we will expect the main propositions of the explanatory theory to show magnitude and direction, but if the theory is qualitatively anchored, then we will expect the predictive propositions to show direction and structural differences.

In the case of an economic system where the interest is on the phenomena of development, the predictive character of the theory should contain explicit or derivable propositions of expected changes at different stages of the process of transition of the economy as the information set tends to alter.

The ability to establish the magnitude of change will be a plus for any theory of development. Thus, theories that have a high degree of quantitative accuracy as well as empirical content are preferable when different theories about the same phenomenon are compared. In terms of theories of development economics, their predictive ability should meet the requirement of direction of change. We, therefore, echo the position of Samuelson, who demands that the signs (direction) of change should be right if economic calculus is used (190, p. 7).

An example may illustrate the point that is being made here. In the case of economic calculus, it is not enough for a theory to say that the means of production and the total output are positively related. If the theory is an explanatory one, it must show why and how increase (decrease) in capital increases (decreases) total output of a country. It cannot end even here. The interconnected chain of the history of decision outcomes requires that the theory should explain how capital and output are measured. A prescriptive theory, on the other hand, will contain an ordered set of optimal rules for increasing capital and the total output. In short, the theory should simultaneously indicate and explain the interconnected processes of the phenomenon of interest.

The Structure of the Main Propositions of Theories

Given that the problems or questions to be studied in a specific area of science are specified and agreed upon by a consensus of the researchers, it is necessary to examine the structure of the main propositions that solve one or more of the problems or answer one or more of the questions. Generally, the class of such questions and problems will deal with "what there is" and "what ought to be." These problems and questions lead to simple questions of "hows" and "whys." These hows and whys define the boundaries of research and admissible theories in the specific area of science.

The question of how and why can be properly answered by advancing a set of basic propositions that are logically ordered either to explain "what there is" (in the case of explanatory theory) or to prescribe rules of arriving at "what ought to be" (in the case of prescriptive theory). The set of ordered propositions constitutes the structure of the main propositions that define the content of the theory. The structure will contain propositions directed either to why and how questions or to ought and how questions. Any theory whose structure of main propositions satisfies the why-how and ought-how questions will qualify for scrutiny and acceptance.

In development economics, these logically ordered propositions should explain the dynamics of socioeconomic change or show how potential socioeconomic changes can be actualized. In this respect, the structure of the main propositions should specify how and why one set of conditions $A = \{a_1, a_2, a_3\}$ produces the set of effects $B = \{b_1, b_2, b_3\}$ and how and why the set $B = \{b_1, b_2, b_3\}$ will produce the set of effects $C = \{c_1, c_2, c_3\}$. What will be the main effects of a cause, and what are the by-products or side effects? In other words, the structure of the main propositions should establish a logical chain of causes and effects in such a way that the intervening mechanism of change is explained or prescribed systematically. The said task may be accomplished by establishing logical propositions that explain the various periods of history as well as providing the basis of quantitative and qualitative motion in the economic sphere. The logically ordered basic propositions then will serve as a framework for the discovery of the laws of socioeconomic change.

The discovery of the laws of socioeconomic transformation is indispensable in the explanation of the phenomenon of development. The developing countries are very different from each other in many respects. Ethnic composition, social organization, economic actualities and potentialities, cultural milieu and potentials, and the historical experiences vary from country to country. The fundamental laws of transformation should be able to explain the causes of past and currently prevailing diversities. These laws also should help to establish the process of change from one period to another and depict the course of reproduction of economic systems from one period to another, as suggested by Hollis and others (81, p. 178). The essence of scientific discourse is to discover laws that can explain the diversity, preferably by a single principle. It is no wonder that Adam Smith was fascinated by Newton's theory of gravity, which can explain diverse phenomena by a single principle. For Adam Smith, the discovery of such a law in economic organization was of basic concern, because he was trying to explain the transition of societies that were very different.

Given the fundamental laws of transformation of socioeconomic systems, the theories should contain propositions that can be tested empirically either by the principle of verification or by the principle of falsification. These propositions should be such that specific operations can be performed. Otherwise, they would remain metaphysical abstractions and cannot qualify as scientific theories.

Prescriptive Conditions

Let us now turn our attention to prescriptive conditions. Examining the framework of prescriptive criterion brings us to prescriptive theory. (A full discussion on the prescriptive theory and its implication for development economics is in Chapter 5.) The aim of prescriptive theory is to develop propositions that are directed toward "improving" reality by actualizing the desired potential. A prescriptive theory should be scrutinized for acceptance on the basis of the set of conditions outlined in the previous section. The validity of propositions of a prescriptive theory is tested differently. In testing the validity of prescriptive theory, two sets of conditions must be satisfied: ex ante conditions and ex post conditions. The ex ante conditions involve the consistency, problem specification, and structural propositions. These three conditions must also be met by explanatory theories. Additionally, the ex ante conditions for a prescriptive theory must include the conditions for what is to be actualized. These conditions must contain an empirical content whose congruence with an ex post reality must be tested.

The satisfaction of the ex ante conditions is sufficient in applying the rules of behavior as prescribed by a prescriptive theory. It is, however, not sufficient for either the validation or the scientific acceptance of the theory. The validity of prescriptive theories is tested by the actual outcomes after the application of the prescriptive rules contained in them. In other words, if a theory is designed to actualize a potential as contained in the main propositions of the theory, then the test for scientific acceptance of the theory lies in whether the practice of the theory results in actualizing the potential. The empirical content is said to be in congruence with reality if it corresponds to the outcomes. This is the ex post condition for the validity and acceptance of a prescriptive theory.

Generally stated, a prescriptive theory must be examined by how well it identifies the necessary and sufficient conditions for actualizing the desired potential as contained in the main propositions of the theory. A seemingly awkward example may be pulled from development economics. An increase in either physical capital or human capital may be a sufficient condition for an economic development, but it may not be a necessary condition to achieve such. In other words, the same level of economic development, as conceived, may be achieved by changing the institutional configuration of economics, law, and politics.

It must be clearly emphasized that a theory qualifies as a prescriptive theory only if the main propositions specify the potential, and its ex ante empirical content, as well as the rules that are necessary and sufficient to actualize the potential. It is then tested to see whether it satisfies the ex ante conditions before being accepted for application. The scientific acceptance and validity of the theory then depend on satisfying the ex post conditions, which require that the ex ante empirical content of the main propositions of the theory be in congruence with the outcomes.

JUSTIFICATIONS FOR CATEGORIZING DEVELOPMENT THEORIES

In order to epistemologically examine the scientific status of theories of development economics along the line of the suggested criterion, we shall categorize the theories of development. Before doing so, we shall first give the reasons for the formation of categories of development theories.

A number of claimed theories in development economics share an underlying methodology in spite of the differences in their appearances. Critical examination reveals that some of these development theories originate from the same source. For example, Gunnar Myrdal suggests that the source of modern theory of capital accumulation is the Marxist theory (154, p. 19). Another example is the stage-based theories, about which it is claimed that, epistemologically, the theories conceive history on a linear scale. Likewise, different prescriptive theories share the philosophical perspective that manipulation of subjective factors can change the course of social progress. Epistemologically, the underlying principle of all prescriptive theories is not the explanation of reality but improvement of the reality that defines the environment of human existence and social life.

Historians and philosophers of science like Thomas Kuhn and Imre Lakatos have also suggested that progress of the sciences is of a cooperative nature. At different stages of the development of sciences, the members of the same scientific discipline share the same philosophical perspective and world outlook. These ideas also hold in theories of development economics. The system of shared beliefs, problems of interest, techniques, and methods is called a paradigm by Kuhn and "research program" by Lakatos. They suggest by way of conclusions that the proper unit of analysis and evaluation is the "paradigm" in the case of Kuhn or a "research program" in the case of Lakatos, instead of individual theories.

Lakatos, dealing with the structure and progress of science, holds that "the history of science is the history of research programs rather than of theories" (120, p. 137). Within the same research program, we may add, theories can be grouped by subject matter. Also, given the phenomenon of concern, theories about the phenomenon may be classified further according to the underlying assumptions and the logic of analysis. As applied to development economics, we must note that the theories do not seem to qualify as establishing well-defined paradigms. It is useful to view theories of economic development as constructing an edifice of thinking, under the umbrella of economic reasoning, which will assist whosoever is privileged to draw correct conclusions and to design appropriate actions for improving economic reality.

Although theories in development economics do not qualify as well-defined paradigms, theories in development economics may be viewed as constituting a research program. Within this research program, theories about development phenomena may be grouped. Individual economists subscribing to a particular theory share certain premises, preconceptions, and beliefs as a group. Collectively, they also debate with and against other groups on the fundamentals of the phenomena of interest, epistemics, and validation of the results of the theories on development phenomena. In this respect, we will create categories of theories of development that then will be evaluated as a group instead of evaluating the theories of development as a single paradigm, as has been done with the neoclassical scientific research program in economics. It is, therefore, an epistemological imperative, almost surely, to categorize the development theories and examine them in groups.

4

Explanatory Theories in Economic Development

Most of what may be considered scientific laws in the social sciences is ⁓ derived from history and from actual accumulated experiences of human beings and their activities in nature and society. Such activities are because of decisions and choices, which, in turn, are reflections of thought and action. The history of human endeavors, therefore, is the accumulated account of the results of past decision and choice events, the outcomes of which are, in most cases, unwilled and uncontrollable. Even when the outcomes are certainly known and controllable, their cumulative linkage effects on future decision-choice events and corresponding outcomes are unforeseen.

Human history, therefore, is a collection of outcomes of past events of success-failure experiments that have, either consciously or unconsciously, been undertaken in the process of creating the right material support for human life and happiness. It forms the empirical terrain in which theories in social sciences are anchored. Given the empirical terrain, stretched over distant past, an analysis is conducted to see whether some regularities among these events can be ascertained to aid the understanding of past events and how the outcomes of these past events confirm the essential force of thought and human cognition for decision and choice activities. Such an analysis usually takes the form of organizing and arranging the past according to an established or acceptable logical process.

The enterprise of organizing and arranging past events is equivalent to what is referred to in modern times as "data analysis." The logical process for abstracting the regularities in historical data is evolutionary and always arises from the social milieu in which the history is created. At different times in the history of human knowledge, different types of logical rules have been applied to assist in the critical analysis of events that collectively constitute the history at the relevant point in time. The logical process allows one to disentangle complexities, discover links among the events, see how they fit, and, so, relate to different aspects of human experience. It also assists us to isolate the most important and significant variables that may be used to describe the organic motion of history. In this enterprise, every logical process encounters the formidable force of the problems of accuracy of historic data. In the current discussion, our objective is not to examine the accuracy of recorded and nonrecorded history; rather, we want to explore the sociology of knowledge as revealed by explanatory theories of economic development as well as other theories that might be implied by accumulated human thinking on economic development.

HISTORY AND ECONOMIC DEVELOPMENT

Economic development is a process whose map shows the contours of intertemporal successes and failures of human decisions and choices. The state of economic development of any given society, therefore, is an accumulated history of success-failure experiments in decision and choice fields of human endeavors in the past. It is a history of generations of human achievements. It is, however, a special history. As such, some historiographical method is required to explain the development process or, at least, to facilitate its understanding.

Excluding the controversies of historiographers, we shall examine how the debates of epistemologies of post-Hegelian dialectical materialism and idealism have affected the analysis, interpretation, and explanation of economic development and growth through the construction of explanatory theories about the phenomenon of economic development. We shall keep in mind, however, that development is a process and that the history of economic development in a nation and among nations constitutes the empirical realm and test of the valid contributions of the theories to knowledge. Viewed from this perspective, we can impose categories on the available theories of economic development. Two such categories have dominated: *stage-based* and *factor-based* theories of economic development.

We shall examine the relative contributions to knowledge of these two categories of explanatory theories about the phenomenon of economic development. In addition, we would like to know the usefulness of these theories in providing meaningful guidelines to improve the quality of human decisions about the development process.

STAGE-BASED THEORIES

We now turn our attention to stage-based theories for explaining economic development. Every theory of explanation must have *explanandum* (that which is to be explained). It must clearly indicate the phenomenon that the theory is intended to explain. The explanandum is a system of ideas that indicates the phenomenon under explanation. As such, it must contain the essential questions that the theory is set to answer. In the case of stage-based theories of explanation of economic development phenomenon, a set of questions that constitutes the description of the central object for explanation must be indicated.

Given the explanandum of economic development with a clear indication of the questions to be answered, an explanation is offered. The explanation is a class of sentences that contains ideas that must advance an account of the phenomenon indicated in the explanandum. This class of sentences is referred to as *explanans*. For the stage-based theories to qualify as an acceptable system of explanation for the phenomenon of development or as a system of explanatory answers advanced to respond to questions about development, they must be logically grounded in the cognitive process of knowing.

In this enterprise, the explanandum must be rationally and scientifically deduced from the empirical base contained in the explanans. The empirical base of explanatory theories of economic development is economic history that contains the information on the basis of which the explanandum must be abstracted. The explanans that constitutes the explanation of the phenomenon of economic development and provides answers to its hows and whys must contain some general laws that relate to the development process. In addition, the theories must contain empirically testable content to allow one to verify how well the theory squares with history. For explanatory theories of development to be fully adequate in explanation as well as in answering questions implied by the explanandum, the explanans contained in them must constitute a logical basis for prediction and prescription. From the viewpoint of development of the material basis of life, it is the prescriptive force (but not predictive power) that provides scientific theories of economic development with their social importance and usefulness. In this respect, we are advancing a different position from that of Friedman concerning the concept of "usefulness" that he relates to prediction (22, 52). Here, usefulness of a theory relates to prescription rather than prediction because the objective of a theory is taken as an improvement of reality and, hence, its prescribed rules provide the daring force of social utility.

Within this framework, the stage-based theories of economic development project economic history, by abstraction, as passing through definite phases. The phases are defined as stages. The stages are time ordered. Common elements and regular patterns of these stages are observed in different human societies, it is claimed. The basic tasks of the stage-based theories of economic development, therefore, are to ascertain the characteristics of different stages for identification, distinction, and recognition and to provide the logical process of explanation that shows how an economic system moves from one stage to another — in other words, to identify by abstraction the laws of transformation of an economic system through different development phases or stages.

From the logical system of the explanation of development, the explanandum of concern may be stated as stylized facts that may be abstracted from history as its empirical land mass that is bared for epistemological exploration and conquest. The relevant stylized facts may be stated as follows:

The quality and quantity of goods and services for the satisfaction of human wants have continually changed with time in history.

The tools and methods of production have also changed.

The institutional framework and the institutional configuration of societies have gone through changes in history.

There are relationships among types of goods produced, methods and tools of production, and the degree of the complexity of the corresponding institutions prevailing at various stages.

To develop the explanans to these stylized facts that constitute the factual ideas about the phenomenon of economic development, the methodology of historicity is applied. The process of economic development, within the explanatory framework of stage-based theories, is conceived as passing through clearly distinguishable stages. This is exemplified by the Scottish school, which believes that, historically, economic development has occurred in stages.

A typical example of such a position and characterization of defined stages was advanced by Adam Smith, who described the sequential nature of economic development as constituting a process passing through hunting, pastoral, agricultural, commercial, and manufacturing stages (219a). The main preoccupation of the Scottish school, in this respect, is the analysis and explanation of the transformation of the feudal stage into the capitalist stage. The category formation of development process into stages is a useful scientific approach, but it is only the beginning; in fact, it may be viewed as a part of data analysis of history.

The success in achieving a category formation only satisfies the *first task* of constructing stage-based explanatory theories of economic development. Although the completion of the task of the stage (category) formation is necessary, it is not sufficient for explaining the development process. The sufficient condition is embedded in the solution to the problem of categorial conversion. A categorial convertibility in stage-based theories of economic development demands that an explanatory theory must contain statements about the laws of transformation that show how any economic system moves from one stage to another. This is the solution to the problem of stage transformation, which is the *second task* of explanatory theories on the phenomenon of economic development.

Stated differently, we may summarize the problems of stage-based explanatory theories of development as category (stage) formation and category transformation. The Scottish school did not accomplish the second task. To accomplish the task of categorial convertibility, it must be realized that logic and science are the tools. Logic is the conceptual tool by which philosophy copes with the complex problems involved in category conversion. Its force is projected by nominalism, constructionism, and reductionism. Based on these, science is called on to derive the conditions of categorial convertibility. Any stage-based explanatory theory of development must deal with this dual charter of the development process: it must establish distinguishable stages, and it must provide the logic of transformation.

It was this recognition that led Karl Marx and Friedrich Engels (138) to provide a more coherent and elaborate method to deal with the problems of category formation and category transformation of stages of economic development by using the science and philosophy of dialectical and historical materialism. Marx and Engels emphasized human material conditions as determining, in the last analysis, the direction of history and, hence, the direction of economic development. These conditions assert themselves in the historic scene through the established and emerging institutions of society that are unquestionable products of the development process.

The methodological technique within nominalism, constructionism, and materialist reductionism, supported by dialectical logic of transformation, is such that one assigns a category as the initial stage of identifiable reality from which the economic system is converted from stage to stage. In a general theory of category formation and transformation, the initially identifiable economic stage will be equivalent to the primary category of reality from which other categories are derivable.

The logical process of stage-to-stage transformation is such that for every true proposition contained in the explanans about the new stage consequent of the transformation, there should be corresponding true propositions about the initial stage such that the explanans could not contain acceptable and empirical content unless the propositions about the initial state meet the conditions of factual correctness.

To lay bare the intricacies and complexities of the logic and methodology of the transforming process, one must understand that in materialist reductionism of a forward-backward recessive process, one deals with the task of how the concepts that are factually proper to a derived stage may be logically reduced to the concepts that are factually proper to the economic stage that is held to be primary in the transforming process. In constructionism, however, using the material concepts and basic characteristics that are factually proper to the primary economic stage, one creates a picture regarding how the concepts that are also factually proper about the derived stage can be formed. The concept proper may be translated as factually correct.

In this analysis, an economic stage is said to be derived from a primary stage if we can establish a transforming relationship between concepts of the two stages that are factually proper and correct. Finally, it must be noted that in nominalism, only the actual or concrete economic stage that has been factually established to exist can be held as the primary or initial stage. From this primary stage, all other potential and actual stages are considered to be surrogates of the primary on the basis of a higher logical plane.

The construction of Marxist theory of economic development is an important attempt to provide answers to problems of category (stage) formation and transformation. This Marxian attempt has been very controversial, and rival theories based on different epistemological paradigms have been advanced. One such theory is developed by Schumpeter. The Schumpeterian theoretical system is motivated from an important appreciation of Marxian analysis where the internal dynamics of the system propel the economic system forward rather than being propelled by an external mover. Like Marx, the Schumpeterian explanatory logic is methodologically historical. The constructed explanans is in some aspects complementary and in other aspects rival to Marx's theoretical construct. It is a deliberate attempt on the part of Schumpeter to adopt certain strengths of the Marxian explanatory logic of history to construct a theory of economic evolution that he believes is not possible using either the Walrasian or Marshallian apparatus. This epistemic position is stated in an explicit or implicit way in a number of places by Schumpeter but is explicitly made clear in the preface to the Japanese edition of his *Theory of Economic Development* (204, pp. 165–67, 205).

Schumpeter, like Marx, accepts a fundamental position that:

There was a source of energy within the economic system which would of itself disrupt any equilibrium that might be obtained. If this is so then there must be a purely economic theory of economic change which does not merely rely on external factors propelling the economic system from one equilibrium to another. It is such a theory that I have tried to build and I believe now, as I believed then, that it contributes something to the understanding of the struggles and vicissitudes of the capitalist world and explains a number of phenomena, in particular the business cycle, more satisfactorily than it is possible to explain them by means of either the Walrasian or the Marshallian apparatus. . . . This idea and this aim are exactly the same as the idea and the aim which underlie the economic teaching of Karl Marx. In fact, what distinguishes him from the economists of his own time and those who preceded him, was precisely a vision of economic evolution as a distinct process generated by the economic system itself. (204, p. 168)

Despite the same idea and aim of both Schumpeter and Marx regarding the phenomenon of economic development, the Schumpeterian theoretical construct and its logical power stand on their own.

A theoretical work that is purposefully constructed to oppose the theoretical system of Marx is that of Rostow's position, which stands out clearly. It earned the reputation as a rival theory to the Marxist theory. We shall evaluate these three theories as representatives of three different world views and approaches to the construction of stage-based explanatory theory of economic development.

We shall examine and present the differences on stage formation. We then shall examine the differences and similarities in the philosophical basis of their explanations to the process of economic development. The differences in category formation regarding the stages of the economy on the part of Marx, Schumpeter, and Rostow are presented as taxonomy in Table 4.1 (see 133, 136, 182, 205, 207).

TABLE 4.1
Interstages in History of Economic Development
According to Marx, Schumpeter, and Rostow

Marx	Schumpeter	Rostow
Primitive communal	Primitive capitalism	Traditional
Slavery	Entrepreneurial capitalism	Preconditions for takeoff
Feudal	Bureaucratic capitalism	Takeoff
Capitalism	Socialism	Maturity
Communism	Bureaucratic socialism	Mass consumption

The identification and characterizations of these stages by Marx, Schumpeter, and Rostow constitute not only abstractions from history but also a true attempt to satisfy the conditions of category formation as a first demand of stage-based explanatory theory of economic development. From the position of nominalism, the factual correctness of all these stages as fitting human experience is unimportant. The most important element for initializing the construction of a stage-based explanatory theory is the stage that is held to be primary. This stage must satisfy the conditions of concrete existence or factual correctness. The rest of the stages may be actual or potential. Their current nonexistence is irrelevant for the development of the theory

Given the abstracted stages, the next problem facing Marx, Schumpeter, and Rostow is to develop transformation relationships that constitute the explanans for the explanandum. The explanans must indicate the movement of the economic system from one stage to another. The task is to satisfy the conditions of category transformation. This requires the construction of a transformation operator that acts on the initial stage and transforms it into another stage by way of an explanation. The construction of the transformation operator must lead to the establishment of a law of motion that shows how the qualities of the stage are altered: in other words, to answer the question as stated by Schumpeter, "How do such changes take place, and to what economic phenomena do they give rise? . . . where economic life itself changes its own data by fits and starts?" (205, p. 62). We shall examine how successful this theoretical task was accomplished by Marx, Schumpeter, and Rostow by their epistemological constructs.

We note that the constructions of Marxian and Schumpeterian explanans, unlike that of Rostow, require an intrastage classification that is associated with the internal dynamics of each stage that induces qualitative self-alteration. The changes that take place within any given stage may be identified and described in terms of changes of equilibrium states with defined characteristics. Within each Marxian state, there is a set of Marxian equilibriums, and within each of the Schumpeterian stages, there is a set of Schumpeterian equilibriums. Each Marxian equilibrium is characterized by a temporary bargaining harmony in terms of class antagonism relative to income and work distributions between the exploiters and the exploited. The Schumpeterian equilibrium, on the other hand, is characterized by a temporary entrepreneurial harmony relative to production and competitive conflict in innovation and markets, where the system settles down to a well-defined routine of circular flow. Within each state, there are, two clearly identifiable sets of Marxian and Schumpeterian equilibriums that define the transient paths along which the economic system is propelled by its internal force. These Marxian and Schumpeterian characterizations as logical abstractions from their works are important in understanding the transient process from a capitalist stage to socialist stage, as well as developments within stages.

The comparative structure of the intrastate classification is provided in Table 4.2.

To examine the degree of success of each of the three explanatory constructs, we shall first identify what Marx, Schumpeter, and Rostow considered the key aggregate factors in establishing the transformation operator and then examine how these key factors are translated into laws of quantitative and qualitative motions. These key factors are summarized in Table 4.3.

Given the identified stages of economic development and the key factors of explanation, we will examine, compare, and contrast the relative epistemological contributions of Marx's, Schumpeter's, and Rostow's theories of economic development.

The Essentials of Marxist Theory of Economic Development

Given the five stages as presented by Marx, the construction of a theory that explains economic development requires Marx to overcome two important theoretical difficulties: constructing a logical process that

TABLE 4.2
Classifications within Stages of Economic Development
According to Marx, Schumpeter, and Rostow

	Marx Intrastages	*Schumpeter Intrastages*	*Rostow Intrastages*
Type	Equilibrium	Equilibrium	None
Defined	Bargaining, simple reproduction and income-distribution game among classes	Routine circular flow with a well-defined configuration of "combination" and mutual interrelations among economic variables under stationary conditions	None
Characteristics	Maximum surplus-value and constant factor shares established by relative class bargaining strength with a) known methods of production technology (capital deepening), b) known size of the means of production (capital widening), c) known configuration of institutions of social organization with defined social power and class relations	Zero entrepreneurial profit, zero credit, no new money creation, and exhaustion of profitable inventions for innovation with a) defined output and resource bundles with known markets where demand and supply balance, b) routine methods of production and business operations, c) known configuration of production institutions with known "combination of productive means" and defined number of competitive producers with full employment of factors, d) established entrepreneurial class with zero entrepreneurial activities and no "new combination"	None

TABLE 4.3
Key Aggregate Factors Producing the Transitional
Processes in Marx's, Schumpeter's and Rostow's Theories

Marx
Class division and class struggle
Changes in production techniques (tools, etc.)
Changes in relations of production
Conflicts in the form and content of the social organization
Schumpeter
Division of capitalists into entrepreneurs and nonentrepreneurs
Entrepreneurial innovations
Changes in combinations
New credit creation beyond the circular flow
Competitive struggle among firms over abnormal profits
Government regulation
Rostow
Intrusion by a more developed society
Enterprising men as critical mass
Human motives leading to political change

explains how the socioeconomic system moves through the identified stages and constructing a logical process to explain how qualitative changes take place in the system at any given stage and how the changes affect the stage-to-stage movements of the economic system — in other words, to explain within-stage changes and between-stage changes and link both explanations to obtain an organic theory of development.

The resolution of the above two theoretical difficulties will generate the explanans to the explanandum concerning the development process. To advance the theory, the descriptive characteristics of each stage must be crisp for identification and recognition when one stage is completely transformed to another. The first theoretical difficulty to be overcome in the theory involves developing a logical construct of an explanation to the interstage changes. This requires the development of a law of motion that governs the economic system. The law of motion will provide the logic of the transforming process. It must, however, be general and derived from the socioeconomic fabric of the social organism, with clearly identified institutions of production and consumption.

The second theoretical difficulty concerns intrastage changes. Overcoming this difficulty requires the construction of another law of motion that traces the path of fundamental changes in the quality of the internal organization and arrangements of the socioeconomic system. Finally, out of the two theoretical difficulties, there emerges an important question as to whether the interstage and intrastage movements are fundamentally interconnected.

Viewed from this angle, we can outline the explanandum of Marx's theory of development as follows:

Intrastage and interstage movements of economic organism are observed.

Each stage is defined by its content, which gives it character and quality; the content is encapsuled in the form, which is composed of a system of ideas, traditions, and ideologies; and the content is composed of quantitative and qualitative properties, internal processes, and methods, techniques, and relations of production.

Each stage has a distinct form and institutions through which it externally expresses the character of the content.

The logical basis of Marx's explanatory theory of socioeconomic development of societies is the materialist dialectics and historicity. The logical construct of the explanation combines principle of materialism, principle of knowability, principle of dialectics and historicity, and principle of contradiction as a dialectical category. The basic thrust of the logical construct rests on four interdependent systems of reasoning. The principle of materialism is called upon to establish the material basis and the existence of the socioeconomic organism and the stages through which it passes. The principle of knowability is used to identify the qualitative and quantitative (content) properties of the stages as well as the structure that encapsules them. The principle of dialectics and historicity is called upon for the establishment of experience and the transformation processes as a general law of economic development. Last, the principle of contradiction is invoked to establish how the transformation process emerges in order to explain the intrastage and interstage movements and changes while the logic of science is brought to connect the explanations of intrastage and interstage changes to obtain a general theory of transformation and, hence, of economic development.

On the basis of these four principles, Marx advances an explanatory theory of development. The theory also constitutes the essential logic of economic dynamics. First, Marx's theory shows that changes in the content are intrastage transformation, while changes in the form constitute interstage transformation. The next step is the examination of the relative movements of intrastage and interstage and the relationship between the two movements; this is done by a critical examination of known stages of the economic organism. It is then argued that the content is unstable and under continual changes. The form, on the other hand, is relatively stable; however, it goes through periodic changes. A change in the form establishes a new stage of socioeconomic development completely different from the previous stage.

To ascertain the factors that cause the form to change, a unity between the content and the form is established. The form is not viewed as external to the content. The form and the content exist in unity. It is the unity of the internal organization of the socioeconomic system and the external expression of that unity that allow complete identification of the stage of the economic organism. The form cannot exist without the content, and the content exists within the form. They are, however, opposites that constitute a unity. They exist in a conflict, because the content is continually in a state of flux. The form as an external expression of the content can exist only with a stable content.

When the character of the content defining the existing stage of the economic system has so changed that the content runs counter to the form, one of two things must happen: the form is destroyed, or the content is again changed to that quality that is consistent with the form that contains it. The first event leads to the creation or emergence of a new form that is consistent with the new content. Alternatively expressed, the contradiction between the content and the form seeking to dissolve the unity of the content and the form defines the force of interstage movements and the equation of motion that governs them. The second event rarely occurs, and its occurrence violates the law of forward motion that defines development.

The law of interstage movements and transformation is the consequence of those forces that generate intrastage changes leading to alterations in the content of the economic system. Within the Marxist theory, such forces are internal and anchored in human decisions and experiences. Generally, it is the contradictions between nature and the human will to survive and create comfort from natural environment and the contradictions among human beings acting as hostile classes to improve their relative positions at least cost that generate forces of change and, hence, establish the laws of quantitative and qualitative changes that bring about the intrastage motion.

The struggles to improve individual and class economic relative positions generate class conflict. The social unity required by material production and the class struggle produced by distribution of the articles of production (income) create contradictions in the unity of the economic organism. The resolution of the conflicts and contradictions brings about some important quantitative changes in the means and methods of production. Such changes are intrastage, take place in the content, and continue for a long period of time.

The accumulated intrastage quantitative changes generate a new content by altering the qualitative characteristics of the existing content. In the process of intrastage changes, a point is reached when the content is no longer compatible with the form that encapsules it. This creates an uncontrollable contradiction where the content and the form can no longer exist in harmony. The social forces generated by the new content of the economic organism pressure the old form to collapse. In place of it, a new form that is compatible with the new content emerges. In other words, the resulting contradiction between the content and its form and the resolution thereof lead to the transformation of forms of the economic system in the Marxist explanatory theory.

The Essentials of Rostow's Theory of Stages of Economic Growth

We shall now turn to the essentials and core ideas of Rostow's stage-based explanatory theory of economic development. Essentially, Rostow's exposition is not directly about economic development. He does touch on it in many places. Because Rostow presented his theory (182) as an alternative theory to that of Marx, we shall place Rostow's theory under a similar examination. Rostow intended to develop a theory that could explain the stages of economic growth without using class conflict as a driving force of change.

As a rival to Marxist theory, Rostow subtitles his book *A Non-Communist Manifesto*. In it, he claims that "the stages-of-growth are assigned to get at these matters and . . . they constitute an alternative to Karl Marx's theory of modern history" (182, p. 2). Having identified five different stages of economic growth as rival categories to those of Marx, Rostow attempts to advance a theory that explains certain observed characteristics.

Rostow's theory is developed on the following characteristics:

Resources of production are used in a specific way in different periods in history.

Limitations on production possibilities are imposed on the economic system by the way in which the resources of production are utilized. Production horizons of traditional societies have substantial limitation, because most of the resources of production are used in agriculture.

A new era in economic development starts with a major breakthrough in production possibilities, made possible by varying applications of economic resources — in other words, the way resources are used.

Each economic system has a corresponding social and political system that may or may not be equipped to exploit the impulse to expand. In this respect, a change in the social and political system is a prerequisite for an economic revolution.

Higher rates of saving and capital spending are closely related to higher stages of economic growth.

Rostow faces the same two theoretical difficulties confronted by Marx, even though the category formation of stages was different. These two theoretical difficulties must be overcome in order for Rostow's logical construct to constitute an explanation to the economic development process. The two theoretical difficulties to be overcome are the problem of constructing a logical process that explains how the economic system moves through the stage categories and the problem of developing a logical construct that will explain, in the same stage, how economic activities reach critical levels, how the critical levels produce changes, how these changes lead to "massive and progressive structural transformations in economies and societies," and how "a political, social and institutional framework that exploits the impulse to expand" arrives on the historic scene.

Rostow's solutions to the two theoretical problems constitute his explanans to the categorial conversion that establishes the development process. The initial requirement for the theory to be advanced is that the description of each stage must be sufficiently crisp for identification and recognition when stage transformation occurs. There are a number of criticisms of Rostow's category formation of the stages (47, 51, 115, 142). These are, however, not our focus here. We shall accept the stages as proffered by Rostow and proceed with our analysis.

Given Rostow's stage classification, the first theoretical problem is the development of a logic required for the explanans of the interstage changes. To accomplish this, a construction of a transfer process that traces the transient path between stages is necessary. The transfer process is basically the law of motion that must govern the interstage dynamics of the economic system. This transfer process is also the transformation process. Its construction must be general and be based on the socioeconomic fabric of the society, with well-defined institutions of production and distribution.

The second theoretical difficulty in Rostow's system of explanation is intrastage in nature. This problem involves constructing an intrastage transformation process that explains changes in institutions and human motives and how such changes are linked to delicate balances in social choices and decision making that lead to fundamental changes in the quality of the stage. The solution involves constructing a general law of motion that governs the internal dynamics of each stage. Additionally, Rostow must demonstrate how the equation of motion or the transformation rule governing the intrastage changes is linked to "massive and progressive structural transformations in economics and societies." The structural transformation is viewed here as changes in form and, hence, stages.

Given the stages as identified, Rostow develops an explanation based on an epistemological position that rests more on an individualistic inductivism. In the construction of the explanans, Rostow sees the movement in history and, hence, stage transformation as explained in terms of human motives. He suggests that "in terms of human motivation many of the most profound economic changes are viewed as the consequences of non-economic human motives and aspirations" (182, p. 2). The explanatory ideas of human motives and aspirations are then combined with intrastage classificatory factors of "leading sectors" whose collective growth becomes instrumental in moving the economy forward and, hence, transforming the stages as identified.

To answer the question as to how "human motives" are inspired or arise to make a breakthrough in each stage and propel the economy to higher stages, Rostow points to political and other institutional factors, the changes of which affect the configuration of "human motives." Regarding the question of how the political factors tend to change, Rostow anchors his answer in forces external to the economic system, such as intrusion by more developed foreign forces or power. In this respect, the ultimate cause of interstate motion or development as we may want to imply is an outside society. In other words, just as Thales' intellectual predecessors invoked the supernatural, within the ambit of the principle of metaphysics, in order to explain nature, Rostow invokes superpower in a political sense and within the sphere of the principle of metaphysics to explain changes in political institutions in which human motives are entrenched.

Rostow, on the other hand, relies on more efficient investment allocation decisions to explain how the "leading sectors" become instrumental in propelling the economy through stages. The trend of Rostow's argument suggests that increased investment in the leading sectors widens "the scale of productive economic activity" to a critical point within a stage. When the critical point is reached, "a massive and progressive structural transformation in the economies and societies" occurs. In a more or less simplified (but accurate) summary, the argument is that an intrusion of an economic and political superpower forces changes in political, economic, and cultural institutions that house human motives and motivations distributed over choices and decisions and how these choices and decisions are balanced. Changes in these institutions that are produced by forces from outside the system then lead to changes in human motives and motivations. Changes in human motives and motivations alter choices and decisions because the old choices and decisions are incompatible with the new institutional configuration that has risen from the impressions of external forces. Changes in these choices and decisions lead to changes in resource allocations that tend to produce changes in the leading sectors. Changes in these leading sectors collectively lead to changes in the scale of productive activity until a critical level is reached. Changes in the scale of productive activity and the reaching of the critical level lead to massive and progressive structural transformation in the economy and society, thus, propelling the economy from stage to stage.

The Essential Logic of Schumpeterian
Theory of Economic Development

We shall now consider the essential logical structure of Schumpeter's explanatory theory of economic development. From the onset,

Schumpeter tells us that his objective is to "construct a theoretical model of the process of economic change in time, or perhaps more clearly, to answer the question how the economic system generates the force which incessantly transforms it" (204, p. 165). Alternatively stated, Schumpeter seeks a pure theory that would explain "economic evolution as a distinct process generated by the economic system itself" (204, p. 166). To do this, he must construct a logically consistent explanans whose propositions must show how the economic system destroys old forms and creates new forms with different qualitative characteristics. Schumpeter calls this explanans "a scheme of possible modi operandi" (204, p. 231). The critical question faced by Schumpeter, therefore, is to craft a mechanism to explain not "how capitalism administers existing structures" but "how it creates and destroy them" (207, p. 84) after projecting that "the social process is really one indivisible whole" and that "social facts are, at least immediately, results of human conduct, economic facts results of economic conduct" where the economic conduct is "directed towards the acquisition of goods" (205, p. 3).

Schumpeter's main concern is to construct an explanans to answer the question as to how capitalism transforms itself through defined developmental stages. In his *Theory of Economic Development*, capitalism is conceived as a "commercially organized state, one in which private property, division of labor and free competition prevail" (205, p. 5). Economic development, on the other hand, is viewed as "spontaneous and discontinuous changes in the channels of the flow, disturbance of equilibrium, which forever alters and displaces the equilibrium state previously existing" (205, p. 63). In other words, economic development is viewed in a manner where the system experiences qualitative and quantitative transformations within states. The explanation of forces of transient process between equilibrium states is the solution to the second problem of transformation that we have characterized as intrastage changes.

Schumpeter's theoretical explanation of intrastage transformation must, then, be linked to a constructed logical explanation of interstage changes to show how the capitalist system transforms itself from primitive form to socialist form. The organic construct of Schumpeter's explanans may be seen in terms of the logical steps of Marxian explanans, where the principles of materialism, knowability, historicity, and dialectics are assembled to show how "changes take place and to what economic phenomena do they give rise" (205, p. 58). Schumpeter evokes the principle of historicity to establish the subject matter of economic development by acknowledging that development is a map of historic facts. He suggests that "economic development is . . . simply the object of economic history which in turn is merely a part of universal history, only separated from the rest for purposes of exposition" (205, p. 58).

The principle of materialism is called into play to establish not only the material reality of each defined stage and its qualities but also the material foundation for convertibility of stages. It is then recognized that materialism becomes dialectical and, hence, dynamic when the economic system is viewed in terms of, not equilibrium states, but decision processes that constitute the living soul of socioeconomic reality. In line with this thought, Schumpeter suggests that: "Every concrete process of development finally rests upon preceding development. But in order to see the essence of the thing clearly, we shall abstract from this and allow the development to arise out of a position without development. Every process of development creates the prerequisites from the following. Thereby the form of the latter is altered" (205, p. 64). He accepts not only the material bases for intrastage and interstage transformations but also dialectical process that will ensure such material basis for conversion of stages.

The principle of dialectics is, thus, called upon to assist in the establishment of the logical transformation of categories of intrastages and interstages. Epistemologically, therefore, Schumpeter first rejects the existing "static method of analysis" as being incapable "to predict the consequences of discontinuous changes in the traditional way of doing things; [because] it can neither explain the occurrence of such productive revolutions nor the phenomena which accompany them" (205, pp. 62–63). It is then observed that "there was a source of energy within the economic system which would of itself disrupt any equilibrium that might be attained" (204, p. 166). Implied in this statement are principles of self-motion and contradiction.

The principle of knowability is used to identify the contents of intrastages and interstages and the structures that encapsule them so that the nature of equilibrium and type of economic system can be isolated and identified when the system is transformed. The principle of knowability, therefore, involves the logical specification of the essential properties of the content of each stage and the nature of the form that contains it so that the loss of old properties and acquisition of new properties can be identified when stages are transformed.

On the basis of these principles, Schumpeter constructs an explanatory theory of capitalist development and then links it to its transformation to socialism. He suggests that even though socioeconomic decisions are driven by economic motives, the principal factors of economic development are noneconomic. These noneconomic factors are to be found in the configuration of social institutions. From the institutional structure that defines the boundaries of decisions and the protective strata of the content, he isolates institution of entrepreneurs and entrepreneurial decision activities. To pull out the law of motion governing the capitalist system and generated by its internal dynamics, Schumpeter acknowledges the fundamental requirement of categorial convertibility, where the category held as primary must satisfy the ontological conditions of factual correctness. He also acknowledges qualitative leaps and that dialectical processes are nonlinear in the transformation of kinds of stages. He states, "Development . . . is a distinct phenomenon. . . . It is spontaneous and discontinuous change . . . which forever alters and displaces the equilibrium state previously existing" (205, p. 64).

These propositions allow Schumpeter to satisfy the two fundamental demands of category formation of ontological conditions of concrete existence of at least one of the categories that can be used as a primary stage from which the subsequent stages may be logically derived and the knowability conditions that allow identifiability of categories or stages as actual or potential in the transient process induced by the internal energies of the economy. From these conditions of concrete existence of the primary category and identifiability of stages when the old stage loses its set of properties and acquires a new set, Schumpeter abstracts an origin of evolution of kind, a dialectical source of change to establish a law of motion generated from the internal conflicts of competing forces in the social organism to ensure intrastage and interstage conversions.

From the social conditions of production and distribution, Schumpeter acknowledges that dialectical transformation and the corresponding dialectical moment require the existence of social self-motion and that this self-motion of the economy results from the fact that the society is under a plenum of decision forces in tension whose resolution propels the socioeconomic system forward. He, thus, accepts the scientific and methodological character of Marx. In fact, he indirectly accepts the first three logical building blocks of Marxian explanans as outlined above but rejects the Marxian class struggle as the dialectical source that generates the force of motion and transformation of intrastages and interstages. He suggests that development is a historic map of success-failure process of past and present decisions of production and investment on new activities broadly defined to break the cycle of equilibrium routine of economic activities by risk taking. The logic of economic dynamics based on conflicting forces within the social system provides us with the required tools for interpreting this map, which is made up of intrastage and interstage transient processes.

The intrastage transformation is effected through the decision processes of introduction of new goods, introduction of new methods of production, opening of new markets for either existing or new goods, conquest of new sources of supply of new materials or half-manufactured goods, and carrying out of the new organization of any industry (205, p. 66) These five decision elements and processes in the social setup, given the institutional arrangements of politics, law, and economics, constitute the set of Schumpeterian innovative decisions that he calls "new combinations." The necessary requirements for bringing about intrastage transformation given each stage (equilibrium) are innovative decisions involving the "new combinations" in all aspects of production activities. The carrying on of such innovation decisions is the responsibility of "the producer who as a rule initiates economic change" (205, p. 65), because "innovations in the economic system do not as a rule place in such a way that new wants arise spontaneously in consumers and then the productive apparatus swings round through their pressure" (205, p. 65).

The innovations are distinguished from inventions and logically linked to the class of producers called "entrepreneurs" who, by a gift of special personality, take risks and implement decisions on new combinations of productive means. The driving force of the innovation decisions is the abnormal profits to be made when success occurs in the process of intraequilibrium changes, not possible in equilibrium states, when the system is transformed from a lower level of equilibrium to a higher level, broadly defined. From the set of innovation decisions and the entrepreneurial group, Schumpeter enters into the world of dialectics and calls into service the principle of contradiction.

Here he evokes the concept of competition, as a contradiction in the category of dialectics, among capitalists over abnormal profits in the disequilibrium process to establish the origin of evolution of kind through dialectical movements of stages. The competitive struggle among capitalists over abnormal profits brought about by entrepreneurial innovative activities and supported by equal credit availability seeks to eliminate the pure economic profits (surplus value in Marxian terminology) and interest income generated from productive investment induced by innovations. This process of capitalist competition will continue until a new equilibrium is established, given the general institutional arrangements of capitalism where full employment, zero credit, and economic stability are ensured.

At the new equilibrium with almost zero profit and investment at the level of replacement, the entrepreneurs look for "new combinations," which often are unevenly distributed through time or appear in "swarms." New innovations are introduced that bring in a wave of new firms and investments that are financed largely by new credit creation from the banks, leading to important disturbances of the "circular flow." The carrying-on of "new combination" through the implementation of innovational investment decisions is the capitalist's weapon of struggle against another to generate and maintain abnormal profits while competition through the rise of new firms and disappearance of inefficient ones is an instrument that eliminates profits as the socioeconomic systems adjust to the new equilibrium. The entrepreneurial innovations create abnormal profits, while capitalist competition eliminates these abnormal profits. The elimination of these purely economic profits motivates a search for and implementation of new "combinations," which engender innovative activities.

A dialectical logic of stage transformation, an origin of evolution of kind, is established in Schumpeterian explanans to the explanandum of economic development process. Here, the joint process of innovation and competition "incessantly revolutionizes the economic structure from within, incessantly destroying the old one, incessantly creating a new one. This process of Creative Destruction is the essential fact about capitalism" (207, p. 83). In this way, an intrastage transformation from within capitalism with a well-defined law of motion is specified and ensured, leading to an explanatory theory of an internally generated process of economic dynamics that involves transformation of quality, quantity, and form. Differently stated, Schumpeter suggests that, "In a society with private property and competition, this process is the necessary complement of the continual emergence of new economic and social forms and continually rising real income of all social strata" (205, p. 255).

Changes in quality, as may be abstracted from the Schumpeterian construct, arise from within the capitalist system through innovation-driven investments, new-investment driven by abnormal profits, and profit-driven competitive struggle among capitalists. Together, they constitute the dialectical force that explains development within stages by showing how the capitalist system moves from one equilibrium to another with a higher level of technology, organizational efficiency, factor productivities, output, and lower levels of costs.

The "law of the falling rate of profit" or the tendency for abnormal profits to be eliminated by conflicts of competition in entrepreneurial capitalism is the driving force to innovate through new investments. Innovation in more efficient techniques of production, cost-saving techniques, and efficient social technologies are the instruments for the capitalists to wage battle among themselves over actual and potential abnormal economic profits. Innovations are introduced to solve the problem of the falling rate of profit in order to maintain abnormal profits. The presence of innovation-induced abnormal profits invites more competition by creating new firms and revolutionizing existing firms that tend to eliminate the entrepreneurial pure economic profits. Thus, a principle of contradiction between innovation and competition is not only established by Schumpeter but also evoked as a dialectical moment that explains the qualitative changes in the content that then induces a creative conflict with the form that contains it. Thus, intrastage transformations that propel the entrepreneurial capitalism forward and bring about its development are ensured.

To logically link intrastage changes to interstage changes to advance an organic theory of economic development, Schumpeter once again relies on the institutional dynamics and internal contradictions of entrepreneurial capitalism. He observes that the very nature of entre-preneurial innovation that generates abnormal profits and invites capitalist competition also alters the essential contents and structures of institutions of values, decisions, and social norms to bring about social and cultural conditions that are inimical to the survival of the entrepreneurial capitalist system. The success of capitalism also is its destructive force, where "entrepreneurial activity impresses the stamp of its mentality upon the social organism. In any cultural history, therefore, the entrepreneurial factor will have to come in as one of the explaining elements" (204, p. 270).

The internal dynamics of institutions of capitalism that foster the growth and existence of entrepreneurs, entrepreneurial innovations, and a higher standard of living for all classes also create hostile conditions for the disappearance of the entrepreneurs and the capitalist class into which they fade. The resulting conditions of the success of entrepreneurial innovation lead to the "destruction of the protective strata" that provide the political, legal, and ideological protection for the capitalists, the entrepreneurs, and their private activities and, thus, hasten the dissolution of entrepreneurial capitalism by undermining the roots of essential institutions.

The working mechanism of "creative destruction" that bring about transformation of stages as set up by Schumpeter is such that: "The very success of business class in developing the productive powers of its country and the very fact that this success has created a new standard of life for all classes has paradoxically undermined the social and political position of the same business class whose economic function, though not obsolete tends to become obsolescent and amenable to bureaucratization" (209, p. 449). He further suggests that: "The fundamental impulse that keeps the capitalist engine in motion comes from the new consumer goods, the new methods of production or transportation, the new markets, the new forms of industrial organization that capitalist enterprise creates" (207, p. 83).

The essential elements of fundamental impulse lubricate the capitalist engine for intrastage transformation to higher order of material level that also constitute the destructive elements of wear and tear as they alternatively present themselves as weapons of competition that adds to the force of intrastage transformation. For it is "the competition from the new commodity, the new technology, the new source of supply, the new type of organization [new combinations] — competition which commands a decisive cost quality advantage and which strikes not at the margins of the profits and outputs of the existing firms but at their foundations and their very lives" (207, p. 84).

From these dynamics of the instruments of competitive struggle among capitalists and how they relate to profits, abnormal profits, losses, disappearance of old enterprises, and emergence of new enterprises, Schumpeter suggested an important element that connects the intrastage transformation process to the transformation of form of entrepreneurial capitalism to bureaucratic capitalism as the content alters from equilibrium to equilibrium. The important elements are uncertainty of profit and the risk of total losses of productive assets induced by competition. At any stage of the process of transformation, the "perennial gale of creative destruction" threatens the material foundation of life and survival of entrepreneurs and capitalist class into which they melt. Schumpeter suggests that: "The businessman feels himself to be in a competitive situation even if he is alone in his field or if though not alone, he holds a position such that investigating government experts fail to see any effective competition between him and any other firms in the same or a neighboring field and in consequence conclude that his talk, under examination, about his competitive sorrow is all make-believe" (204, p. 30). The "perennial gale of creative destruction" induced by innovation and competition imposes a particular rational behavior on the entrepreneurs, firms, and capitalists in a rapidly changing environment of business competition to restrict competition.

In the Schumpeterian logical world, entrepreneurial capitalism is a process where competition among capitalists promotes the introduction of "new combinations" through implementations of investment decisions in *innovations* that are carried on by entrepreneurs. Innovations generate abnormal profits, which, in turn, invite more and intense *competition* for the innovators. Competition depletes the entrepreneurial *abnormal profits* and then threatens the productive assets that embody the innovation by creating *risky environments*, which then induce a process of *new innovations*. The existence and threat of entrepreneurial risk in a rapidly changing environment and the need to protect entrepreneurial activities, abnormal profits, and capital associated with innovations force entrepreneurs, firms, and capitalists "to resort to such protective devices as patents or temporary secrecy of processes or, in some cases long-period contracts secured in advance" (204, p. 31).

To overcome the dangers of competitive capitalism, the innovators, firms, and capitalists consolidate and form megagroups. The business megagroups develop routine management of bureaucrats and technocrats whose decision activities are simplified by rules, made less risky and innovationally conservative with new values, culture, and personality completely different from those consistent with entrepreneurial capitalism. The new values, culture, personality, and large firms create a risk-averting business and social environment that is hostile to the entrepreneurial innovative process, thus, marginalizing the entrepreneurs and individual capitalists whose activities diminish in importance and are finally ousted.

Entrepreneurial capitalism, with its institutional configuration of law and ideology, and laissez-faire government that rewards and encourages the innovative process of individual entrepreneurs, a subclass of capitalists, loses its content through the process of creative destruction. The old content is replaced by a new content with bureaucratized giant firms managed by hired and depersonalized technocrats who encourage depersonalized ownership. The new content no longer is consistent with the form of entrepreneurial capitalism, which gives way to a new social form of *bureaucratic capitalism* with its own value system, cultural norms, ideology, and institutions of law and politics that form its protective strata.

The process of content changing includes:

an increasing obsolescence of the entrepreneurial function as the function is depersonalized by the created large concerns and taken over by collectives;

the destruction of the protective strata that includes the precapitalist social groups and the corresponding values and personalities;

the collapse of the institutions that support individual proprietorship, innovativeness, and incentive structure; and

the emergence of a new value and thinking system that brings about ideological restructuring of the relationships among private property, individual achievements, rewards, and nation and also creates hostile elements against entrepreneurial capitalism as well as the collective personality that represents its disposition.

In providing a theoretical explanation for the movement from bureaucratic capitalism to socialism, Schumpeter sought a new law of motion based on antagonistic forces in the social setup of bureaucratic capitalism. Here, the antagonistic forces are generated by conflicts between large firms and the state. The large firms seek to maintain their abnormal profits not through new innovations but through intensive exploitation of the market with their acquired market power. The state as a product of entrepreneurial capitalism seeks to maintain certain qualities of competition of the old form so as to promote innovation, increasing diversity of goods, and lower prices. The large firms not only are innovationally restrictive but also develop strategies for generating and managing success in business, as measured by profits.

The strategies involve predatory competitive practices, where monopoly and oligopoly tendencies develop to create conditions of imperfections and unfairness in the market that give impressions "that private profits, both in themselves and through the distortion of the economic process they induce are always a net loss to all excepting those who receive them and would therefore constitute a net gain to be reaped by socialization" (204, p. 23). Furthermore, "at any point of time they seem to be doing nothing but restricting output and keeping prices high" (204, p. 32).

These perceptions, which find imprints from the operations of bureaucratic capitalism, invite state regulations in all markets of inputs and outputs with the hope of correcting the ills of imperfect competitive struggle induced by bureaucratic capitalism. New rules and regulations are legislated, setting into motion alterations of the content of the legal structure, which affects the decision-making process, the environment of business, the political structure, the content of economic structure, and the ideological system that provides its protective belt. The state's objective is to rid the economic system of unfair competition, predatory business practices, and consumer exploitation.

As old strategies and techniques of trade restrictions are constrained by the evolving legal structure, the large firms and business enterprises of the bureaucratic capitalism design new strategies and resort to novel techniques to restrict competition and trade. The new strategies and techniques designed to restrict trade and create unfair and imperfect competition invite more state intervention through market regulations and controls, creating a process of creative conflict. Each round of this process heightens the contradiction between the business sector and the public sector, while each resolution alters, in a significant way, the content and moves the system to a new qualitative level.

In such a process, the state and the business sectors operate in an antagonistic decision mode where they exist in creative tension that provides the dialectical moment for propelling the system through the developmental stages by means of the principle of mutual negation and destruction. In one of his essays, Schumpeter illustrates the nature of the creative conflict that induces transformation of kind by stating: "The capitalist process itself produces, as effectively as it produces motorcars or refrigerators, a distribution of political power, an attitude of the public mind, and an orientation of the political sector that are at variance with its own law of life" (204, p. 176). He further adds that:

The very success of the business class in developing the productive powers of its country and the very fact that success has created a new standard of life for all classes has paradoxically undermined the social and political position of the same business class whose economic function, though not obsolete, tends to become obsolescent and amenable to bureaucratization. . . . The concentration of the business class on the task of the factory and the office was instrumental in creating a political system and intellectual class the structure and interests of which developed an attitude of independence from, and eventually of hostility to, the interests of large-scale business. The latter is becoming increasingly incapable of defending itself against raids that are, in the short run, highly profitable to other classes. (209, pp. 448–49)

The constructed Schumpeterian explanans suggests that it is the conflict between the state and business concerns in the social decision space that institutionally generates the law of transformation. The social interests (or, at least, the perception of them) that motivate the state's decision to regulate and control come into conflict with the business interests that motivate decisions to promote imperfection and trade restriction. This conflict strips the bureaucratic capitalism of its adaptability and flexibility, calcifying and transforming it into *centralist socialism*, where the "organization of society in which the means of production are controlled, and the decision on how and what to produce and who is to get what, are made by public authority instead of by privately-owned and privately-managed firms" (207, p. 421). In this way, the bureaucratic capitalism alters its content by its internal force, bringing about the transformation of its form such that there is "the migration of people's economic affairs from the private into the public sphere" (207, p. 421).

The content of the bureaucratic capitalism becomes so much altered that a conflict arises between the form and the content in a way that induces mutual negation. A resolution of the conflict takes place where the structure and form of bureaucratic capitalism collapse to give way to a new form, which Schumpeter calls "socialism," with new political, cultural, and institutional arrangements that are in harmony with the new form. The new form comes with a political arrangement where the state acquires the authority in decision space that allows it to determine production and distribution of the social output. It brings with it a new culture, personality, ideology, and thinking system that create a new protective stratum.

EVALUATION AND CRITICISMS OF THE SCIENTIFIC STATUS OF THE STAGE-BASED THEORIES

We have presented the basic logical constructs of three differently structured stage-based explanatory theories of economic development, as expounded by Marx, Schumpeter, and Rostow. Scientifically, they have the same objective, but their epistemological bases are different. In terms of category formation, they project economic development and, hence, history in a dynamic setting. Marx, Schumpeter, and Rostow attempted to characterize the evolution of society and its history by what they considered points of critical turns. The structures between points of critical turns are referred to as stages on the evolutionary path of the socioeconomic organism.

The logical basis for Rostow's category formation is the level of economic activity defined in terms of growth or what may be referred to in Marxian terminology as the level of productive forces. Contrary to Rostow's classificatory scheme, the logical basis for Marx's category formation is ownership relations to the productive forces and power relations to the distribution of results of production rather than to productive forces. Schumpeter's classification scheme is based on power relations as they involve economic decisions in production and distribution spaces, the size of the decision unit, and the degree of state involvement. We shall not take issue with any specific category formation.

We want to point out, however, that every category formation has its epistemological usefulness and deficiencies and, hence, is subject to criticism. It is always possible that more than one useful system of categories may be formed from historical data. Subsequently, although we do not want to discourage criticisms of stage classification of history, we want to point out that such criticisms should not be overemphasized and overstretched. Epistemologically, most of the criticisms of Rostow's stages are both philosophically and theoretically irrelevant. Having said this, it may be suggested that classification of stages of history based on either production relations such as ownership and distribution or power relations in economic decision space is an explicit acknowledgment that production takes place within the ambit of a society, no matter how small such a society may be. Moreover, it is only in society where individuals relate to one another and to the collective to decide and generate collaborative effort, but not in an individual isolation, that levels of productive activity in society are changed to bring about what Rostow calls "massive and progressive structural transformation in economies and society" (182) of which individuals are integral parts.

In a general scheme of things, the logical basis of Rostow's classification implicitly assumes existing institutions of ownership and distribution of a society and its production organism. In this respect, Schumpeter, like Marx, was explicit from the onset that "we shall primarily think of a commercially organized state, one in which private property, division of labor and free competition prevail" (205, p. 5). Although Rostow seems to suggest that his category formation of stages of economic evolution is an alternative to Marx's, nonetheless, Rostow's category formation can, in all theoretical purposes, be considered as intrastage categories within each of Marx's stages. Rostow indirectly acknowledges this point in his diagrammatic representation of stages of economic growth (182, p. xx), where different economic systems with different institutional arrangements of ownership and distribution are presented. In this respect, much of Rostow's own criticisms of Marx are purely ideological, epistemologically empty, and scientifically irrelevant to the explanation of economic evolution and development that we seek.

Categories are aggregates constructed to bring into focus certain patterns that are inherent in the data or a set of microprocesses. Many patterns may, therefore, be formed, depending on the point of emphasis, the objectives, and the problem of science at hand. The first epistemological requirement demanded of any system of category formation is that one of the categories must satisfy the ontological conditions of concrete existence or factual correctness. The second requirement demanded by the epistemological condition of knowing is that the rest of the categories must, at least, have potential for existence and that each category must satisfy the conditions of identifiability. The current existence or nonexistence of a category is irrelevant to develop an explanatory theory of evolution of kind.

The epistemological demand of category-based explanatory theory, given the categories or stages in the case of economic evolution, requires that the category that satisfies the ontological condition of factual correctness be held as the primary category or initial stage and all other categories must then be shown as derivative from it. In other words, the dynamic process of interstage and intrastage transformations must be initialized. All other stages are real and concrete only insofar as they are derived from the primary stage.

Evaluation, Appraisal, and Criticisms of Rostow's Theory

Upon examination of the explanans of Rostow's system, one becomes uneasy with the number of theoretical difficulties and logical inconsistencies. These difficulties and logical inconsistencies may be abstracted from the systematized steps of Rostow's logical sequence of explanation of stage evolution of economic development. Rostow's explanatory theory is, more or less, data analysis of randomly selected points of history with transitional process externally induced.

The problem of economic development as specified by Rostow is general, encompassing the structure of history as societies interact with nature for survival, livelihood, and comfort. Just like Marx, Rostow audaciously attempted to explain socioeconomic development of societies. The problem as structured by Rostow meets the general conditions of manageability and clarity. In terms of problem specification, the goals and objectives are clear.

The logical structure of Rostow's explanation is defective. It does not satisfy the condition of generality. At least, the system fails to explain the British case, which he admits in his discussions. Here, Rostow assumes the British case to be unique and, hence, outside his system of explanation. Thus, Rostow, indirectly or directly, assigns the first mover to Britain, whose actions explain the economic development of the rest of the world social systems. When it comes to answering the question as to how the British acquired the power to be a first mover, Rostow, entangled in a theoretical difficulty, exits out of his logical system and enters into plea with the logic of dialectics to forcefully pull out a transfer function that will explain the transient process of the "great mover" of history.

Rostow makes a great attempt as an alternative to Marx. However, he produces an important logical contradiction and an explanans that seems to be plagued with flaws. For example, what epistemological interpretation should one assign to Rostow's statement: "Now as we have seen the British case of transition was unique in the sense that it appeared to have been brought about by internal dynamics of a single society, without external intervention; that is, there grew up within an agricultural and trading society an industrial middle class, which progressively transformed the politics, social structure, and values of the society, notably in the three decades after Waterloo" (182, p. 15).

Rostow's statement is more of an experiential assertion rather than an explanation of a process with a transfer function that shows the transient structure between stages. The forces that brought about qualitative transformation of how individual members relate to each other and to the British society that generated a new social milieu leading to the emergence of an industrial middle class with a new value system must be explained if a law of motion is to be indicated. The quoted statement is a tacit acceptance of Schumpeter's position that "there was a source of energy within the economic system which would of itself disrupt any equilibrium [stage] that might be attained" (204, p. 166).

This explanation must then be linked to a second order explanation of how this new British value system tends to influence choice and decision in a particular direction among all possible directions. If Rostow is going to dabble in dialectics of change, then he must meet a basic consistency principle to which all dialectical logicians must adhere. First, he must come to the recognition that when history becomes dialectical in a materialist sense, the characterization of the economy into stages must be logically transformed into processes, which then become the lifeblood of reality that must satisfy the ontological conditions of factual correctness. Similarly, when the material basis for category formation, such as the stages of growth, becomes dialectical, it establishes the true basis for stage transformation.

In this respect, Rostow fails to show that an explanation of stage-to-stage transformation is a categorial conversion that becomes complete when its explanans suffice for explanation, by means of admitted rules for specifying the transient process, of all the propositions belonging to the explanans. Laws of transformation, in dialectical sense, are those that make evolution of stages possible. He, thus, fails even to explain the British case on the basis of which he dismissed the logical system of Marx regarding category formation and the explanans.

Viewed in this respect, a number of criticisms against Rostow become concretized. One such criticism is the linear characterization of history. On this point, Kuznets warns us that stage-making "approaches are misleading when they succumb to a linear conception of history and imply that all economies tend to pass through the same series of stages" (116). It is important to be cognizant of the requirement of the principle of dialectical evolution that stages of economic development are not conceived to be unidirectional, linear, or even continuous. In the logic of transformation of kinds and, hence, stages (as may be classified in history), linear and continuous transformation are incompatible. Every categorial conversion represents a qualitative jump in a linear sense; thus, interstage transformations are finitely linear discontinuities whose positions are manifested by leaps. The intrastage transformation, however, progresses in a nonlinear way, which is also admitted by Schumpeter in his analysis of intrastage transformation through business cycles. These basic logical requirements for explaining the dynamics of quantitative and qualitative changes of the socioeconomic system were not met by Rostow.

In Rostow's explanation of how other economies besides Britain have passed or are passing through some or all the stages that he has identified, he makes an exit out of the logical world of dialectics and assigns the explanatory force of stage transformation of these economies to an external mover without which these economies would remain or would have underdeveloped. This approach of evoking a supereconomy and supernation in order to explain intrastage changes in production relations, or what Rostow prefers to call "value system," that lead to interstage transformation amounts to no explanation of scientific significance.

If superpowers are viewed as an explanatory device, as Rostow does, for intrastage and interstage transformations and, hence, account for development phenomena, then there is nothing to prevent the most vicious and oppressive superpower emerging, whose greed may bring about lack of development and, hence, constitute an explanation of underdevelopment. There are plenty of human experiences attesting to this. The Western slavery of Africans is a good example. In other words, the same use of the presence of a superpower to explain positive economic growth can be used to explain negative economic growth, thus, producing contradiction in Rostow's logic of forward motion. It is, therefore, not surprising that he returns to explain the emergence of internal self-motion, which he assigns to Britain by the presence of a threat of superpower. Rostow says:

The general case is of a society modernizing itself in a nationalist reaction to intrusion or the threat of intrusion from more advanced powers from abroad. The British experience of freeing itself from the Church of Rome, Spanish power, quasi-colonial relationship to the Dutch . . . and of this is a not wholly unfamiliar story of reactive nationalism.

. . .

It is possible, then, that British nationalism, transcending caste loyalties created by a series of intrusions and challenges to a lesser island off a dominant mainland, may have been a major force in creating a relatively flexible social matrix within which the process of building the preconditions of take-off was hastened in Britain. (182, pp. 34, 35)

This position on Britain is inconsistent with the initial claim of British self-motion.

The general thrust of Rostow's logic is to deny, in a set of contradictory explanatory statements, the evolution of kind or transformation of stages where the stages lose their old properties and acquire new ones through the internal dynamics of the society. By introducing a superpower as an explanatory force of intrastage and interstage transformation, Rostow joins the intellectual predecessors of Thales who invoked supernature in order to explain nature. As such, the energies of Rostow's enterprising men as a critical mass who are destined to bring about stage-to-stage transformation will stay frozen under the ice of ignorance until an arrival or the feeling of an arrival of a superpower. Similarly, the human motives of specific societies that will bring about political change as well a changes in economic relations and value system will lay dormant and in conditions of passivity until the indicated conditions of superpower theologically arrive in that society to act like missionaries to rescue these societies from economic and social primitivity.

Inevitably, when superpowers are used as an explanatory force of economic development, a high degree of colonialism and imperialism is indicated. Thus, just as Marx seeks to provide intellectual ammunitions for the workers to alter their relationships with the owning class of the productive basis of societies, so Rostow ideologically seeks to provide an intellectual ammunition for imperialists and colonialists to hold onto their colonies as well as provide an important ideological justification for the developing world to accept the dominance of a superpower or potential superpower in the name of economic development. It must be emphatically pointed out that the current political movements in Eastern Europe, the Soviet Union, and South Africa, which became explicit in the 1980s, do not provide any support to the logical position of Rostow. They actually work against Rostow's principle of superpower intrusion and in favor of the materialist dialectics of internal self-motion, the logical foundation of Marx and Schumpeter's analysis of stage transformation.

Despite the fact that Rostow's explanans lacks logical consistency and acceptable legitimacy of explanation, we must acknowledge that the logical construct deals with the questions of why, how, and ought. It also contains an empirical content that suggests a hypothesis that wherever we find growth, we can also find a foreign or superpower intrusion. If the main ideas of Rostow's explanation are accepted, then we also must be willing to predict that whenever there is a superpower intrusion, economic growth or stage transformation can be expected. Alternatively stated, Rostow's logical system fails to meet the consistency principle and the conditions of explanation. The explanans satisfies the conditions of structural propositions, existence of empirical content, and prediction. In view of Rostow's position, it may be suggested that Gerschenkron's analysis of attitudes, entrepreneurship, and development is more insightful than that of Rostow (59, pp. 52–71). The same may be said for Schumpeter's works (205, 207).

Finally, Rostow's introduction of key sectors is more or less arbitrary. If he had scientifically read Marx, he would have come across Marx's introduction and analytical use of "key sectors." He also would have observed the analytic beauty of Marx's explanans in the process of seeking logical completeness within the dialectical logic. Marx writes: "Under all forms of society there is a certain industry which predominates over all the rest and whose condition therefore determines the rank and influence of all the rest. It is the universal light with which all the other colors are tinged and are modified through its peculiarity. It is a special ether which determines the specific gravity of everything that appears in it" (132, p. 302). It was the realization of this basic idea that led Marx to analyze the capital-producing sector as a vehicle for intrastage and interstage transformations.

Evaluation, Appraisal, and Criticisms of Marx's Theory

We must now turn our attention to evaluate, appraise, and criticize Marx's stage-based explanatory theory of socioeconomic development. The essentials of the Marxist theory of economic development presented above include elements of our evaluation and appraisal. We explicitly stated the epistemological basis of Marx's explanans. Central to the logical construct are the principles of materialism, dialectics, and contradiction. We shall, however, add some clarity.

In Marx's logical construct, the economic basis is held as the primary factor from which all other important factors that influence stage transformation are derivatives. The maintenance of social life requires collective economic production, and collective work calls for a distribution of the results of production. Production and distribution, in turn, require human organization of resources and cooperative effort in order to deal with the harsh realities of nature, which invariably overwhelm an individual production in isolation. The cooperative effort within the epistemics of materialist dialectics may be peaceful or forced.

The demands of effective organization of production give rise to a political organization that structures and guides the process of production and distribution. The stability of the organizations of politics and production is created by systematizing the evolving social norms into a dynamic system of values that constitute a system of rules and regulations for economic, political, and social behaviors in the fields of decisions and choices. Some of these rules constitute the legal structure of the society. The effectiveness of these rules and regulations on human decision behavior and the survival of the economic and political organizations require the establishment of an organization of armed forces for the internal enforcement of the rules and values and against external threat to the socioeconomic organism. As viewed, the political, social, cultural, and legal characteristics of societies are housed in the economic structure and its progress while they, in turn, form the protective strata for its morphology. This is the first proposition that

Rostow referred to in his summary of what he called the "seven Marxist propositions" (182).

From the methodological position of historical materialism, this basic proposition translates into a minimal logical sequence of important building blocks for establishing categories as conceived by Marx and explaining intrastage and interstage transformations. The first steps in the logical sequence of the building blocks are:

1. The primary goal of human beings is survival and maintenance of life of individuals and the collective; all other goals are derivatives.

2. The primary instrument for achieving the goal and its derivatives is the material production, broadly defined; all other instruments are derivatives.

Given these two building blocks, another cognitive step is taken to extend the logical process by recognizing that an organization of production and the consequent political, legal, and religious suborganizations require all kinds of decision making and choices among alternatives, all of which may have different individual preferences that may compete with one another. The members of these suborganizations are drawn individually to one another and into groups or classes by their own economic self-interest as tied to the primary goal and the derivatives thereof. In so doing, all kinds of economic and other relations are formed. The next logical building block may be stated in accord with the principles of materialism and conversion of categories:

3. The primary relation in society is economic; all other relations are derivatives.

It is then recognized that history is a map of past decisions and choices in the arena of production and other activities that are derivatives. The understanding of economic dynamics, therefore, provides an instrument in interpreting its map, the human history. Production decisions are made by those that hold the power to do so. In the process of material production set in cooperative effort, the power to make decisions is determined by the ownership of the means of production. Such ownership determines the dominant group, whose past and present decisions shape the course of economic development (and, hence, social history) in a bitter struggle among the groups or classes of the social organism. Because the power of decision making in the arena of choice is vested in those that own and/or control the means of production, they also determine the relations of production and the distribution of the results of production against the will of the other classes. This leads us to a fourth building block in the logical system.

4. The primary factor that determines economic relations, decision-making power, and, hence, the distribution of the results of production is the ownership of the means of production; all other factors are categorial derivatives.

Given the power distribution over classes in a production process, each class develops a value system based on its experiences from class interactions. Such value systems provide each class with the subjective foundations in assessing the relative positions in meeting the primary goal and its derivatives. They also provide the foundation for judging the fairness of the system of production and the relative distribution of output and effort. The dominant value system and the imposed relations of production are those of the owning class. This value system is basically composed of views in theory and practice concerning the nature of organizations of production and politics, forms of state, relations among classes, acceptable codes of conduct, legal order, and organization of enforceability. The dominant value system constitutes the legally enforceable social milieu in which individual as well as collective decisions and choices are made. The fifth building block of the logical sequence may then be stated as follows:

5. The primary value system that determines the social milieu for all kinds of decision making regarding production, politics, relations, law, and so on is that of the owning class; all others are derivatives.

It was, perhaps, the recognition of history as a map of outcomes of past decisions in the field of production and derivatives thereof, and the value system of the owning class as determining a definite social milieu for choices and decisions, that led Marx to categorize stages of development on the basis of ownership and type of production relations. The social milieu that defines the boundaries of socially tolerable decisions and choices and at the same time shapes social history is derived from the material needs of society in support of the primary goal and its derivatives. The same logical awareness within the materialist epistemology led Marx to state that:

In the social production which men carry on they enter into definite relations that are indispensable and independent of their will; these relations of production correspond to a definite stage of development of their material powers of production. The sum total of these relations of production constitutes the economic structure of society — the real foundation on which rise legal and political superstructures and to which correspond definite forms of social consciousness. (132, p. 11)

These definite forms of social consciousness that are derived from production with cooperative effort and that form part of the social milieu weigh heavily on the direction of decisions and choices and, thus, exert preponderating influence on intrastage and interstage transformations as well as the direction of economic development.

The weight given to economic factors does not deprive other noneconomic factors that are derivatives by categorial conversion of influencing the stage transformation process. Because these are derivatives by categorial conversion, their existence and influence are traceable to material production in support of life. Thus, in the last analysis of social change and development, the economic factors assert themselves as necessary even though a host of other factors may play a decisive role. It was an attempt to clarify these relative logical roles of economic and noneconomic factors in explaining socioeconomic development process that led Engels to state in his letter to J. Bloch, written September 21–22, 1890, that:

According to the materialist conception of history the determining element in history is ultimately production and reproduction in real life. More than this neither Marx nor I have ever asserted. If, therefore, somebody twists this into the statement that the economic element is the only determining one, he transforms it into a meaningless, abstract, and absurd phrase. The economic situation is the basis, but the various elements of the superstructure — political forms of the class struggle and its consequences, constitutions established by the victorious class after a successful battle, etc. — forms of law — and then even the reflexes of all these actual struggles in the brains of the combatants: political, legal, philosophical theories, religious ideas and their further development into systems of dogma — [values] also exercise their influence upon the course of the historical struggles and in many cases preponderate in determining their form. There is an interaction of all these elements, in which, amid all the endless host of accidents (i.e. of things and events whose inner connection is so remote or so impossible to prove that we regard it as absent and can neglect it), the economic movement finally asserts itself as necessary. Otherwise the application of the theory to any period of history one chose would be easier than the solution of a simple equation of the first degree. (139, p. 475)

Having categorized the stages of development on the basis of the logical building blocks 3, 4, and 5, Marx observed that these five logical building blocks are necessary but not sufficient to develop an explanans to a socioeconomic transformation process. To complete the logical building blocks, Marx then observed that the methodology of materialist dialectic recognizes differences among categories, between quality and quantity, and between energy and mass, just as it recognizes the differences between brain and mind. It is further observed that these differences exist under tension.

As applied to the socioeconomic organism, materialism recognizes differences of classes in societies and differences in corresponding class value systems. These differences are defined by production relations and their derivatives and exert tension in classes and their corresponding value systems as decisions regarding production and distribution are undertaken in a society. The value systems of classes by which economic states are individually and collectively judged by each class are always in conflict regarding what are socially good decisions. Classes, therefore, are in a continually bitter struggle against one another to either control the decision-making power or influence the direction of social decisions in the field of production activities or derivatives thereof. This conflict is dynamic and provides the dialectic that converts categories.

Within this analytic framework, the principle of class struggle as the defining equation of motion for converting categories of relations and stages of development is pulled out by Marx. The sixth logical building block from Marx may, thus, be stated as:

6. The conflict among class value systems regarding decisions in the production process and judgment regarding the fairness of distribution, application, and enforcement of rules and regulations of behavior leads to struggles among the various classes for control over institutions that have been established to organize production and its derivatives. This class struggle is the force that moves history and provides the force of category conversion and, hence, provides the logic to explain the development process.

The logical building block 6 is the second of what Rostow has referred to as "the seven Marxist propositions" (182, p. 146). From an epistemological standpoint, only the first two propositions specified by Rostow are useful. The five other propositions are irrelevant as far as the explanans of Marx is concerned. The epistemological basis for the construction of the explanans of Marx is materialism. The minimum requirement for its application to social dynamics is not only the absolute and independent existence of matter but also the absolute and independent existence of society and the will of its members. Society, composed of individuals, classes, and interest groups (to use the modern term) with different value systems, tastes, and preferences, is a plenum of forces that are in unity and, yet, in antithetic mode to each other. Alternatively stated, societies constitute masses that are endowed with the powers of self-motion in terms of social change. These powers of self-motion provide the driving force for intrastage and interstage changes that explain development processes.

In the construction of the logical system for explaining socioeconomic developments induced from within the society, two types of equation of motion forming categories of motion are advanced to explain the process of social transformation. They are motions regarding quantity and quality. An external mover like Rostow's superpower intrusion not only is inconsistent but also falls short of logical plenitude. The rise of a superpower must also be explained within the same logical system for it to be acceptable as part of the explanation process.

In view of this, the explanans of Marx is not only logically complete and closed, it is also internally consistent, thus, meeting the completeness and consistency requirements of a scientific theory. The problem as specified, like that of Rostow, is general and manageable. The goal is not the discovery of origins of things but, rather, explanation of the mechanism for socioeconomic development. Alternatively stated, Marx sought to logically construct a law of socioeconomic development. In other words, the objective of the constructed explanans to the explanandum of economic development is not to explain how the socioeconomic system manages its existing forms but how it internally destroys old forms and creates new ones through qualitative and quantitative transformations.

The empirical content of Marx's theory of development of socioeconomic systems is specified in terms of factors that affect the direction of the class struggles. These factors involve quantitative relationships among the growth of technology, capital accumulation, concentration of production and wealth, relative values of distribution of income among classes, and relative "miserification" of the masses as the class struggle proceeds. The specifics of the empirical content are not our concern here. We only want to point out that Rostow, unlike Marx, dwells only on some aspects of the qualitative characteristics of factors and their relationship to the concept of class struggle. This idea was pointed out by Kuznets as: "Basic to Rostow's original analysis, in *The Stages of Economic Growth*, was his sketch of a dynamic theory of production that emphasized the composition of investment and the growth of particular sectors in the economy. This theory of production allowed Rostow to identify certain 'leading sectors,' the growth of which is thought to be instrumental in propelling the economy forward" (116, p. 241).

Within the explanans of Marx, the growth of institutions, the formation of interest groups, and their struggle to shape the directions of social decisions are explained. This cannot be done with any logical consistency within the explanans of Rostow. In particular, Rostow's theory does not allow us to account for the enactment of laws such as child-labor law, the rise of institutions such as price and wage control boards, the formation of interest groups such as trade unions or chamber of commerce, and so on. In fact, Rostow's superpower intrusion is explainable within the logical structure of Marx's explanans (133).

The main assumptions of Marx's logical construct are the logical building blocks 1 and 2 that may be compactly stated as the primary goal of human beings is survival and maintenance of their lives, and the primary instrument for achieving this goal is material production that is social in nature. These assumptions are not only appropriate but also in congruence with reality. The structural propositions involve questions as to why production and growth of production take place, how such production and growth take place, and what ought to be the course of history regarding human progress.

Within the demands of scientific theories, Marx's explanans satisfies the predictive conditions. The predictions include the concentration of production, increased perfection in technology, growth in capital accumulation, brutalities, wars, human misery, and growth in output. All these point to one important predictive power of Marx's explanans and fall within the dialectical methods as indicted by Nkrumah (161). Society is a plenum of forces as well as constituted by processes. When the content runs counter to the form that contains it, the form is changed to propel the socioeconomic organism forward. To conclude, we must point out that any criticism directed against formation of stages in economic development in order to construct either explanatory or prescriptive theory of category conversion is a futile exercise. The identification of the concept of developed and underdeveloped economies is itself an act of category formation whose transitional process may be considered as an explanandum requiring the construction of an appropriate explanans. The constructed explanans constitutes the theory of economic development. The theory of economic development, therefore, is not only to indicate the key factors in the transient process but also to discover the mechanism through which these key factors operate to effect socioeconomic development and, hence, a social transformation. It is also important for us to understand that every effective social transformation first proceeds by throwing into chaos the content, which then becomes opposed to the form, the content's protective stratum. Second, the protective stratum is set ablaze, for complete disintegration. Third, in the place of the old form, a new protective stratum is erected to house and protect the new content.

Evaluation, Appraisal, and Criticisms of Schumpeter's Theory

We shall now turn our attention to evaluate, appraise, and criticize Schumpeter's theory of economic development just as we have done with those of Rostow and Marx. The evaluative conditions are those that constitute the composite elements of the rational-historical criterion, as specified in Chapter 2. The outline of the essentials of Schumpeterian explanans includes some elements of our appraisal. Let us state the explicit propositions contained in the explanans in terms of logical building blocks. Basically, the Schumpeterian construct indirectly or directly accepts the first three logical building blocks of the explanans of Marx. From here, it is then recognized that economic development is a map of outcomes of production, investment, and innovation decisions. The production decisions are made by the members of the capitalist class. The innovation decisions are made by entrepreneurs as a capitalist subclass. The investment decisions are undertaken by the capitalists and entrepreneurs regarding replacement, expansion, and innovation. Of all of these decisions, Schumpeter singled out innovation as the centrally autonomous force of transformation of stages and entrepreneurs as the mode of transmission of this force. The innovative investments and the corresponding capital accumulation are the results of innovations in the environment of competitive struggle in production. These lead to the following important three building blocks of Schumpeter's explanans regarding intrastage changes:

1. The primary mechanism of economic transformation and, hence, development is the process of innovation, which takes place in key sectors.
2. Innovations are transmitted through capital investments, which they induce.
3. The innovative capital investments are undertaken by entrepreneurs.

The mechanism of economic transformation that qualitatively moves the entrepreneurial capitalism through equilibrium states depends on the volume of innovative investment decisions. The degree to which these investment decisions are implemented depends, in turn, on the incentive structure contained in the institutional and cultural arrangements given the conditions of business risk and sociopolitical environment that foster the rise and growth of entrepreneurs. This incentive structure is profits, which entrepreneurial innovations create over and above costs. We can now state the next logical block in the Schumpeterian explanans.

4. The rise and growth of entrepreneurs, entrepreneurial decisions, and risks taken are motivated by abnormal profits to be made given the sociopolitical environment.

The entrepreneurs and their activities and values affect the direction of "social climate" in which they operate. Each successful innovation as measured by profits brings in other capitalists who are followers and creates competition and capital widening. Competition from other capitalists tends to eliminate the abnormal profits as well as drive it to zero in equilibrium states. Another sequence of logical building blocks may be stated:

5. Entrepreneurial innovations create abnormal profits, which are entrepreneurs' reward.
6. The innovation-induced abnormal profits invite competition from other capitalists, which tends to deplete and eliminate the profits and create risk.

7. The elimination of abnormal profits or the perception of increased risk induced by competition tends to motivate new innovations, which invite more and intense competition.

8. The instruments and weapons for competitive struggle by entrepreneurs and capitalists are innovations and innovative investments.

It is useful to point out, contrary to the perception left in Schumpeter's analysis and the interpretations by others, that innovation is not introduced by entrepreneurs, innovative investments are not carried on by innovators, and capital widening is not undertaken by capitalists who follow the innovators for either their own sake or to promote social interest of improved methods of production with economic growth and development. Rather, innovations, innovative investments, and capital widening are tools of competition among capitalists over distribution of profits net of the total social wage bill. Technological progress (physical and social), economic growth and development, the disappearance of existing enterprises, the emergence of new firms, and the decrease and increase of the social output are unplanned, unwilled, and incidental outcomes of this process of capitalist struggle over the surplus value (profits).

In this process ("creative destruction"), as competition becomes intense and destructive, profitable innovation becomes expensive, and business risk increases and megagroups are formed. The objective is to combat the destructive effects of competition and the process of individual innovations and, at the same time, exploit their creative effects. The dialectics of the process of creative destruction, however, is such that this objective cannot be accomplished without ruining the creative process of competition. The destructive component of competition eliminates old and ineffective enterprises while its creative component replaces them with new and more efficient ones. This affirms the dialectical law of disappearance of the old and emergence of the new.

The strategies undertaken to restrain the destructive component of competition are such that depersonalized management and innovative process arise, and along with them come bureaucrats and technocrats who are less risk takers. The old form of entrepreneurial capitalism collapses and gives way to a new form of bureaucratic capitalism. We arrive at another sequence of the logical building blocks of Schumpeter's explanans.

9. Competition among capitalists over profits constitutes the force that brings about the conversion of economic states by eliminating technologically inefficient producers and replacing them with more efficient ones and, hence, provides the explanatory power of the economic development phenomenon.

10. As competition among capitalists intensifies, the business environment becomes more uncertain and risky, entrepreneurial profits and productive

assets become threatened, and existing enterprises face possible elimination. In response, megagroups of business operated by bureaucrats and technocrats are formed to overthrow the personalized entrepreneurship and management, replacing them with centralized bureaucracy.

The rise of bureaucratic capitalism shifts the center of conflicts and contradictions from among capitalists to the state and megagroups of business enterprises (i.e., between the state and the business sectors) relative to perceived public and private interests. A new process of socioeconomic transformation with its own internal dynamics is born. The understanding of this process of transformation is provided by Schumpeter through the following sequence of logical building blocks:

11. The operation of bureaucratic capitalism is such as to restrain the destructive effects of competition and individual innovations by adopting all kinds of trade restrictions and predatory competitive strategies. This leads to the destruction of the creative component of competition.

12. Bureaucratic capitalism gives rise to an intense conflict between the large business organizations (business sector) and the state (public) over the relative importance of private and public interest broadly defined (including economic insecurities that translate themselves into group interest), which then exerts pressure on the direction of sociopolitical decisions.

13. The conflict is expressed in the general decision space where the state, reasoning from its perception of the creative component of competition, seeks to regulate and control the conditions of competition and production through the legal structure, in accordance with perceived public interests, broadly defined, and the firms, reasoning from their perceptions of the destructive component of competition, design strategies to evade the rules and regulations to manipulate conditions of competition to generate and maintain large profits at least effort in the marketplace.

14. The conflict between the state and business concerns regarding perceived relative importance between public and private interest induces a process of socioeconomic transformation that alters the content of bureaucratic capitalism, the form of which collapses to give way to socialism as defined by Schumpeter.

These 14 logical building blocks constitute the essential core of Schumpeterian explanans to the explanandum of the phenomenon of economic development. The explanans advances a theoretical explanation based on the production of internal energy from the socioeconomic organism. The internal energy is postulated to be generated from competing social forces under tension whose resolution brings about destruction of old socioeconomic forms and creation of new ones; Schumpeter calls it the process of creative destruction. The creative destruction is a process; it is also a revolution. It is a revolution against the existing social form. It is also a revolution in manufacturing its replacement. Finally, it is a contestant for any potential in natural arrangement of all possible social forms.

The explanans epistemologically acknowledges the critical emergence of quality from quantity in the transition of the quantitative process. Thus, changes in the quantitative values of key economic parameters within given institutional conditions lead to changes in the basic structural institutions that house the key socioeconomic variables. In this respect, development emerges out of the conditions of less development as a process that is characterized by categorial leaps and nonlinear motion. The conditions specify the circumstances that give rise to the content of social consciousness. Social consciousness, in turn, shapes the direction of decision making that contains the incipient change necessary to effect a transformation of quality of any defined stage through the institutional structure of the society. The philosophical basis for Schumpeterian logical construct is induced by methodological individualism to which von Mises has given impressive account (146, 147), where the individual rather than the social collective becomes the instrument of transmission.

The explanans of Schumpeter is logically complete in some senses but is not internally closed. To close the logical system, however, one needs to explain how the internal energy of the socioeconomic system gives rise to inventions and entrepreneurial personality. From the logical process of transformation of kind induced by self-motion, this is, perhaps, the greatest weakness of Schumpeter's theory of economic development. It is epistemologically not enough to simply distinguish inventions from innovations and select innovations as instruments of struggle, as Schumpeter does. How inventions tend to arise in the transient process must be explained and then linked to innovations, which are the vehicles for connecting new technologies and know-how to the production process. Innovation is a process of diffusion of new inventions broadly defined, and invention is a process of creating new knowledge that defines a new framework for creation of minor inventions, improvements, and applications.

In this respect, a statement by Kuznets is instructive:

A major technological innovation is the application of an invention, a new ingenious combination of existing knowledge, to satisfy a large latent demand that could not be satisfied until the invention — the technological breakthrough — had been made; and indeed, until it spread, and in spreading elicited the hundreds of minor inventions and thousands of improvements which by their cumulative impact drastically reduced relative cost (and thus satisfied the demand, which is largely only in response to a much reduced relative price). A technological innovation that has a major economic impact is a combination of three components: an invention that provides a framework around which a whole succession of minor inventions and improvements can be built; a supply of material capital and, more particularly, of human capital (such as inventors, engineers, and organizers), whose engagement and concentration on the problems of the major invention will assure its effective improvement and diffusion; and a large potential demand, often revealed by an obvious bottleneck in the production process of a recent growth industry. (118, pp. 326–27)

It is also important to note that in the framework of Marx's explanans, inventions and innovations come under technical composition of capital that is actively sought to replace labor as the class antagonism proceeds. Thus, just as actual and potential wars induce a search for more and powerful munitions through inventions and innovations, so also is the existence of class conflict and war. Such a logical connection is unavailable to us in the Schumpeterian theory.

The general core of the explanans of Schumpeter is internally consistent, where great patience is exercised to ensure that no rule of dialectical logic is intentionally violated. The metaphoric attribute of Hegelian hero assigned to entrepreneurs by Schumpeter is logically consistent insofar as it operates through the contradiction of competition that creates new forms and destroys the old. However, the assignment of special psychological motivation to the entrepreneurs, such as a "fight for the sake of fight" rather than for financial gains of innovation, is logically defective and falls outside the acceptable logic of internal self-motion.

The problem of economic development is specified in its generality but within manageable theoretical bounds. The empirical content of the theory is cast in terms of factors that shape the resultant resolution of the capitalist competitive struggle over distribution of profits. These factors involve quantitative relationships among the volume of new technologies, number of bankruptcies, capital accumulation, concentration of production, number of new firms, increased number of products, growth of national output and wealth, degree of government controls, and so on. The accompanying structural propositions of the theory center around the mechanism by which development is transmitted and forms of institutional change from one to the other regarding the evolving history of socioeconomic progress. The main propositions establish some congruence with reality that allows either verification or collaborativeness.

Schumpeter's theory also satisfies the predictive conditions required by the constructed composite rational-historical criterion in assessing the scientific status of theories. The main predictions include quantitative changes of some key aggregate variables (78) that are followed by qualitative jumps. The quantitative changes include increased national output; level of technology; growth in capital accumulation; number of bankruptcies; number of takeovers, buyouts, and new firms; and increased product diversity. The qualitative changes include increased size and quality of firms, monopoly formation, increased government regulation and control, and changes in socioeconomic attitudes and values.

The analytical structure of Schumpeter's theory of economic development is cast in a rational-historical framework where the explanans is induced by methodological individualism. The individual choice-decision processes in the production space act as vehicles for socioeconomic transformation, given the institutional bounds. The actions of the collectives such as the government and large firms are, at best, constraints on the individual activities in the decision space. The social activities in the consumption space are dragged along the transient process by the choice-decision outcomes in the production space, where the outcomes are the results of contradictions in the innovation-competition process. In other words, supply creates its own demand. The conflicts resulting from competition and innovation, from individual and the collective regarding relative interests, from individual entrepreneurs and large firms, and from the large firms and the state are tapped by Schumpeter as modes of accessing the logical power of dialectics at work in isolating the mechanism of change in order to induce an explanation of the socioeconomic development process as we travel along the transient path.

A NOTE ON EPISTEMICS OF MARX AND SCHUMPETER

There are important and interesting similarities and differences in the theories of Marx and Schumpeter about economic development. If there is any theory of economic development that can claim a rivalry or an alternative to that of Marx, it is that of Schumpeter. The explanandum is the same for both Marx and Schumpeter, that is, "to answer the question how the economic system generates the force which incessantly transforms it" (204, p. 165). The answer requires a construction of "purely economic theory of economic change which does not merely rely on external factors propelling the economic system from one equilibrium to another" (204, p. 166). Schumpeter suggests "that this idea and the aim are exactly the same as the idea and the aim which underlie the economic teaching of Karl Marx [whose vision is to produce a theoretical construct of an] economic evolution as a distinct process generated by the economic system itself" (204, p. 166).

The relative reflections on the two theoretical constructs of Marx and Schumpeter may be divided into two. We have available the epistemological basis of the theory itself and the main and supporting propositions contained in the constructed explanans to the explanandum of the phenomenon of economic development. By this bifocal approach, we would be able to throw a light on the intellectual creativity and the creative insights that Marx and Schumpeter bring to enlighten us about the phenomenon of the process of quantity-quality transformations that induce economic development of societies.

The abstracted similarities and differences reflect their differential views about the structural features and ideological essentialities of the social point of reference and the economic stage assumed and held as primary in the evolutionary process. Additionally, the similarities and differences arise from their views on the concept of science and acceptable scientific and epistemic methods to deal with economic theory of social development where chaotic, complex, and seemingly confused historical material is organized into a simpler logical system for illuminating our understanding of the mechanism by which a higher level of development is forged out of a lower level.

By examining the epistemological basis of their theories, we shall come to appreciate their relative views on science and scientific methods as applied to human action. The comparative examination of the main and supporting proposition of their theories, on the other hand, will assist us to understand what they isolated as key aggregate factors that define the mechanism for socioeconomic change. In addition, we will come to understand their relative social consciousness and ideologies. We shall first take up the epistemics and then examine the explanans. Table 4.4 provides a quick comparative structure of the explanans of Marx and Schumpeter.

TABLE 4.4
A Taxonomy of Explanans of Marx and Schumpeter

Marx
1. The primary goal of human beings is survival and maintenance of life of individuals and the collective; all other goals are derivatives.
2. The primary instrument for achieving the goal and its derivatives is the material production, broadly defined; all other instruments are derivatives.
3. The primary relation in society is economic; all other relations are derivatives.
4. The primary factor that determines economic relations, decision-making power, and, hence, the distribution of the results of production is the ownership of the means of production; all other factors are categorial derivatives.
5. The primary value system that determines the social milieu for all kinds of decision making regarding production, politics, relations, law, and so on is that of the owning class; all others are derivatives.
6a. The conflict among class value systems regarding decisions in the production process and judgment regarding the fairness of distribution, application, and enforcement of rules and regulations of behavior leads to struggles among the various classes for control over institutions that have been established to organize production and its derivatives. This class struggle is the force that moves history and provides the force of category conversion and, hence, provides the logic to explain the development process.
6b. The primary mechanism of economic transformation and, hence, development is the process of class struggle in the arena of socioeconomic production and distribution.
7a. The struggle among classes is a struggle over the fair distribution of real income as a primary category of instruments of livelihood and other derivatives thereof.

The struggle over the equitable distribution of real income is the primary category of antagonistic relation between workers and owners of capital; all other relations are derivatives thereof.

7b. The mechanism through which the class struggle is waged is the labor-capital process and the established institutions.

8. Labor is the primary factor for capital's creation, and all other factors are derivatives thereof. Capital and its accumulation are the material factors by which socioeconomic transformations of stages are effected.

9. The variation in the technical composition of capital (i.e., the process of capital deepening) replaces labor, creates unemployment and economic insecurities, weakens labor's bargaining position, reduces labor cost, improves profit margin, and strengthens the bargaining position of owners of capital.

10. The positive variations in the value composition of capital (i.e., the process of capital widening) create employment and increase total output and surplus value.

11. The conflict is expressed in the general decision space where the working class, reasoning from the perception of its interest, seeks to control the institutions of decision that affect the labor process; the capital owning class reasoning from the perception of its self-interest seeks to control the institutions of decision making that affect the capital process.

12. The class conflict between workers and the owners of means of production, relative to the perceptions of their interests, and operating through the capital-labor processes induces socioeconomic transformation that propels the economic system through the specified stages and, thus, explains the internal dynamics.

Schumpeter

1. The primary mechanism of economic transformation and, hence, development is the process of innovation, which takes place in key sectors.

2. Innovations are transmitted through capital investments, which they induce.

3. The innovative capital investments are undertaken by entrepreneurs.

4. The rise and growth of entrepreneurs, entrepreneurial decisions, and risks taken are motivated by abnormal profits to be made given the sociopolitical environment.

5. Entrepreneurial innovations create abnormal profits, which are entrepreneurs' reward.

6. The innovation-induced abnormal profits invite competition from other capitalists, who tend to deplete and eliminate the profits and create risk.

7. The elimination of abnormal profits or the perception of increased risk induced by competition tends to motivate new innovations, which invite more and intense competition.

8. The instruments and weapons for competitive struggle by entrepreneurs and capitalists are innovations and innovative investments.

9. Competition among capitalists over profits constitutes the force that brings about the conversion of economic states by eliminating technologically inefficient producers and replacing them with more efficient ones and, hence, provides the explanatory power of the economic development phenomenon.

10. As competition among capitalists intensifies, the business environment becomes more uncertain and risky, entrepreneurial profits and productive assets become threatened, and existing enterprises face possible elimination. In response, megagroups of business operated by bureaucrats and technocrats are formed to

TABLE 4.4, continued

overthrow the personalized entrepreneurship and management, replacing them with centralized bureaucracy.

11. The operation of bureaucratic capitalism is such as to restrain the destructive effects of competition and individual innovations by adopting all kinds of trade restrictions and predatory competitive strategies. This leads to the destruction of the creative component of competition.

12. Bureaucratic capitalism gives rise to an intense conflict between the large business organizations (business sector) and the state (public) over the relative importance of private and public interest broadly defined (including economic insecurities that translate themselves into group interest), which then exerts pressure on the direction of sociopolitical decisions.

13. The conflict is expressed in the general decision space where the state, reasoning from its perception about the creative component of competition, seeks to regulate and control the conditions of competition and production through the legal structure, in accordance with perceived public interests, broadly defined, and the firms, reasoning from their perceptions about the destructive component of competition, design strategies to evade the rules and regulations to manipulate conditions of competition to generate and maintain large profits at least effort in the marketplace.

14. The conflict between the state and business concerns regarding perceived relative importance between public and private interest induces a process of socioeconomic transformation that alters the content of bureaucratic capitalism, the form of which collapses to give way to socialism as defined by Schumpeter.

Epistemics of Marx and Schumpeter Compared

Both Marx and Schumpeter accept the historical method as an important tool for organizing a theory that will show how the key factors work together to define the mechanism of change. The historical method that allows rational organization of data is then supported by a materialist conception of evolution of kind, more so with Marx than with Schumpeter. They recognize that socioeconomic change takes place through a mechanism that is internally subjected by the system's own energy. Such energy is derived from social forces under tension, from the competing forces within the social organism as the members, either individually or collectively, seek to act in the choice-decision space. The resultants of these forces shape the direction of change and the path of economic development.

Economic development is, thus, viewed relative to time, where such a development is defined by changes in quantity and quality. The quantitative changes are more or less gradual and accumulate to a point where qualitative leaps are established for a complete socioeconomic transformation. Economic development, therefore, is a "spontaneous and continuous" process, to use Schumpeter's terminology (205, p. 63). The socioeconomic transformation is seen by both Schumpeter and Marx to be affected by the internal contradictions of social forces that continually seek to destroy the form and establish a new one through the nonstationary process of creative destruction. It is precisely the contradictions inherent in the competing social forces under tension in the decision-choice space (to use a modern term) that produce the internal energy necessary to provide the impetus for stage transformation and, thus, push the social organism forward without externally impressed force. External forces and factors only establish signals for change and operate through the internal factors that establish the true basis for socioeconomic development. The nature of operations of internal factors reflects social experiences that shape the individual and collective consciousness that induces directions and patterns of decisions and choices whose outcomes define the transient process of development.

We are, thus, convinced that both Marx and Schumpeter accept the dialectical logic and its two basic principles — law of identity and principle of contradiction — as essential methodological approaches to understanding social dynamics and the mechanism for socioeconomic transformation. Different realizations of socioeconomic development are the consequences of dialectical processes, which proceed in accord with objective social laws where such laws operate through the contradictions among poles. The logical problem faced by both Marx and Schumpeter, therefore, is to isolate the social poles for the contradictions that will establish the dialectical process that will produce the dialectical moment for the laws of transformation that govern the dynamics of the socioeconomic system.

In solving this logical problem, it is essential for both Marx and Schumpeter to understand (as it is important for us to understand) that not every means of resolving the identified contradictions of the social forces can establish the true mechanism of change and, hence, an economic theory of social development. Development is conceived to be born out of tension in the decision space involving human actions. Decision making is composed of forces under tension, and decision outcomes are children of tension of opposed social forces and tendencies that establish the direction of development. These are understood by both Marx and Schumpeter. They also accept that the world is a world of processes but not states. These processes on the part of the social organism are due to self-motion generated by human actions; without self-motion, dialectical change would be impossible and dialectical logic would lose its epistemological stand and its methodological appeal.

The theoretical establishment of the social forces of contradictory poles and the means of resolving them are different for Marx and Schumpeter — Schumpeter accepts the methodology of Marx but rejects Marx's class-based conflict to establish the dialectical moment that induces the process of change. Both Marx and Schumpeter accept that development is a map of decision outcomes and that the people constituting the social entity are the reality and backbone of this map. Development is a victory that emerges out of the people's effort to alter their social circumstances, and it is by the people's actions, guided by their consciousness, in the choice-decision space that the map is shaped in the direction that reflects their social exigencies.

Of all these, one important point emerges. There is a methodological unity in the constructed explanans of both Marx and Schumpeter where the essential force of the theoretical explanation of socioeconomic development centers around the mechanism of transformation rather than factors utilized in the mechanism. There is, more or less, an epistemological agreement between Marx and Schumpeter on the nature of science and the application that is required of its logic to understand social dynamics.

The Explanans of Marx and Schumpeter Compared

The major theoretical differences between Marx and Schumpeter are contained not in their epistemological outlook but in the constructed explanans. The differences are particularly captured in what they considered as the essential contradictions that provide the mechanism of change and the source of internal force of motion that leads to the development of the capitalist system as well as transforming it to a socialist stage. As we have pointed out, Marx isolated contradiction of social classes and their economic relations regarding distribution of power, income, and effort as the internal source of energy that produces the force of change. The class conflict defines the creative destruction that brings about quantitative changes and, finally, a qualitative leap.

Schumpeter, on the other hand, isolates competition among capitalists over the distribution of actual and potential profits net of total wage bill as the conflict or contradiction that defines the source of internal energy that induces the transformation process of the social organism and propels it on to higher levels of development. Even though Schumpeter tried hard to avoid the class-based conflict as a source of energy to induce social motion, it would be demonstrated that not only is the internal energy of self-motion in Schumpeterian explanans class based but also the competition, conflict, and social contradiction are class induced. This places Schumpeter in a Marxian explanatory world with ideological spin and emphasis on classes different from those of Marx.

To create the logical poles of contradiction, Schumpeter separates the capitalists from the rest of the society and groups them into two classes of elite and nonelite. The elite class is composed of those that lead in the production sphere — he calls them "entrepreneurs." The nonelite class is composed of those capitalists that follow the daring actions of the elites. They are the nonentrepreneurial capitalists. In modern terminologies, the entrepreneurial class is the class of risk-takers from within the social subclass of capitalists. The nonentrepreneurial class is composed of risk-averters from the same social subclass of capitalists who exploit the fertile fields of profits by competition after the profit gates of production have been opened by entrepreneurs through the introduction of new combinations. Thus, implied in Schumpeterian dynamics of socioeconomic change is a class struggle that he directly denies.

The basis of class division on the part of Schumpeter is different from that of Marx. Marx's class division is based on income and power relations in the whole society. Schumpeter's class division is based on externally induced psychological characteristics of investment-decision behavior of the capitalists and encompasses only a small segment of the society. An important theoretical difference emerges when these classes are used in the explanation process. In the explanans of Marx, the whole society becomes the mover of history and the force behind socioeconomic development. In the explanans of Schumpeter, socioeconomic transformation and history are the responsibilities of the capitalist class. The workers are dragged along by the forces of capitalist innovation and competition. The workers appear as passive participants of the economic transformation and, thus, are projected to make no contribution to the force that propels the system.

In the constructed explanans of Marx, capital accumulation serves as an instrument on the part of the capitalists to fight the antagonistic relations among the capitalist class and the working class while labor power enters as a weapon on the part of workers. Capital deepening (what Marx calls "technical composition" and Schumpeter calls "innovation in capital") is employed to reduce labor input and, thus, to weaken the ability of labor to wage effective class struggle in the class conflict-resolution process. Technical progress and innovations are by-products of this process. Capital widening (what Marx calls "value composition" and Schumpeter calls "competition-induced investment") is employed to increase the profit size through increased output at constant technique. Increased volumes of capital and productive capacity are the results of this process. The theory of Marx also projects capital deepening and widening (i.e., the whole process of capital accumulation) as tools and strategies for carrying on competition among the capitalists over profits. Socioeconomic development is a by-product but neither the goal nor the objective of these processes.

In the explanans of Schumpeter, innovations ("technical composition" in Marx's terms) are strategies on the part of entrepreneurs (the risk-taking capitalists) to establish and maintain a competitive edge over other capitalist competitors (nonentrepreneurial capitalists) in a bitter struggle over the market distribution of profits. Capital accumulation enters the process as a medium through which the innovation is carried on, and technological progress is a result of this process. After a successful entrepreneurial innovation, capital widening on the part of risk-averting capitalists occurs through increased competition, which leads to the depletion of the individual profit shares. Capital deepening is a weapon of competition on the part of entrepreneurial capitalists (risk-takers), and capital widening is a weapon of competition on the part of nonentrepreneurial capitalists to wage the war of competition against one another. Capital accumulation is the result of this innovation-competition process. It enters as a two-sided sword that creates and eliminates the capitalist profits. Socioeconomic development is neither a goal nor an objective of this process; it is simply a by-product.

The innovation-competition conflict between the two subclasses of capitalists and its resolution are expressed by Elliott as a process where "by incorporating new technologies and other sources of qualitative changes, entrepreneurial innovations create surpluses of revenues above cost. . . . Competition tends to eliminate these surplus values, but innovation creates them" (205, p. xxxv). This innovation-competition process of creative destruction takes place in the production decision space where the competing participants are the members of the capitalist class. The energy generated from this decision process only destroys the form of entrepreneurial capitalism and in its place creates a new form called "bureaucratic capitalism" (72, pp. 23–24) and then dissipates out of sight without affecting the needed and continuous transformation from bureaucratic capitalism to socialism. A new and different energy is, thus, required to produce the force that must govern the transient process between bureaucratic capitalism and socialism.

In Marx's explanans, however, the defined class antagonistic relations generates a continuous flow of internal energy that transforms the capitalist system through stages and then to socialism. A new source of energy that will induce a new law of transformation is not needed. The Schumpeterian explanatory logic, however, requires a new source of contradiction and energy to induce a different law of transformation that will govern the dynamics between bureaucratic capitalism and socialism. The new source of internal energy is generated by the conflict or antagonistic relation between the class of members who operate in the business sector of bureaucratic capitalism and the class of members who operate in the public sector regarding the relative importance of social and private interests.

From the understanding of the analytical structure of Marx, the government represents the interest of the capitalist class and, hence, must be replaced by an alternative that represents the interest of the masses, in particular, the workers, in order to establish socialism. Conceptually, Marx sees socialism as an outcome of the process of class movements that express broad and profound cultural, political, and institutional changes. Contrary to Marx, Schumpeter sees the government as representing not the interest of the capitalist but that of the public. The government regulates and controls the environment of the market for social interest as the business sector fights to maintain the private interest inherited from entrepreneurial capitalism. Through the process of private-public interest conflict, socialism is born out of the bureaucratic capitalism. Socialism is viewed by Schumpeter as "that organization of society in which the means of production are controlled and the decisions on how and what to produce and on who is to get what, are made by public authority instead of by privately-owned and privately-managed firms" (207, p. 421). Socialism is, thus, an outcome of a bitter struggle between the class that represents public interest and the class that represents private interest.

Available to the class that represents public interest is the weapon of political power, which is exercised to alter and shape the legal structure that defines the legally acceptable bounds of environment of socioeconomic decisions. Available to the class that represents the private interest is the weapon of economic power, which is used to constrain the exercise of political power over the shape and form of the legal structure. Marx sees the political power as being controlled by the capitalist class and exercised in the favor of the interest of the capitalists over public interest, thus, ensuring the capitalist victory in the class conflict. Schumpeter, on the other hand, sees the political power as controlled by a public interest group that is supported by its intellectual elite, where such a power is exercised against the interests of the capitalist class and in favor of public interests to ensure the final collapse of bureaucratic capitalism.

Epistemically, no important differences arise whether the major properties of capitalist behavior as identified by Marx are seen by Schumpeter as inevitable and complementary outcomes of the process of creative destruction, while Marx views them as operational flaws of the system whose self-corrections induce social transformations. There is a lot to learn about their methodological approach, conception of the problem of economic development, and the manner in which the problem theoretically can be studied for our understanding. One may undoubtedly find a lot to criticize about both theoretical constructs and their conclusions. These criticisms will reflect only our preconceptions regarding institutional relevance and social utility of capitalism and the results of its dynamics. However, the important theoretical emphasis by both Marx and Schumpeter on institutions of values, customs, laws, politics, and ideology that define acceptable boundaries of decisions whose outcomes specify the direction of economic development cannot be taken lightly.

Abstractly, both Marx and Schumpeter affirm a proposition that development is transmitted through a medium and propelled by self-generated force. In social organisms, this medium is the institutional configuration through which the organism derives its life-supporting blood, and this force is the energy produced out of contradictions inherent in the social organism involving decisions of production and distribution of efforts (costs) and fruits (benefits). No external force or mover is required to induce a continuous change of stages, no matter how strong the force may be. External forces can facilitate the process of transformation and, hence, socioeconomic development by helping to define the conditions of change. Their operative effectiveness is through the internal forces that are self-generated. The nature of the system's dynamics is described by Schumpeter as:

No therapy can permanently abstract the great economic and social progress by which business, individual positions, forms of life, cultural values and ideals, sink in the social scale and finally disappear. . . . [Additionally, these outcomes are operational necessities, because] in a society with private property and competition, this process is the necessary complement of the continual emergence of new economic and social forms and of continually rising real incomes of all social strata. (205, p. 255)

The factors emphasized in constructing the mechanism for change reflect the relative consciousness and ideology of Marx and Schumpeter that show their vision concerning their views about the basic structural characteristics of the state of society, about what is and what is not analytically important in order to understand its life at a given time. The exclusion of the roles of labor, property, and power relations by Schumpeter and their inclusion by Marx is an important reflection of their relative ideological stands and their vision of future social forms.

Marx and Schumpeter see different factors as important in constructing their explanans for the socioeconomic transformation, even though they express a methodological unity. In other words, they conceive of a common apparatus by which to construct the main and supporting propositions contained in their explanans. Each of the explanans, however, is an illumination of the problem of economic development. Anyone stands to appreciate their organic efforts only if one remembers that explanatory theories are logical reflections on accumulated data or experience; as logical reflections, they are formed through the process of human practical interactions with things and processes and are developed by scientific and philosophical investigations. They emerge out of social exigencies and are intimately influenced by social currents, ideology, prevailing social order, and the social class to which the theorist associates his or her identity. Social theories are telescopic cognitive mirrors whose images reflect illusions and realities that are conditioned by ideologies and science.

Thus, it may be concluded that even though Schumpeter abstracts away the class nature of his explanans, his theory is class based. His view that "being an entrepreneur is not a profession and as a rule not a lasting condition, entrepreneurs do not form a social class in the technical sense, as, for example, land owners or capitalists or workmen do" (205, p. 78) is an assumption whose justification cannot find a support in the ontological conditions of factual correctness. It is a theoretical illusion arising from a misconception of classes in terms of preconceived ideas of the social organism. Entrepreneurs belong to a class, and this class is Schumpeter's subject of analysis in relation to the dynamics of economic development. His class-conflict analysis is advanced to justify the interest of capitalists whose activities, he claims, constitute the essential force of economic development. Marx's class-conflict analysis is advanced to justify the interest of the working class, whose labor process, he claims, constitutes the essential force of economic development. It is important to note that Schumpeter's innovational process and the role of entrepreneurs in development is contained in Marx's explanans and can easily be pulled out and made explicit within Marx's class-conflict process. It may, however, be said that the theories of Marx and Schumpeter are formed by the development of scientific and ideological processes that generate intense contradictions, which give birth to truth and illusions. This intense contradiction has always called for an effort of reconciliation on the process of scientific discovery by all reflective people. Both Marx and Schumpeter identified the key sectors of the economy as the capital-producing sectors. The key sectors are those through which the mechanism for change is primary or the greatest. On the ideological front, just as Marx seeks to provide intellectual munitions for the workers to alter their relationship with the owning class of the productive basis of societies, so Schumpeter ideologically seeks to arm the capitalist class with intellectual weapons to wage war against the state so as to contain the working class in its position. In Marx's analytical structure, harmony is created between the working and owning classes in a partnership. When such a harmony occurs, the state institutes an apparatus function to navigate the socioeconomic system through production-consumption conflicts, where both profits and losses are socialized. In Schumpeter's analytical structure, harmony is created by forging an alliance between the business sector and the state. When such a harmony occurs, the state institutions and apparatus function to support the capitalist class, leading to a socioeconomic organization where there is capitalism for the working masses and socialism for the owning class and where business profits are privatized and losses are socialized.

5

Factor-based Theories of Economic Development

In the construction of scientific theories, the main objective is to create order from confusion and produce simplicity from complexity by isolating the essential factors that can be used to explain a given phenomenon. The technique is not different from that of category formation where factors are categorized into essentials and nonessentials. In general, the growth and progress of scientific knowledge are based on the principle of differentiation and category formation of essential and nonessential "causal" factors. The human mind, as a derivative of the human brain, anatomizes the unknown, tears apart is components, and exposes its mysteries by dissecting the "whole" into various complements of kinds in an attempt to discover relationships among the components, if any, and the mechanism of the processes that govern its behavior.

Within this tradition of scientific enterprise, economists have, for many years, been struggling to dissect socioeconomic development process. The objective is to identify the essential factors or key factors of this process through which the economic development could be understood and explained. The underlying strength of the inquiry may be summarized as:

The whole process of economic development can be categorized into its causal constituents (factors).

In the economic development process, some factors of economic production are key in the sense that either they develop prior to other factors or their linkage effects or their causal effects are the greatest.

Within this framework, economists of different persuasions have abstracted different categories of factors with which the economic development process may be examined and understood. Any theory of development whose main logic centers around a factor or a set of factors of production as a key of analysis is classified here as factor based. The factor-based theories of the phenomenon of economic development may be classified into three groups: physical capital, human capital (labor services plus their skill levels), and technology. We shall take each of these positions separately.

In order for any factor-based theory to constitute an explanation to the economic development process, the *explanans* not only must indicate the key causal factors but also must contain a law of motion that explains how the economic system is qualitatively and quantitatively propelled forward. For the explanans to be complete, it must show how the indicated factors bring about new institutions and force the collapse of the old ones. In other words, it must provide a mechanism where the old forms give way and new forms arise in the process to replace them. Furthermore, it must depict the transitional mechanism of the development process. In a sequence, we shall examine the capital-based, human-capital-based, and technology-based theories.

CAPITAL-BASED THEORIES

One of the factor-based theories is what may be called a "capital-based approach" to the analysis and explanation of economic development. The approach is built on the observations that quantity and quality of productive capital were improved prior to other factors in the economically advanced societies of today; penetration of productive capital into different socioeconomic systems destroyed the stagnant character of traditional economies and replaced them with a character of new system of production; and introduction and increasing volume of productive physical capital have been most effective in changing traditional institutions for organizing production and, hence, to propel economies forward.

There are two types of capital-based approach to the understanding and explanation of the phenomenon of economic development — the Marxist and non-Marxist approaches — which have several similarities and differences. We shall examine their epistemic differences and similarities and evaluate their contributions to the understanding of the development process.

The Marxist Theory of Capital as a
Subtheory of the Development Process

In this section, we shall put into a proper perspective the Marxist concept and the role of capital in the development process. Our objective is to focus on the epistemics of the theory but not on the whole content of the theory. The current examination of Marx's concept and role of capital in explaining development is based on four of his writings (132–135). In the previous chapter, we outlined the methodological essentials of Marx's stage-based theory of economic development from the broad perspectives of socioeconomic transformation. The quantitative dynamics of intrastage transformation in the Marxist theory is through capital as a factor of production and capital as a strategic instrument of class struggle.

Marx may be considered the pioneer in isolating capital as a productive factor and establishing its fundamental role in economic development in a given mode of production. Having spoken of the rise of private property and primitive accumulation, Marx illustrates the dynamic role of capital in the transformation of feudal societies into capitalist societies. Marx goes to great length to explain and answer the questions of how and why the means of production, the capital, acquires its dynamic character as a causal factor in the process of socioeconomic transformation.

In terms of intrastage transformation, Marx's analysis of the role of capital in the capitalist economic system is the most interesting and profound. This is not to underestimate the analytic role of capital in Marx's explanation of the dissolution of the feudal system of production and the rise of the capitalist system of organizing social production. We shall, thus, focus on the analytic role of capital in Marx's explanans of intrastage changes of capitalism. This explanation easily applies to category transformations in the systems of Rostow and Schumpeter. Marx's theory of capital is an integral part of his stage-based explanatory theory of socioeconomic transformation. It cannot be otherwise.

Having established that, in the last analysis, economic factors not only determine the direction of history; it is also argued that they constitute the vehicle by which the conversion of socioeconomic categories is caused and explained. Marx establishes economic factors as the primary category on the basis of which the equations of motion for the transient process of the socioeconomic organism must be conceived and derived. The problem remained to be solved by Marx is to select the key economic factors and show their role in the dynamics of change as well as their effect on the outcome of the class struggle.

To pull out the pivotal economic factors from the set of economic factors, it is observed that the logical building block 6 (as specified in Chapter 4) establishes a class struggle that reflects a class conflict and contradiction in the value systems of the classes. The conflict and contradiction generate a dialectical force for the conversion of categories of economic relations. The manner in which the class conflicts are engendered is explained by analyzing the class conflict over the distribution of output between wages for workers and profit ("surplus value" in Marx's terms) for the owners of capital. The primary instrument available to the workers for waging the struggle is their labor power, while the primary instrument available to the owning class for waging the struggle against the workers is capital. Thus, Marx identified two pivotal economic factors — labor power and capital — in an attempt to explain the development process.

It is then observed that under conditions of freed labor, the owners of the means of production do not exercise direct control over labor as they do under the conditions of serfdom and slavery, where serfs and slaves are looked upon as mere instruments of production who have no share in the output except that part needed to replace their lost energy. Because labor cannot be forced, institutions of exchange develop between owners of labor and owners of capital. This, in turn, gives rise to special relations of production and institution of legal support. In this framework, workers and potential workers have the right to withhold their labor, and the owners of capital also have the right to employ, dismiss, and lay off workers in accordance with the established and acceptable rules of exchange of factors. Under serfdom and slavery, there was no such legal claim on the output of production except that of the owners of means of production, but under conditions of freed labor, the workers have a claim to some part of the output. Although the rules of the game of exchange are more or less defined, the proportion that goes to labor must be negotiated. Such proportion depends on the relative bargaining strength of the workers versus the owners of capital.

The bargaining strength of the workers depends on the ability of the workers to act individually and/or collectively in withholding their labor power from the owners of means of production for any given economic condition. Similarly, the bargaining strength of the owners of means of production depends on technical conditions of machines and the size of the unemployed labor force, given the existing economic conditions. Another important logical building block is, thus, established in the Marxist system.

7. The struggle among classes is a struggle over the fair distribution of real income as a primary category of instruments of livelihood and other derivatives thereof. The struggle over the equitable distribution of real income is the primary category of antagonistic relation between workers and owners of capital; all other relations are derivatives thereof.

In this antagonistic relation between workers and owners of capital, Marx observed that workers and capitalists are also brought together in unity by the production and consumption, which also place them in an antagonistic mode that seeks to destroy their very existence against their will (132, 133). The workers and owners of the means of production are mutually interdependent by the nature of production and consumption. The same nature of production and consumption sets the workers and owners of capital against one another in a conflict through the process of distribution of the output of production. Consumption requires production. Production requires consumption. The two together engender cooperation and conflict. In a market setting, the strategies of workers and the owners of capital for resolving the conflicts over the distribution of the output of production are mutually destructive, yet, by the very nature of the institutions of exchange, the conflicts are unavoidable. Against this background of production unity, consumption antagonism and class mutual annihilation, Marx postulates the weak bargaining position of workers without the ownership of capital. He observes that it is by the effort of labor that capital is created, and yet, labor becomes totally dependent on it for its survival. After capital is created, it becomes the instrument of livelihood for labor as well as an instrument by which labor is controlled by those who own the capital.

Marx observes that capital accumulation acquires a strategic role in strengthening the bargaining position of the owners of the means of production over output distribution and production decisions. Under these observations, capital is then isolated as an object of inquiry to establish its dynamic role in intrastage and interstage transformation and to explain socioeconomic development of societies (132–134). This leads to another important logical building block in the Marxist system of explanation:

8. Labor is the primary factor for capital's creation, and all other factors are derivatives thereof. Capital and its accumulation are the material factors by which socioeconomic transformations of stages are effected.

Having identified capital and its accumulation as causal factors for economic development, changes in institutions, real income growth, quality of life, and so on, Marx has to explain, within the logic of dialectics, how internal accumulation of capital takes place and how it imposes its own law of change on the economy, society, and the development process.

In demonstrating the dynamic character of capital and how it is linked to the law of transformation, Marx introduces the concept of "organic composition of capital." He argues that "the most important factor in this inquiry [into the phenomenon of socioeconomic development] is the composition of capital and the changes it undergoes in the course of the process of accumulation" (133, Vol. 1, p. 575). The composition of capital is divided into value composition (quantity of capital) and technical composition (quality of capital). The technical composition refers to technically allowable complementary labor or the embodied technical substitution of capital for labor. In the modern terminology, it is the capital-labor ratio. The variation in the technical composition is the vehicle by which labor is displaced from work and replaced by capital. This process leads to what Marx refers to as an "industrial reserved army" of the unemployed. It is also a process by which the owners of capital control labor cost per unit of output, as well as production decisions. The component of the technical composition of capital then becomes the leverage for the owners of the means of production to negotiate the labor cost and increase the excess over and above labor cost and, hence, the relative proportion appropriated by them. The excess over and above labor cost is what Marx calls the "surplus value." This leads to an additional important logical building block in the construction of Marx's explanans for socioeconomic development and transformation of stages.

9. The variation in the technical composition of capital (i.e., the process of capital deepening) replaces labor, creates unemployment and economic insecurities, weakens labor's bargaining position, reduces labor cost, improves profit margin, makes funds available for techical innovation, and strengthens the bargaining position of owners of capital.

The variations in the technical composition result form the fundamental changes in the tools of production, which, in turn, affect innovations, and the existing relations between workers and the owners of capital. The driving force of capital deepening or changes in the technical composition of capital is the increase in surplus value per unit of output. Whether total surplus value will increase or not depends on the increase in the total volume of output. This total volume of output may be increased in two ways. Besides reducing labor cost, an increase in the technical composition of capital may lead to an increase in output per unit of labor input as well as an increase in the overall output, even though a reduction in the work force may have resulted.

Output may also be increased by expanding the volume of capital, given its technical composition. In the Marxist construct, the volume of capital and its changes are the value composition and its variations. The value composition and its increases, for any specified technical composition, provide the vehicle by which the owners of capital increase output and total surplus value. The strategy of expanding output and surplus value requires increases in employment, which must be drawn from the "industrial reserve army" at a relatively lower market unit cost, given the existing economic conditions. The required increases in employment, output, and surplus have been extensively discussed by Marx under the simple and extended reproduction (132, 133). We only want to point out the logic of the dialectics at work. The same capital accumulation that displaces labor also employs labor. The same capital accumulation used by the owners to increase the surplus value per unit of labor input also becomes the vehicle that can weaken the bargaining positions of the owners. The same capital that reduces the total remuneration to labor also acts as an instrument of labor's livelihood.

Surplus value and its increases are the driving force for accumulation of capital, which in turn drives output, employment, and the creation of new institutions to mediate between the laboring masses and the owners of capital. It may be noted that capital plays a similar dialectical role in Schumpeterian logical system as in Marxian logical system with an important ideological spin. In this Marxian framework, capital is accumulated to create surplus value, which then becomes the powerful instrument for financing the articles of capitalists' consumption and further capital accumulation as an important strategy to control cost and behavior of labor, improve productivity, and increase total output and, hence, the surplus value. We have now arrived at another important building block in the chain of Marx's logical construct.

10. The positive variations in the value composition of capital (i.e., the process of capital widening) create employment and increase total output and surplus value.

It is the recognition of the dual financial role of surplus value that leads Marx to examine the theories of surplus value that also form a powerful logical thread in the construct of Marx's explanans of the socioeconomic development process (134). In this construct, capital is accumulated for surplus value (profit), which then offers possibilities of further accumulation and further increase in output and surplus value. In the process of class conflict leading to accumulation, growth, and intensification of the struggle over distribution of output and production strategies, outmoded institutions, customs, and rules of decisions give way. New institutions, customs, and rules arise to support the new form and environment of production and distribution decisions. Insofar as at least part of the profits is reinvested to deepen capital as well as widen it in the economy in which it is produced, capital accumulation as a strategy of controlling labor also becomes the powerful driving force for quantitative and qualitative transformation of the economy and propels it from less- to more-developed stages.

New institutions that rise include institutions of science and technology that induce inventiveness, institutions of credit and finance that define lending and borrowing, institutions of law that restrict and control the allowable decision space, and institutions of marketing that facilitate the exchange process. Within the Marxist explanans, these institutions arise from the class conflicts and their derivatives in addition to tensions and conflicts that are generated from discrepancies between results of social decisions that are at variance with the dominant value system. The organic composition of capital and its positive variation, therefore, are the instruments for bringing about intrastage changes. The demands of efficient use of capital bring about revolution in the attitude to work and the utilization of time and other resources as demanded by the owners of the means of production.

The fundamental assumption on which Marx based his explanation is that societies are endowed with self-motion, which is brought about by the conflict between classes and contradictions (discrepancies) between the results of social decisions and the dominant value system that seeks to stabilize the form. This leads to a situation in social production where the form is no longer compatible with the content and, thus, brings about a revolutionary conversion of categories (in this case, stages of development). The revolutions have two sides: first, they are revolutions against the old forms; second, they are contestants for the new order. It must be kept in mind that every old form has the seeds of new forms as well as the surviving remnants of other previous forms. All these coexist in an unstable tension whose resolutions propel the social system forward. The socioeconomic system is, thus, conceived as a plenum of forces in unity, with some locked in antagonistic modes, while others are set in cooperative modes.

The Essentials of Non-Marxist Capital Theory of Economic Development

We shall now turn our attention to non-Marxist use of capital as an explanatory factor in the development process. There are a number of non-Marxist economists who, from the 1950s to the present, have identified capital as a basic factor for explaining either economic development or lack of it. For example, R. Nurkse suggests that low real income or, perhaps, lack of development "is a reflection of low productivity, which in turn is due largely to lack of capital. The lack of capital is a result of the small capacity to save, and so the circle is complete" (165). Similar ideas are echoed by Rosenstein-Rodan (180), Nelson (158), and many others, whether the discussion is on balanced growth, big push, or leading sectors.

These non-Marxist capital-based theories about development or underdevelopment phenomena are basically either drawn from or motivated by sections of Marx's explanans. Gunnar Myrdal has also pointed out that these so-claimed non-Marxian capital-based theories of development are borrowed primarily from the explanans of Marx. He states: "Marx's assumptions, so widely adopted by Western economists, that the effect of industrialization and, indeed, of investment generally — in the final instance Marx's changes in the 'modes of production' — spread quickly to other sectors of the economy and to institutions and attitudes, may be fairly realistic for Western countries, both now and when they started their rapid economic development" (154, p. 19).

This borrowed Marx's capital-based argument has been an ad hoc introduction by the non-Marxist economists into the logical search for causes of either development or underdevelopment. They attempt, on the basis of capital as a causal factor of category transformation, to explain the process of economic development through the following system of logic. They contend that the introduction of capital into an underdeveloped economy raises the rate of savings and investment. In light of this, the human and nonhuman resources are used more efficiently after the penetration of capital. The existing markets expand, while new markets are created for new products. In other words, supply creates its own demand. Furthermore, profits (surplus value, in Marx's terms) are raised, providing better incentives, and, thus, become the vehicle for more investments in productive capital for increased capital accumulation and further expansion of production and market. Nurkse puts it as:

At least in principle the difficulty [of development] vanishes in the case of a more or less synchronized application of capital to a wide range of industries. Here is an escape from deadlock; here the result is an overall enlargement of the market. People working with more and better tools in a number of comple- mentary projects become each others' customers. Most industries catering for mass consumption are complementary in the sense that they provide a market for, and thus support each other. The basic complementarity stems in the last analysis from the diversity of human wants. (165, p. 11)

The argument continues where it is suggested in the non-Marxist capital theories that the surplus labor of urban areas then can be employed at low wages by the new class of capital owners. This process leads to increases in the profits of the producers as well as the aggregate income of labor and, hence, a possibility of greater production and consumption. This construct is used in the abstraction that most underdeveloped economies are stuck with a low-level equilibrium where either sufficient savings are not generated for accumulation or there are savings in the form of hoarding due to the lack of any mechanism for transforming these savings into accumulation of productive capital. In this non-Marxian construct, the state of underdevelopment is explained by lack of capital.

In an alternative statement, the non-Marxist capital-based explanans suggests that the transformation of stages of development is explained in terms of capital accumulation. The process of economic development under the defined circumstances is projected by injecting capital into the economy. The capital is expected to increase the capacity to save by the capitalist class of these stagnating economies by in- creasing their profits. These profits will increase because of the avail- ability of low-cost labor and cheap raw materials. As the accumulation of capital moves the economy forward on the development path, the unemployment and underemployment will decrease, with an increase in total labor income leading to the expansion of consumer markets. Con- sequently, the underdeveloped economies will be able to reach a rela- tively higher level of real income and saving-investment equilibrium. Capital accumulation, therefore, propels the economy through stages.

In this non-Marxian framework of capital process, it is instructive to note the important work of Schumpeter. The first logical building block of Schumpeter's explanans, as we have structured it, involves a central concept of innovation that is carried on by entrepre- neurs through capital investments. In its bare essentials, the capital process in Schumpeter's logical construct is the driving force for economic development, which can be enhanced by other factors as contained in his "new combinations." He differs from other non-Marxists in that his capital process is part of innovation-competitive process among subclasses of the capitalist class. In this respect, he adopts the methodology of Marx but changes the focus of the analytical use of capital by altering the nature of socioeconomic contradictions.

Schumpeter finds a theoretical meeting point with Marx. Like Marx, he isolates a mechanism through which capital operates as an important weapon of struggle. Unlike Marx, the capital process affects the capitalists only in their struggle over profit distribution. Labor process is completely out of the process of change. Like Marx, Schumpeter subdivides capital as a weapon of struggle into capital deepening and capital widening. Capital deepening ("technical composition" in terms of Marx or what Higgins calls "autonomous investment" [78]) is investments that are carried on through such competitive conditions as new-product and cost-saving technologies. Capital widening ("value composition" in Marx's terms or what Higgins calls "induced investment") is investment stimulated by recent increases in profits brought about by recent new-product and cost-saving technologies.

Unlike Marx, Schumpeter neglects the dynamic role of labor and the labor process, concentrates on the capitalist class, and subdivides it into the class of entrepreneurs (risk-taking capitalists) and the class of nonentrepreneurs (risk-averting capitalists) and sets them against each other in a competitive struggle over distribution of profits induced by price system and market mechanism. By such an analytical process, a class conflict is indirectly induced by Schumpeter. Capital deepening enters the conflict process as a weapon on the part of the entrepreneurial class, while capital widening enters the conflict as a weapon on the part of nonentrepreneurs. In this process, positive variations in capital deepening either create new products or reduce cost and increase profits above normal and, thus, strengthen the entrepreneurial position. Positive variations in capital widening create more output, reduce price, and deplete profits of the entrepreneurs in the competitive process. In the process, technology improves, production efficiency increases, and output grows in each round of the conflict. The automatic management of this creative conflict leads to the rise of new institutions of science, technology, law, credit and finance, and so on. In other words, these institutions arise from the competitive struggle.

In Schumpeter's analysis of capital process in socioeconomic development, capital is a weapon for the capitalist against itself. The capitalist class creates conditions for its own destruction. In Marx's analysis, however, capital is a weapon for the capitalist against the working class. It is also a weapon of the capitalist class through competition against itself. Thus, capital is a two-sided destructive and creative weapon against the working class and against the capitalist class as it enters the process of disappearance of the old and emergence of the new (the process of creative destruction) to propel the society forward. It spares no one, and no therapy can stop either its creative or its destructive force as a weapon in the class conflict. It is simply a devastating instrument that respects no law except its own. It imposes its will on its creator, and it offers itself at the service of anyone that holds it and is willing to obey its own laws of dynamics. When it externally impinges itself on a society, it has no sustained motion except when its laws of dynamics are internalized to create a basis for continuous social transformation that is internally sustainable.

Evaluation of Capital-based Theories of Economic Development

The evaluation of capital-based theories of economic development must be critical as well as epistemologically insightful. We have discussed two approaches to capital-based theories. Evaluationally, the non-Marxist position is basically drawn from Marx's logical system as we have pointed out. There are, however, some basic differences that are worth noting.

In the non-Marxist approach, with the exception of that of Schumpeter, the institutions and the mode of production are assumed to be basically capitalistic with a supporting value system. Such an institutional configuration and the corresponding value system that form the environment of socioeconomic decision making are assumed to be right for growth and development. The only important ingredient lacking is capital, which places the underdeveloped economies in a more or less classical stationary state, endows them with states of inertia, and, thus, deprives them of the dynamics and possibilities of self-development or transformation.

This construct is basically a mechanistic inductive extension of the Newtonian first law of motion, where "every body persists in its state of rest or of uniform motion in a straight line unless compelled to change that state by forces impressed on it." Within the non-Marxist logical frame, capital is the force that must be impressed on these economies, and because these underdeveloped economies are capital poor, such force must be external, which establishes the concept of external movers. This echoes Rostow's position of external mover (see the discussion of epistemics of his stages of development). In the case of Rostow, an "intrusion" of more advanced nations, rather than penetration of external capital, constitutes the external mover to provide the force of change.

Basically, it is unclear whether this non-Marxist position is directed to explain the underdevelopment phenomenon or to prescribe a corrective mechanism. In other words, the objective of the constructs is unclear in all the literature of the non-Marxist capital-based exposition. Epistemologically, it cannot constitute a complete system of explanation to the development phenomenon. The mechanism, through which capital acquires its role as category converter in the non-Marxist approach, is not provided. Schumpeter's approach is exempted from this criticism. Because the forces of motion of the quantitative level are external to these economies, the non-Marxist construct is incapable of explaining sustained growth that may be the result of new institutional arrangements or internally motivated changes in the value systems. Furthermore, the logical construct fails to account for quality trans- formation that may lead to new stages of the economic system. As such, if the objective of the capital-based logical construct of the non-Marxists is that of explanation, then one must look elsewhere for another logical construct. Perhaps that logical construct is the Schumpeterian explanans, which is methodologically Marxian derived. If the objective is a prescription of corrective mechanism, then one must ask for the logical authority by which the prescription is derived.

The implicit assumption of institutions of capitalism has no self- contained logical basis. Its empirical acceptance can be traced only to the Marxian system of explanation. The nature of the non-Marxist saving-investment mechanism is also not logically motivated. It is a mere ad hoc expositional graft. The notion that capital accumulation and penetration must be externally impressed is non-Marxist and antidialectical. It is basically metaphysical materialist in method. The non-Marxist construct seems to suggest that the motivation for increased investment decisions is growth and development. In other words, the capital-owning class has the society at heart and, hence, accumulates for growth and development. This is, at best, ideological and, at worst, empirically unjustifiable. The general self-interest argument suggests that the capital-owning class invests for reasons of increased profits rather than increased growth of aggregate social output and development. We stated this position when we examined the explanans of Marx and Schumpeter.

In Marx's explanans, on the other hand, the driving force of accumulation is the class struggle over distribution of income. Capital accumulation is an instrument of strategy, employed by the capital- owning class to wage the struggle against labor as well as to increase total profit. These are achieved through capital widening (value composition) and capital deepening (technical composition) or what is referred to in modern terminology as "embodied technological progress." Socioeconomic growth and development are just by-products of this class conflict. Institutions of law, finance, politics, and so on are the results of this class conflict, based on self-interest. Thus, category transformation and quantitative and qualitative changes are explained by resolutions of internal conflicts that generate the forces that propel the socioeconomic system forward and explain the development process. The same argument holds with the explanans of Schumpeter except that the class conflict is between subclasses of the capitalist class.

It is logically inappropriate for one to suggest that Marx incorporated into his logical construct "the basic idea that technological progress is the main spring of economic growth, and that innovation is the main function of the entrepreneur" (78, p. 87). The correct logical posture is that technological progress, holding value composition constant, increases in value composition, holding technical composition constant, and innovation by entrepreneur are instruments for waging class struggle and competition among capitalists. Economic growth is a by-product. The system of Marx's explanation presents a nonlinear process in growth and development where capitalism goes through crises, taking the form of economic fluctuations where economic growth and development are viewed within the class struggle as a destabilizing phenomenon consequent of stage-by-stage resolution of conflicts. This also holds for the approach of Schumpeter.

The capital-based theories of development satisfy the condition of empirical content where output growth is related to capital accumulation. The main propositions also satisfy the conditions of falsification or verification. Predictive conditions are also met in the sense that if x units of capital are of productive accumulation in the sense of Marx, then it is predicted that real national income will increase by y percentage. Although Marx's explanans meets the conditions of structural proposition regarding why, how, and ought, the non-Marxist capital-based expositions fail this test except when one links them to the logical construct of Marx, but then one is immediately caught in logical inconsistencies. The Schumpeterian approach may be exempted from this criticism.

Again, although Marx's explanans clearly satisfies the problem-specification condition in terms of generality and manageability, the non-Marxist logical construct, although manageable, cannot claim generality in terms of category transformation of socioeconomic stages. Furthermore, the *explanandum* of the non-Marxist capital-based theories seems to be the growth of output in a linear-time trend. How development seems to be related to output growth is either completely neglected or casually mentioned. The explanation of socioeconomic transformation in terms of category convertibility, the rise of new institutions and the collapse of outmoded ones, decay and restructuring of political order, social value systems, and conflicts in decision environment as related to distribution, production, and consumption is neglected. The non-Marxist capital-based theories, therefore, cannot be considered a serious explanatory theory of the development process and cannot be considered a rival theory to that of Marx.

Having said this, we observe that there are a number of criticisms levied against capital-based theories. It is claimed that human societies are so different that it is impossible to discover any general law of explanation that is applicable to all in terms of socioeconomic transformation. Hence, capital accumulation is unacceptable in providing a

general law of transformation. This objection is based on an individualistic empiricist epistemology that is an antiscientific generalization.
Methodologically, every science deals with a similar phenomenon
among categories. An apple and a stone, for instance, belong to different
categories of objects, but the law of gravitation explains their downward
movements.

Another criticism presented against capital-based theories is that
they are derived from the experience of the industrial revolution of
Europe (57). The underdeveloped countries, it is suggested, are substantially different from the economies of Europe in many respects. The
theories based on the European experience, therefore, cannot explain
the development phenomenon of the underdeveloped world of today.
Gunnar Myrdal has pointed out that the initial conditions in Europe
were institutionally different at the dawn of the industrial revolution
(154). Consequently, the capital-based theories are not considered very
relevant to the explanation of the development phenomenon of
presently developing economies.

Essentially, the same criticism has been raised by dependency
theorists from another angle. They argue that the current global
economic and political interdependencies have changed the international economic relationships in such a way that the underdeveloped
countries have no meaningful and viable possibility of experiencing
economic growth like Europe (11, 198). Usually, the trade imbalances
and the increasing real-income gap between the developed and
underdeveloped economies are cited as proofs.

This criticism is epistemologically invalid and empirically non-
supported. First, the theory cannot be falsified or invalidated because
its empirical realm is derived from the European experiences. This
criticism is based on vulgar inductivism, which demands that every
case has to be accounted for before arriving at a general law. There is no
area in the scientific enterprise that can afford the luxury of such vulgar
inductivism. Every derivation of a general law in areas of scientific
theory is based on finite observations. The utility of a general law and
applications thereof do not require that the initial conditions must be
the same. Recent data about underdeveloped economies show that the
growth rates of these economies are almost identical to the early periods
of industrialization of the European economies (127).

Moreover, these criticisms are epistemologically ill-conceived. Criticisms must be constructed on the basis of the indicated explanandum
and the constructed explanans. The first question that must be
answered and criticized is what is the explanandum. The second set of
criticisms must be directed against the constructed explanans regarding the logical consistency, the correctness of the problem specification,
the appropriateness of the maintained assumptions, the existence of
empirical content of the main propositions, and whether these main
propositions meet the conditions of factual correctness, as well as

prediction. The third criticism must be directed to examine whether the explanans can constitute a logical basis for policy actions or prescriptions.

THE ESSENTIALS OF HUMAN-CAPITAL THEORY OF ECONOMIC DEVELOPMENT

We now turn our attention to another factor-based theory of phenomenon of economic development, the human-capital-based explanatory theory of the development process. In this approach, human capital is defined as the mental and physical know-how of the society to produce economic goods and services. One may refer to this as the knowledge base of the society or the mental labor in the Marxian term. The social knowledge base or the mental labor is the totality of skills, methods, and techniques of all kinds that are collectively possessed by the members of the society. It is, therefore, the knowledge in the possession of the population as well as the social capacity and training of the population to effectively utilize it to satisfy the configuration of its needs and wants. It defines the quality of the societal labor input. The growth of such knowledge is viewed as investment in human capital (100, 151, 228, 229).

The knowledge base of a society has three important functions. It enables the labor force to use the existing physical and nonphysical tools of production — in other words, to provide the commodities that will satisfy social needs and wants. Second, it provides the know-how to create new tools and products for production in order to satisfy other needs and wants. Third, it provides the required know-how to create the workable institutional configuration for organizing social production and distribution, as well as creation of value systems that are compatible with work and wealth creation. Viewed in this way, investment in human capital is linked to increased productivity through invention and innovation and, hence, output growth and economic development. It is directly responsible for bringing into being the Schumpeterian "new combination."

The Methodology of Human-capital-based Theory of Economic Development

A theory constructed around investment in social knowledge as a key factor to explain development or underdevelopment is referred to as human capital based. The proponents of human-capital-based theory attempt the explanation of the process of economic development and growth on the basis of human capital as a driving force of production. Essentially, the objective of the theory is to establish a causal relationship between the quality and quantity of human capital and the direction and rate of economic development. On the phenomenon of underdevelopment, it is an attempt to explain why certain societies have not realized the desired economic development despite costly investment in physical capital. On the phenomenon of development, the attempt is to show that human capital and its investment are important factors in explaining economic development. At the very least, as a driving force of socioeconomic development, human capital and its investment must be given a causal role.

Concentrating on the recent experiences of developing economies, it is argued in the theory that societies that invest more in human capital than physical capital have a higher rate of economic growth. The core of the human-capital-based explanation of economic development or lack of it is summarized by Meir:

The slow growth in knowledge is an especially severe restraint to progress. The economic quality of the population remains low when there is little knowledge of what natural resources are available, the alternative production techniques that are possible, the necessary skills, the existing market conditions and opportunities and the institutions that might be created to favor economizing effort and economic rationality. An improvement in the quality of the "human factor" is then as essential as investment in physical capital. An advance in knowledge and diffusion of new ideas and objectives are necessary to remove economic backwardness and instill the human abilities and motivations that are favorable to economic achievement. Although investment in material capital may indirectly achieve some lessening of the economic backwardness of the human resources, the direct and more decisive means is through investment in human beings. (142, p. 610)

Essentially, when either the availability or the attainability of natural resources is assumed, then the argument reduces to the following main propositions:

The societies that have invested heavily in humans and, hence, with improved human capital have developed first and faster.

The individuals and societies with better education and training are more productive and have higher real incomes.

The history of economically advanced societies reveals that knowledge of production technique precedes its application and that improvement in physical capital is less likely unless human capital has improved.

Many developing countries have not achieved the right potential for sustained economic growth despite the fact that they have borrowed economic resources, particularly physical and financial capital, from more-developed countries, and when these societies are examined, it is found that there is low-level investment in their human capital.

These main propositions form the explanatory basis of the human-capital-based theory of economic development or lack of it, where a positively causal link is made between the level of human capital and its rate of investment, on the one hand, and the level of development and its rage of change and sustainability, on the other hand. On the basis of these main propositions, the driving force of economic development is directly and empirically abstracted as human capital and its investment. Thus, economic growth and development are explained in terms of human capital.

Essentially, the methodological position of human-capital-based theory is that of metaphysical materialism, where the creation of the knowledge base of any society is assumed to be possible irrespective of its historical conditions. This would seem to indicate that the improvement in the quality of a population and, hence, its labor force is a function of human will rather than being determined by the objective material needs and wants of societies, social exigencies, and the nature of the historical processes they reflect.

Because improvements in the state of human capital and investment in humans are not determined by historical conditions, the theory merely attempts an explanation of development phenomenon by simply showing an empirical correlation between human capital and its investment and growth of production of goods and services. More precisely, an empirical correlation is established between the years of education and either real income or productivity appropriately measured when one examines developed economies.

When this empirical argument is extended to explain the presence of underdeveloped economies, the absence of the proper level and rate of investment in human capital is pointed out. The argument is structured to indicate that only investment in human capital can create new value systems and a new environment for production and consumption decisions and increase the chances of making correct decisions and choices to speed up the econom-ic development process. By investing in human capital, the work force will become more informed and be able to improve the existing production methods and techniques as well as learn about new ones. As such, the accumulated physical capital will be used more efficiently, resulting in higher output growth in proportion to the rate of investment.

Additionally, the social and cultural horizons of the work force will expand as the investment in human capital is increased, leading to an improved attitude to work and efficient time utilization. Musgrave stresses this point in the following words: "Perhaps the most important aspect of the external benefits of education lies in the change in the social and cultural climate, incident to the widened horizons which education entails" (151, p. 33).

In this framework of exposition, it is hoped that the increased level of investment in humans will motivate a change in outmoded political order and other institutions of production that will be conducive to economic growth and development.

An Evaluation of Human-capital-based
Theory of Economic Development

We have presented the main propositions of the human-capital-based explanation of the process of economic development. We have pointed out that the methodological basis of the human-capital-based theory is metaphysical materialism. It is not clear whether the argument is constructed to explain the process of economic development or the phenomenon of the existence of underdevelopment. If construction of an explanation is the objective, then many logical questions tend to arise. For example, the indicated empirical correlation cannot be taken as a causal relation. Even if it can hold as a causal relation, it cannot be taken as an explanation of the process.

For the main propositions to constitute an explanans to the economic development process or lack of it, they must meet the conditions of categorial convertibility. This requires that the construction abandons the metaphysical position in order to incorporate a law of sustained socioeconomic transformation. The argument as constructed is more or less empirical and lacks self-containment as well as logical completeness as demanded by a scientifically acceptable construct of an explanans. The rise of institutions through which investment in human capital can be transmitted to the society is assumed to take place without cause. The existence of these institutions is explained through the methodological position of idealism. The cause of the rise of such required institutions may be ascribed to internal or external forces. If one holds the methodological position of dialectical materialism, one then will ascribe the rise of such institutions not only to the material needs of the society but also to the internal forces of the society in order to resolve certain conflicts within the content, as well as between the form and the content of the socioeconomic organism, as opposed to the methodological position of idealism, where cause is believed to be externally subjected.

The implicit assumptions of the existence of an acceptable institutional configuration and a mode of production require an analytical justification, or they are unacceptable. Such assumptions may be acceptable if the main concern is an empirical correlation regarding quantities in a given category or state. The indicated causal relationship between investment in human capital and economic growth meets the conditions of existence of empirical content. This is not enough, because the process by which the output growth is translated into qualitative improvement of the content of the socioeconomic organism is left unexplained. If one accepts the human-capital-based exposition as meeting the minimum requirements of a scientific theory, then one must also accept that it satisfies the conditions of verifiability or falsifiability in that the main proposition meets the conditions of congruence with reality within its logical confines. Furthermore, the main proposition allows test operations to be performed on it.

In the context of empirical verification of the argument, some development economists have tried to provide suitable measures based on levels of education, technical and managerial skills, level of rationality, and so on in attempts to find indicators of improvement in human capital. Within this attempt, there are some problems, which have been indicated by H. Myint as "The problem(s) of trying to establish a causal quantitative relation between the expenditure of resources invested and the value of capital formation which results from it are multiplied when we move from material capital to human capital" (152, p. 529).

The argument as abstracted from the human-capital position, even though it indicates direction of change, does not explain the process of change. It does not adequately answer the question of how and why increases in human capital, approximately measured, result in higher economic growth and changes in the development state. What motivates and how does the social knowledge base expand to the point where it not only facilitates societal use of the existing physical capital and production know-hows but also defines favorable social climate for the creation of new ones? This question, as critical as it is to the logical construction of an explanans to the explanandum of the development phenomenon in economics, is left undealt with. In other words, the argument fails to satisfy the conditions of structural propositions.

On a positive note, however, one can say that the human-capital argument draws attention to the important role of labor and its quality in the socioeconomic development process. It is a point that is completely overlooked by Schumpeter, and it is a point that may help connect inventions and innovations to the capital process as it is projected in Marx's explanans. It is a position that corroborates the old view that labor is the real source of the wealth of nations. This view must be expanded to include the quality and quantity of labor and how labor acts on nature to create wealth and productive capacity of a society as well as development. The capital and labor processes must be logically connected in order to craft an organic theory of socioeconomic transformation that is inherently generated and self-sustaining.

It is this recognition that leads Marx to distinguish mental labor (quality) from physical labor (quantity). It is also on this basis that Marx insists on valuing real wealth and capital in labor units. Within the Marxian framework, the driving force of development is not quality of labor and its human capital; rather, it is conflicts in institutions and classes that create the driving force for investment in human capital and the efficient utilization in the process of resolving these conflicts. Investment in human capital, therefore, has a cause that is internally generated. When the explanatory role of human capital and its investment (mental labor) in economic development is viewed in this light and as part of a logical chain in the explanation, then we speak of Marxist human-capital-based analysis. Within the construct of Marxian explanans, human capital constitutes a part of the organic explanation of economic development and social change based on antagonistic interests of social classes. The investment in humans leading to improved quality of labor is an instrument of struggle at the disposal of labor as well as at the disposal of the owners of the means of production.

Within Marx's logical system, a socioeconomic development is a labor process. It is not only a revolution in the mode of production, it is also a revolution in the organization of production and instruments of production. The labor process is the technology and a vehicle by which a socioeconomic change and a category transformation of society are effected. Development, therefore, is a continuous updating and error-correction process on the part of labor, based on decision-information-interactive processes where conflicts in the self-interests of classes and individuals provide the internal force for transformation of stages and converting of categories, where results are the unpredictable outcomes of labor's own activities in nature and society.

The introduction of mental labor in Marxian epistemological process has a specific objective. The objective is to establish that the technological know-how of production, capital creation, and organization of production, inventions and diffusion of know-hows, and their rates of change are anchored in the accumulated knowledge of society, where such knowledge provides an indication of success-failure experiences of labor. Labor is the technology of social transformation as well as the technology for labor's self-transformation. The improvement in quality of labor is induced by the material conditions and relations in society. Thus, a law of motion for social transformation is indicated. This law of motion is associated not only with output growth but also with society, labor, and social institutions of production. In this way, the constructed explanans is logically self-contained relative to the explanation of the process of economic development where labor and capital processes are theoretically connected.

The non-Marxian human-capital-based theory seems to be concerned with establishing statistical causal relation between output-growth and changes in quality of human capital, appropriately measured. It does seem to suggest that improvements in human capital are sufficient conditions for economic growth. It fails, however, to specify whether it is a necessary condition. Alternatively stated, the non-Marxian theory does not establish the necessity of human capital in its explanation of economic development. For example, it does not provide answers to some fundamental questions: How does a user of capital become transformed into a creator of capital? Why do certain societies invest more in human capital at certain stages in their evolution?

In conclusion, the non-Marxist human-capital-based theory of economic development has a number of epistemological problems. It does not provide a convincing logical system of thought on the basis of which the development process of socioeconomic system can be explained. At the very best, it seems to suggest a prescription for economic development where such a prescription is derived from some explanatory theory. Such a theory, we have suggested, seems to be the Marxian system of explanation of socioeconomic development where there exists an explanatory mechanism that ties labor process to capital-creating process, institutional-transformation process, and a process of conversion of categories as defined by stages of development, as well as erections of political-support mechanism, legal-support mechanism, and dynamically compatible system of values.

THE ESSENTIALS OF TECHNOLOGY-BASED THEORIES OF ECONOMIC DEVELOPMENT

We have discussed the epistemics of two of the factor-based theories about the phenomenon of socioeconomic development. The last in this chain of examination is the technology-based theory of economic development. An explanatory theory about the phenomenon of economic development is said to be technology based if the logical construct of the explanans lays claim to the primacy of technology and technological progress. In such a construct, the explanation of the process of category conversion or the transformation of socioeconomic stages is assigned to technical know-how and the rate of changes of such know-how possessed by the societies. Thus, observed differences in levels of economic development and economic growth rates for any given time point among societies are attributed to the primacy of the explanatory factor of technology. The theory emerged mainly from the need to explain and understand the rising gap between developed and underdeveloped economies (217).

In accordance with this theory, the observed income gaps and the rising gaps in socioeconomic development among nations are because of the fact that more-developed countries are continuously creating and using the most sophisticated technologies in all fronts of production. This creates positive linkages and feedback mechanisms, which tend to speed up the development processes of the economically more-advanced economies. It is further suggested that the economic development of certain countries is left behind because the societies are not able to keep pace with rapid innovations in technology or with employment in growth-generating sectors of the economy.

It is generally agreed among proponents of technology-based explanation of levels of socioeconomic achievement of a given society that technological progress is that which produces growth while levels of technology are associated with output or development levels. B. Higgins states the relationship as "an increase in the rate of technological progress rather than mere existence of technological advance which produces economic expansion. . . . The problem is not merely one of introducing some degree of improvement in techniques, it is a matter of raising the rate of technological progress" (78, p. 94).

As we examine the historiographies of development of nations and societies, the core of technology-based theories holds that the rate of improvement in the technological know-how of a society determines the direction of economic development, while the level of technological know-how determines the level of development. The argument is extended to underdeveloped countries by pointing to the idea that the absence of appropriate technology and a lower level of economic growth are simultaneously observed in these economies. The level of technology and its rate of change are taken to account for the higher level and rate of development of developed countries.

The technology-based exposition is made sharper by Kuznets, who states: "But it is precisely backwardness and seemingly greater backlog of technology that make for the significant differences between the growth position of the less developed countries of today and that of the developed countries when they were entering the modern economic growth process" (114, p. 256). In concluding remarks, Kuznets adds that, "The high rate of growth (in modern economies) is sustained by the interplay between mass applications of technological innovations based on additions to the stock of knowledge and further additions to that stock" (114, p. 257).

It is also suggested by proponents of this position that the process of economic growth involves continuous innovations and inventions in technology and its diffusion and applications to production. It is suggested that scientific inventions, innovations, and applications must be combined to create a high rate of technological progress. Higgins summarizes it in this way: "A high rate of technological advance requires both inventions and innovations; that is, it requires that new techniques be not only discovered but also brought into use" (78, p. 194). Kuznets amplifies this statement by suggesting that:

Mass application of technological innovations, which constitutes much of the distinctive substance of modern economic growth, is closely connected with the further progress of science, in its turn the basis for additional advance in technology. . . . It seems fairly clear that mass-uses to technical innovations provide a positive feedback. . . . They permit the development of new efficient tools for scientific use and supply new data on the behavior of natural processes under the stress of modification in economic production. (115, p. 250)

Kuznets also recognizes that technology and the rate of its progress is not sufficient for economic growth. He points out that: "Advancing technology is the permissive source of economic growth, but it is only a potential, a necessary condition, in itself not sufficient. If technology is to be employed efficiently and widely, and indeed, if its own progress is to be stimulated by such use, institutional and ideological adjustments must be made to effect the proper use of innovations generated by the advancing stock of human knowledge" (115, p. 247).

These arguments combine to arrive at the conclusion that the process of economic growth involves continuous invention and innovations in the field of technology as well as their applications to production. Most of the inventions and technological innovations are created in developed countries. These inventions and innovations are not appropriate for developing countries and, hence, cannot be integrated into their production processes, even if they are made available. As a result, the technological gap between the developed and underdeveloped countries keeps growing, and this obviously manifests itself in the disparities in the levels of development. In other words, technological gaps explain the observed development gaps. The underdeveloped economies are left behind, with a widening gap between them and developed economies, because they are not able to keep pace with rapid inventions and innovations in technology or with its employment in the growth-generating sectors of the economies.

The intellectual voices of Schumpeter and Marx must be added to those voices that articulate the role of technological progress in economic development. Technological progress, or innovations in capital and organization of production, is an important part of Schumpeter's new combinations, and innovations are weapons at the disposal of entrepreneurs, as we have pointed out. They play a special role in Schumpeterian explanatory logic of the mechanism through which the phenomenon of economic development can be understood. Technological progress also plays an important role in the Marxian capital process and the dynamics of class conflict on the transient path of economic development.

The Methodological Basis of Technology-based Theories of Economic Development Process

Epistemologically, the logical characteristics of the explanans of technology-based theories are similar to those of the non-Marxist human-capital-based theories. In the implicitly or explicitly constructed explanans of the technology-based theories, a technical know-how system, consisting of scientific knowledge, invention, and innovation, is treated as an historically external factor whose unexplainable force acts externally on the socioeconomic organism and propels it in the direction of the force. The production and absorption of technology, inventions, and innovations are not treated as an internally determined process that is induced by the material needs and all aspects of social conditions of societies. Because technology is treated as an external factor grafted to the social structure, only empirical links are indicated and described between the level of technology and production, on the one hand, and between the rate of technological progress and socioeconomic development, on the other hand. How technology comes to be embodied in societies, how inventions are created, what motivates innovations, and what causes diffusion are left unexplained. Furthermore, how social transformation and category conversion tend to occur are left in a muddle.

The explanandum of the technology-based exposition seems to be comparative growth-rate differences among economies rather than the phenomenon of socioeconomic transformation. The constructed explanans of these technology-based theories is drawn from an empirical correlation based on the most recent period of human history by mostly dwelling on the cross-sectional aspect of the phenomenon. In this way, all the variations in technology-based theory about the development phenomenon tend to avoid the question of evolution and revolution of technology in various societies of the present and the past and how our understanding can constitute an important basis for prescription. It is always useful to keep in mind that correlation is not causation and that causation is not theoretical explanation.

An Evaluation of Technology-based Theories of Socioeconomic Development

We shall now turn our attention to evaluate the core ideas of the technology-based theory. There are two basic versions: the Marxist and non-Marxist versions. Our treatment has been mostly focused on the non-Marxist version, which has many variations. The basic characteristics of the non-Marxist version are its ahistoricity and staticity. Its methodological position leads to a construction of an explanans that fails to acknowledge that the socioeconomic organism is not a world of states but of processes that are the blood of real socioeconomic outcomes. It is, therefore, not until the non-Marxist theory of development phenomenon, based on technology and its progress, is constructed to indicate a mechanism of technological change and show how this change induces socioeconomic transformation that old forms disappear and new forms emerge. The theory does not establish a convincing, logical basis for explaining economic development as a megaprocess.

The essential hypothesis of non-Marxist technology-based theory is that the quantity and quality of technology of society and their rates of change determine or explain the level and rate of economic development. The conceptual framework of this hypothesis contains an empirical content that meets the condition of congruence with reality. The main propositions can also be operationalized and falsified. The empirical verification of the maintained hypothesis is attainable if we can overcome the measurement problem of the concepts of technology and its progress.

There are a number of shortcomings in the non-Marxist technology-based exposition of development. The problem for analysis in these writings is not clearly defined. Also, like the human-capital-based theory, it is unclear whether the inquiry is focused on the importance of technology and its progress on the development process or on the explanation of the underdevelopment phenomenon. In other words, one is not sure what the explanandum is. Neither is one sure whether the exposition is a rationalization to invest in technology. If the explanation of the development process is the focus, then the theory cannot be taken as a serious scientific work. The theory must establish a linkage or a difference between its explanans and the explanandum indicated by human-capital-based theory as well as that indicated by physical-capital-based theory.

If the stress of importance is that which is indicated in the exposition, then the technology-based exposition must find anchorage in a generally established complete system of thinking about the development phenomenon. We think that this general system of thought is the Marxist megatheory, where an explanatory role is assigned to technology and its progress and where the development of technology consisting of scientific progress, invention, innovation, diffusion, and application is also explained as part of the general process of social transformation leading to conversions of social categories.

In its structure, the non-Marxist technology-based exposition theoretically does not advance the abstracted simple empirical correlation between levels of development and levels of technology; it merely suggests an observed empirical correlation that by increasing the quantity and improving the quality of technology, a country can increase the level and the rate of socioeconomic development. It fails, however, to explain and provide answers to a number of important questions: Why and how do different societies have different rates of creation and absorption of technology intertemporally and cross-sectionally? How do technology and its progress act on the society and alter its quality? How general is the technology-based explanation of the phenomenon of development? When all these are combined, we arrive at a conclusion that the technology-based exposition does not fulfill the basic requirements of an explanatory theory and, hence, contains a limited predictive power and scientific utility.

In Marx's analytic framework, technology and its rate of progress are instruments of struggle for all classes. The rate of technological progress depends essentially, but not absolutely, on the intensity of class contradictions and antagonistic economic relations. The technology and its advancement play a specific role in Marx's logic for explaining economic development and transformation of stages. However, the dynamics of the technological subsystem of production including invention, innovation, and applications is explained by antagonistic class relations, where each class juggles for favorable socioeconomic position and influence or dominance in the decision-choice space. Growth of output is not the primary objective of technological advances. The growth of output is a by-product of advances of a technological system that is geared toward the resolutions of conflicts in socioeconomic relations. In this way, the process of technological advances and the rate at which they take place are rooted in history, considered as part of the megaprocess of development, and explained by the internal dynamics of the socioeconomic organism.

Technology and its progress can be embodied or disembodied, both of which are instruments of class struggle. Both types of technologies are interdependent in their creations, progresses, and applications. In fact, they form an inseparable union and, yet, are antagonistic. It was the recognition of the dual character of technology that led Marx to logically separate mental labor from labor in general and technical composition of capital from capital in general. In Marx's explanans, mental labor and its progress are equivalent to disembodied technology and its progress, and technical composition of capital and its progress are equivalent to embodied technology and its progress. Technology is not abstract, and, like any process when it emerges, it acquires its own course. Here, there is affirmation that technology and its progress cannot be isolated from social exigencies of class antagonisms and conflicts among classes to control the machinery of decision making in the realms of production, distribution, consumption, and their derivatives.

SOME REMARKS ON FACTOR-BASED THEORIES

Some concluding remarks are necessary and appropriate in bringing this chapter to a close. We have labored through jungles of ideas, we have journeyed over slippery grounds, and we have sweated over logical confusion. The effort is considered well-spent if some development economists become aggravated and angry. Additionally, time would have been well-spent if a clear and new thinking emerges to clean up the logical mess of development economics that allows every argument to be unscientifically correct, if ideological positions are separated from matters of logical reasoning that will allow headway into a world of scientific theorizing, and if cooperation and continuity can be forged among preconceptions and values that are opposed to one another in the process of logical construct.

For example, it is useful to agree on the nature and structure of the problem of development phenomenon and also on a class of subproblems that an explanatory theory of development must tackle. Every process has a medium of transmission. The mechanism for transmitting socioeconomic development is the actual and potential institutions of politics, law, values, production, distribution, and consumption. These institutions arise from the dynamics of social value systems that generate the environment for decisions and choices whose collective outcomes are usually unknown. The mobilization and organization of resources available to society take place through these established institutions. Thus, any theory of development that assumes the presence of such institutions and deals with growth of investment, technology, and quantity of labor in the abstract cannot and should not be taken as a serious scientific approach to the explanation of the process of socioeconomic change. The explanation of the rise and fall of institutions of different qualities and forms that help to establish the boundaries of acceptable socioeconomic decisions and choices must be part of the theory. This is where Marx and Schumpeter score their greatest points in their creative insights into the explanation of the mechanism of the development process.

We have available to us the social milieu, comprising the value systems of various interest groups, their attitudes, preconceptions, and so on, through which individual and social decisions and choices are made. With any given resource, sustained output growth and its proper utilization to improve the welfare quality occur with sustained progressive innovations and changes in the existing institutional configuration. New institutions arise as a result of conflicts, either among competing value systems or between the dominating value system and the results of choices and decisions. In the process, outmoded institutions crumble under the weight of their own inefficiencies and from the pressure of new ideas and institutions. The emerging configuration of institutions that defines a new order of decision-choice environment is not only a revolt against the previous institutional configuration of an old order but also a contest for a potential institutional configuration that defines a potentially new regime of decision-choice environment.

The growth of output makes materially possible the rise and maintenance of new institutions. The rise of new institutions defines new possibilities of social technology that makes it possible to design a mechanism for efficient mobilization and organization of the existing human and nonhuman resources, creation of new inventions, introduction of innovations, and better applications of existing know-hows to expand the frontiers of production and consumption — in other words, to make possible the introduction of Schumpeterian "new combinations." All these are interconnected and form a unity of the megaprocess, the transformation of society, where the driving force is internally generated by antagonistic class relations. The logical beauty of Marx's explanans is usually overlooked. The scientific power of explanation, where every important process or subprocess is elevated to focus and assigned a role in the logical construct and where logical completeness is sought with intuition and analytical brilliance, is always overlooked by critics who dislike and condemn his ideology and admirers who support his ideology. It is, perhaps, this analytical brilliance that drew Schumpeter to accept Marx's methodology and also state that "It is probably due to this fact [the combination of Ricardian economics and Hegelian logic] that one generation of economists after another turns back to him again, although they may find plenty to criticize in him" (204, p. 167).

In the works of Marx, one sees Marx as a scientist and a philosopher, on the one hand, and Marx as a philosopher and ideologist, on the other. Most critics dwell on his ideological position and either overlook or discredit his scientific works and contribution to epistemics. In this way, we learn very little, or perhaps nothing, from Marx's monumental works on economic dynamics and, in particular, economic development. In defining and asserting his ideological position, Marx understands that philosophies are reflections of social currents; they have to be, because they always arise from social exigencies. He also understands, from his own philosophical works, that logical strength is that which will maintain his constructed explanans and that if the logic is weak, no amount of words will save the theoretical results and convictions to them. So far, there is no rival theory to Marx's on economic development and transformation that is as complete and self-contained in its explanans, not even that of Schumpeter.

This is not to say that the logic of Marx's theory of economic development and transformation cannot be faulted or that the main propositions are corroborated in the sense of Lakatos or pass the test of falsification in the sense of Popper or stand the test of resolutions of all anomalies in the sense of Kuhn or overcome all barriers to scientific discovery in the sense of Kedrov. We are merely emphasizing the idea that all key factors of development process are accounted for in a self-contained system of explanations and that the mechanism by which the key factors operate to effect economic development has been indicated.

6

Prescriptive Theories and the Development Process

We have examined the epistemological foundations of theories of economic development. In the process, we have analyzed the contribution to knowledge made by development theories. Furthermore, we have argued that a substantial portion of the literature on economic development does not fit into the category of explanatory theory. In this chapter, we will examine whether that substantial portion can satisfy the conditions of prescriptive theory of economic development.

The first task is to clarify the concept of prescription and categories of prescriptions. The prescriptions are directed to solve specific micro-problems or macroproblems. These are suggested policies for practice with the hope that development will occur. The literature on prescriptions may be divided into two categories: those that are based on explanatory theories, and those that are logically self-contained theories that prescribe the path by which the potential inherent in nature can be actualized in accordance with the will of human beings. Prescriptions, therefore, may or may not be based on established theory of explanation. As such, we shall explore the relationship between explanation and prescription before we elaborate and evaluate.

EXPLANATION, PRESCRIPTION, AND PRESCRIPTIVE THEORY

The explanatory theory tells us how and why a phenomenon behaves in a certain way. The prescriptive theory identifies a course by which the element or elements of the phenomena can be manipulated in a desired direction. A question that arises is whether there is a relationship between explanation and prescription. Arthur Lewis indirectly reflects on this question when he states that "The approach of the economist qua philosopher, is to try to understand what is going on; the approach of the social engineer is to change the outcome" (123, p. 6). The question, thus, falls back to the fundamental epistemological problems of existence and knowability and whether "what there is" can be changed by utilizing the rules implied in the predictive force of explanatory theory concerning "what there is." Alternatively viewed, the question may be stated as to whether there is a rational connection between explanation and social engineering through prescriptions implied by a theory of explanation.

Prescriptions in economics are about social currents and future possibilities as induced by social exigencies. Prescriptions are rational rules for actions to hasten the disappearance of the old and the emergence of the new. Such rules for engineering a change must have some rational basis. The act of prescribing a future course for economic development is a "social engineering." Social engineering requires that the rules for decisions and choices leading to the transformation from the old to the new be constructed. Such a construction may proceed in two ways. One may accept the predictions and forecasts of an explanatory theory as the rational basis and use the main propositions of the explanatory theory to prescribe rules of behavior in the decision-choice space that would allow the predictions of a theory about a desired phenomenon to be actualized in a new environment where such a phenomenon does not exist. In this way, one is at least probabilistically certain about the future development history.

Just as some philosophers of science consider prediction a necessary quality for explanatory theory, so also, some economists consider explanation as a necessary prerequisite for prescription. This position regarding the relationship between explanation and prescription in economic development instructs us to raise logically prior questions as to whether economists really understand what is wrong and how to right it (i.e., explain and predict) before advancing a prescription. In this context, although explanation is adequate for prescription, prescription is not only inadequate but also not necessary for explanation, as is implied in our discussion on the instrumentalists.

According to this view, the prescriptions must be based on an explicit or implicit explanation of a theory. One of the main tests of a scientific theory is whether or not it yields valid and falsifiable predictions. The prescriptions based on explanatory theory are, in a way, the operationalized predictions. The practice of these explanatory-theory-based operationalized predictions may be viewed as creating the conditions for the empirical falsification of the theory. Contextually, therefore, an explanatory theory is not fully adequate unless its explanatory propositions (the *explanans*), in a time domain, could have served as a rational basis for actualizing the phenomenon (the *explanandum*) under consideration.

The logical structure of the relationships among explanation, prediction, and prescription may be schematically illustrated. Suppose that a set $A = \{A_1, A_2,..., A_n\}$ constitutes the statement of antecedent conditions of a theory. Furthermore, suppose that a set $B = \{B_1, B_2,..., B_n\}$ constitutes the main propositions (general laws) of the theory. If D is an observed phenomenon that is explained by A and B systems, then, given A, the set of propositions in B explains the causal relationship of D relative to A ex post. In other words, A causes D and B provides the reasons. On the other hand, if the occurrence of D is derived from the knowledge of A given B, then A constitutes a prediction of D relative to the main propositions, B, of the theory. The set A constitutes the predictive force for the phenomenon, D, given B.

The explanation implied in the theory of discussion is a causal one. Thus, if D describes a phenomenon of development, then the stated antecedent conditions in A about development may be said to jointly cause development in the sense that there are certain empirical regularities constructed as the main propositions in B of the theory, which lead to the implication that whenever we find the conditions stated in A occurring, the development phenomenon, D, would be expected. The main propositions in B connect the development phenomenon, D, to a set of conditions contained in A but to no other set. The implication to prescription is that if one creates the set of conditions contained in A, one would expect these conditions to result in the outcome of D, whose connection to A is provided by B. We have previously pointed out that the importance of an explanatory theory is found in its predictive power, while its social utility is found in its prescriptive force. Generally, a good scientific explanation should lead to a relatively good explanatory-theory-based prescription.

Some problems tend to arise in relating predictions to prescriptions as one moves from phenomenon to phenomenon and through different areas of science. There are certain predictions from explanatory theory that cannot be operationalized into prescriptions. Furthermore, explanatory-theory-based prescriptions do not provide rules of behavior that would show the practitioner how to create the set of conditions contained in A. It simply suggests that if the outcomes in D are desirable (undesirable), then one must create (destroy) the conditions in A if one wants D to result (disappear), because wherever a set A is found, D follows. The user of explanatory-theory-based prescriptions must first accept the result D as a desirable (undesirable) outcome. One must also accept the main propositions, B, of the explanatory theory as valid. One, however, must find a way to create (destroy) A. The way to create (destroy) A may require another theory. Such a theory may itself be an explanatory one or be engineered.

In this connection, one thing must be made clear: the explanatory-theory-based prescriptions cannot be expected to result in the outcome of something that has not been explained by the theory except such an outcome is by accident. Such an outcome that is not implied in the theory will not satisfy the empirical requirements expected of the theory. As we have argued, prescriptions are viewed as a set of operationalized conditions whose practice must bring into existence the explained consequence. The relationships among explanatory theory, predictions of the theory, and the prescriptions that flow from the theory are shown in Table 6.1.

TABLE 6.1
Explanatory Theory, Explanation, Prediction, and Prescriptions

---

Logical Item D
  Phenomenon to be explained as currently observed (Explanation)
  Phenomenon to be predicted for future observation (Prediction)
  Phenomenon to be realized (demolished) in an environment different from A
     (same as A) (Prescription)

Logical Item A
  Environment in which D is to be explained (Explanation)
  Environment in which D is to be predicted for future observation (Prediction)
  Environment to be created (destroyed) so as to realize (demolish) D (Prescription)

Logical Item B
  Main propositions or laws that explain D in A (Explanation)
  Explanatory-theory-based rules for predicting the future occurrences of D
     (Prediction)
  Operationalized explanatory-theory-based predictive rules (prescriptions) for
     realizing D (Prescription)

For the operationalized rules of prediction of an explanatory theory to constitute a set of prescriptions, the explanandum must be contemplated in an environment different from that of the explanans. Predictive rules do not acquire the qualities of prescriptive rules in the same environment in which "that which is to be explained" is explained. Prescriptions are about something, and this something is a cure directed toward improving or transforming reality.

Generally, there are some prescriptions that are not explanatory theory based but project outcomes that are to be anticipated in the future. The prescriptions of a social engineer, for example, may not be based on any scientific explanation as he designs strategies to effect the future social outcomes. In this case, he selects a goal in the future and devises a course of action to achieve that goal. An illustration with the development process may be used as an example. A development economist may select a goal of industrialization for country X that must be accomplished within t number of years. The task, in this respect, is not to explain the causes of underdevelopment but to design appropriate rules of behavior that would allow a particular type of industrialization to occur. The design of a set of appropriate rules that is not explanatory theory based will constitute a prescriptive theory if certain conditions of science are satisfied.

The preceding argument suggests that prescriptive theory generally must be distinguished from prescriptions whose construct is based on an explanatory theory. On the other hand, prescriptions constructed from an explanatory theory must be distinguished from predictions abstracted from such a theory. The main distinguishing characteristics are offered in Table 6.1. Generally, however, predictions may be neither scientific nor unscientific. The scientific predictions may be viewed as a set of logically derived propositions about either the future behavior or the outcome of a phenomenon. Such propositions constitute current knowledge that is theory based. Unscientific prediction, however, is derived from either empirically based belief, pure speculation, or superstition. Insofar as our understanding of scientific theories is concerned, unscientific predictions do not qualify for scientific scrutiny.

Scientific prediction, as a set of logically derived knowledge about the future behavior of a phenomenon, may be based on empirically valid or invalid explanatory theories. A theory is said to be empirically valid when it has not been falsified in repeated tests. In this respect, predictions derived from empirically valid explanatory theory may become a scientific basis for a valid scientific prescription. A valid scientific prescription, however, does not necessarily constitute a valid prescriptive theory. An empirically valid explanatory theory generates an information set about present physical realities or social currents on the basis of which some aspects of future possibilities may be conceptualized and conceived.

The recipient of such information, although having knowledge of social currents and future possibilities, may not take advantage of that knowledge to design the future as willed. The information from the theory may be taken passively or fatalistically. In order to benefit from the knowledge of an empirically valid explanatory theory, the implied predictions must be operationalized into prescriptions that are viewed as a set of action rules that must be produced by a logical construct into a design. The design itself may or may not be scientific in the sense of meeting conditions of consistency and logical validity.

We shall refer to a set of action, choice, or decision rules that are produced by a logical construct into a design for transforming reality, changing existing conditions, improving reality, or actualizing the potential inherent in nature as a prescriptive theory. Prescriptive theory, as we have specified, lays down rules of correct human "behavior" for affecting the outcomes of future possibilities that, when actualized, would become part of the known reality. Prescriptive theory is about human action. It is also about engineering and transforming the future to coincide with human desires and will. Furthermore, it is about shaping history. It is simply about problem solving.

The primary objective of a prescriptive theory, therefore, is neither to explain "what there is," the known reality, nor is it to predict the occurrences of the known reality in the future. The primary objective of a prescriptive theory is to construct action-based rules for bringing desired outcomes into an environment where these outcomes were not previously observed or in existence. The driving force is the improvement of the quality of human conditions in society and nature.

Prescriptive theory is a rational construct of the model of human decision and choice process. Viewed as such, a prescriptive theory translates into a materialist conception of humans where it is held that it is possible to manage and affect outcomes of human destiny in the sense of actively setting the potential against the actual. This view is stated by Dompere as, "The process of setting the potential against the actual in the practice of decision is dialectical in that it admits of a continual state of motion for both qualitative and quantitative transformations in order to decide on the potential and then actualize the potential" (41, p. 222).

A prescriptive theory may be scientific or unscientific. Furthermore, every prescriptive theory has a knowledge base that is acquired by some logical process. The knowledge base may have been derived from an explanatory theory. In this way, the predictions of an explanatory theory may constitute the basis for constructing a prescriptive theory. The knowledge base for the development of a prescriptive theory also may be derived logically from some information that meets the ontological conditions of factual correctness. Prescriptive theories, like explanatory theories, should qualify as scientific theories if they meet the criteria of science as outlined Chapter 3. As a matter of analytics, they have identical structures in which "explanation, prediction and prescription can be considered as identical in their logical structure" (99, p. 14).

Besides fulfilling the necessary conditions of a scientific theory, a prescriptive theory must contain, within its logical construct, universal conditional laws from which the action-based prescriptions are derived. The main propositions of a prescriptive theory, like those of explanatory theory, are subject to falsification. The channels and techniques for testing for scientific validity are different for the two types of theories. The validity of an explanatory theory lies in its explanatory power relative to the explanandum. The validity of a prescriptive theory lies in its power to actualize the desired outcome. Explanatory theories are cognitive activities about explanandum ex post, while prescriptive theories are about explanandum ex ante. An explanatory theory is about "after the fact," while a prescriptive theory is about "before the fact" in some ontological sense.

Two types of prescriptive theory may be conceived methodologically. The distinction is based on the source of information required for the construction of the prescriptive theory. If the knowledge base of a prescriptive theory is constructed from an explanatory theory, then the resulting prescriptive theory will be called *type A*. If the knowledge base is derived from information that is not from an explanatory theory, the prescriptive theory is called *type B*. The structure and the logical relationship between prescriptive theory, information, and knowledge are schematically presented in Table 6.2.

TABLE 6.2
A Structure of Prescriptive Theory

Logical Item D (known or conceived normatively)
> Type A — Characteristics for identification obtained from explanatory-theory-based description
> Type B — Characteristics for identification obtained from nonexplanatory-theory-based description
> Explanation ex ante — Desired outcome or goal sought or the conceived potential that "ought to be"
> Prediction ex ante — Phenomenon predicted to occur by applying some action rules in an environment in which it is not currently presented
> Prescription ex ante — Desired outcome or a potential phenomenon willed to be actualized

Logical Item A (known or conceived logically)
> Type A — Knowledge obtained through explanatory-theory-based information
> Type B — Knowledge obtained through nonexplanatory-theory-based information
> Explanation ex ante — An environment in which D is conceived to occur
> Prediction ex ante — Environment in which D is predicted to occur now or in the future
> Prescription ex ante — Potential environment to be actualized so as to allow D to occur

Logical Item B (sought or derived logically)
> Type A — Logical construct based on the main propositions of explanatory theory
> Type B — Logical construct based on main propositions derived as explanation ex ante
> Explanation ex ante — Action rules logically conceived for explaining the outcome of D ex ante
> Prediction ex ante — Action rules that establish a causal relationship between A and D and, hence, predict D in A ex ante
> Prescription ex ante — Action rules or main instructions to be followed so that D may be actualized in A

The prescriptive theory of type A may be viewed as providing further evidence in the falsification process of the supporting explanatory theory. The prescriptive theory of type B, on the other hand, may be viewed as ex ante explanation of phenomenon, D, in an environment, A. If the potential, D, is actualized by the application of the set of rules contained in the logical construct, B, then the outcome, or actualization of D in the environment, A, constitutes a verification or falsification of B. The prescriptive theory of type B becomes an explanatory theory for the phenomenon, D, in an environment, A. In this respect, propositions contained in A and B constitute the explanans, while D is the explanandum. A prescriptive theory of type B contains explanation, prediction, and prescription that combine ex ante and ex post analysis of a phenomenon of interest.

In the type A prescriptive theory, the goal or the phenomenon, D, is known to occur in an environment, A. The task of a prescriptive theory of this type is to operationalize the predictive rules of an explanatory theory into an operational engine to achieve the goal or actualize the phenomenon in an environment in which the phenomenon currently is not known to be observed. Because D is known and given, the prescriptive rules are directed toward creating the environment, a set of conditions, A, that allows the phenomenon, D, to occur. The logical construct of prescriptive theory of type A is about action rules to create the environment, A. The logic is based on the principle of causation in that the environment, A, implies the occurrence of D and, hence, the creation of environment, A, will make the occurrence of D possible.

The prescriptive theory of type B is more complex. The construct of the theory involves designing sets of prescriptive rules about both the phenomenon, D, and the environment, A. A set of action rules must be prescribed for the selection of the goal or phenomenon, D. A different set of action rules must be prescribed for creating the set of conditions in the environment, A, so that the selected goal or the conceived potential may be actualized. The logical construct of the main propositions, B, provides the cognitive justification of the causal relation between the selected goal, D, and the environment, A, to be created.

The logical construct must establish a system of logical completeness that allows the environment, A, to imply the outcome, D. Thus, when one follows the prescribed action rules contained within the logical confines of the theory, then D will be actualized in A. The occurrence or nonoccurrence of D is the test of the empirical validity of the prescriptive theory. The falsification or the empirical validity of a prescriptive theory is examined at the ex post application of the prescribed action rules within the logical boundaries of the theory. The logical consistency and completeness are examined at the ex ante application of the prescribed action rules. The ex ante logical test and ex post empirical test constitute the falsification (verification) process of a prescriptive theory.

Generally, prescriptive theories are designed to change the empirical world as we see it, and their validity is always tested against their performance in actualizing the potential as desired or willed. The theory must indicate within its logical construct the process of change and the implementation of the process. Thus, contained in the theory is an empirical law that must be a law of motion. Such a law of motion must indicate a dialectical moment. It is the potential of the implied dialectical moment to actualize the desired outcome that provides the prescriptive theory its scientific importance and social utility.

PRESCRIPTIVE THEORIES AND ECONOMIC DEVELOPMENT

We have discussed theories of explanation of the phenomenon of economic development. In the process, categories and stages were introduced as concepts of classification in time or at a fixed time point. In discussing the development process, it becomes clear that the process of economic development requires transformation of stages or categorial convertibility. Such categorial or stage-to-stage transformation requires a dialectical moment or a transformation function that propels the economy through stages. Any scientific theory of explanatory kind directed toward the phenomenon of economic development must contain within its logical construct the needed law of change or a conversion factor. This law of change then will constitute the prescriptive rules for propelling the economy through stages or for transforming an economy in a category of underdevelopment into a category of development. Here lies the essence of categorial conversion.

Within this framework, prescriptive theory has an important linkage to the phenomenon of economic development. In this section, our main discussion will center on prescriptive theory applied to the phenomenon of economic development. We shall examine the scientific correctness of prescriptive theories of type A and type B. Just as we evaluated explanatory theories, so shall we evaluate the prescriptive theories as applied to the phenomenon of economic development. Three different theoretical structures will command our attention: perfectly competitive market-based prescriptive theories, interventionist prescriptive theories, and theory of development planning.

Competitive Market-based Prescriptive Theory of Economic Development

The theory of perfectly competitive markets with its extensions is a rational construct intended to explain the working mechanism of capitalism with regard to allocation and distribution of inputs and outputs to meet the needs and wants of a closed society. The assumption of closure may be relaxed. The major assumptions of this theory with regard to the understanding of economic transformation center on institutions and ideology. The institutions of private ownership of the means of production and the supporting political and legal structures are assumed to be in place or, at best, taken for granted. The ideology of individualism is assumed to be the fundamental principle on the basis of which all individual and social decisions are made in the price-output space. Given the assumptions about institutions and ideology, other critical assumptions of a technical nature are made in order to construct the theory and subject of the main propositions to an empirical test (49, 190, 206).

The theory of a perfectly competitive market is directed to present an explanation of observed characteristics of the capitalist economic organization and its assumed institutional organization and corresponding ideology at work. The theory's main propositions center around how inputs are distributed among private producers, what outputs are produced by them, and how the outputs are distributed among individuals for consumption and use within the framework of markets and price mechanism. At the core of the main propositions of the theory is the hypothesis that under institutions of private ownership of the means of production and the fundamental moral postulate of individualism, allocation, production, and distribution are efficient where prices are imputed by a freely working and undisturbed market mechanism.

By the principle of logical extension, the theory advances a position where the market mechanism, given the assumed conditions, can create and sustain economic development. Additionally, the proponents of the theory hold the view that the institutions of perfectly competitive markets under private ownership of production are the only ones through which the economic resources can be allocated efficiently to support and sustain economic development. The market mechanism under the institutions of private ownership of the means of production with the assumed conditions engenders economic development.

The prediction that follows from the theory of perfectly competitive market as an explanation of development may be abstracted. The abstraction leads to a statement that the institutions of private ownership of the means of production working through a perfectly competitive market and supported by the ideology of democratic individualism are predicted to led to development over time. The proponents of this position seem to suggest that perfectly competitive capitalism, composed of institutions of private ownership of means of production, institutions of perfect markets with autonomous price mechanism, and ideology of individualism, effects development.

*Methodology and Prescriptions Based on the
Theory of Perfect Competition*

Certain prescriptions based on the theory of perfectly competitive markets are advanced to promote economic development in areas where sustained development is not present. The operationalized predictive rules as prescriptions to actualize the desired objective may be stated as follows:

Privatize the ownership of the means of production and establish institutional support.

Promote the thinking and ideological system of individualism and self-interest.

Establish and/or improve the working mechanism of the system of markets in which information and signals are distributed among economic agents.

Restrain government interference in the price mechanism that serves as a mode of allocation and distribution of inputs and outputs for production and consumption.

Limit the role of a government to the elimination of the factors that hinder the free functioning of the system of markets and price mechanism.

The design of these prescriptive rules is based on the precept that the market mechanism and the price system are universally true in promoting economic development. Other critical institutions necessary for promoting economic transformation are methodologically taken to be neutral with respect to decision activities in the field of economic evolution. The theory of perfectly competitive markets is accepted by its advocates as constituting adequate grounds for explaining an economic development phenomenon. The proponents have come to accept that the theory provides critical insights for understanding the phenomenon of economic development. They believe that the logical generalizations contained in the theory of perfectly competitive markets offer adequate predictive grounds to enable one to anticipate new development occurrences. They are also convinced that the main propositions of the theory provide sufficient grounds for accepting the existence of causal laws between institutions of private ownership of means of production and competitive markets, on the one hand, and economic development, on the other hand. All other institutions are not predictively and prescriptively relevant because they are induced and dragged along by institutions of private property.

The scientific attitude of the subscribers to the theory of perfectly competitive markets is a hostility to all other theories and possible theories of economic development. They have taken the set of the main propositions of perfectly competitive markets as a paradigm-theory. By this paradigm, they craft prescriptions of economic development. In other words, the prescriptive theory advanced from the knowledge base of the theory of perfectly competitive markets is paradigm governed in the sense of Kuhn and, hence, dogmatic in method of prescription. This paradigm-governed prescription has become a conservative social dogmatism rather than a scientific belief. However, the logical test of the theory of perfectly competitive markets does not seem to meet the requirements of the canons of induction of causality.

Evaluation of Competitive-market-based
Prescriptions for Economic Development

In evaluating the scientific strengths of prescriptions based on the theory of perfectly competitive markets, we must point out that the prescriptions tend to follow ideological lines rather than economic rationale. There are a number of epistemological questions and problems with the set of prescriptions advanced from this theory for activating economic development in societies where economic development is viewed as lacking.

The prescriptions advanced are based on the assumed conditions but not on the main propositions of the theory. Furthermore, as the theory of perfectly competitive market is intended to explain the working mechanism of a market solution under private property ownership of the means of production, to the "what, how, and for whom" questions of social production, it provides no explicit explanation for the phenomenon of economic development. As a matter of fact, it also does not directly answer questions about economic development, nor does it have predictive force regarding possible occurrence of development.

Epistemologically, therefore, there is no logical channel for extending predictions contained in the theory to prescriptions required for actualizing economic development in environments in which such development is not present. The lack of a meaningful channel of logical extension between predictions and prescriptions leads the policy advocates to follow ad hoc prescriptive rules that have no anchorage in the scientific component of the theory. They insist on privatization without the instructive rules as to how privatization can generate the dialectical moment required for conversion of categories of underdevelopment to categories of development. The advocates stress the role of market but fail to prescribe how the markets are created and how the system of markets is linked to the conditions required for transformation of categories.

The market mechanism, supported by institutions of private ownership, is prescribed as a transcendental metaphysical entity that must be worshiped. It is stripped of its historical significance and evolutionary dynamic role. Within the prescriptive rules, the market is not viewed as a product of human activity in the decision space of social endeavors. It is disconnected from all relevant institutions of the management of society. As conceived and prescribed, the institutions of perfectly competitive markets and private property are implicitly assumed to be sustainable in any organizational form of society. Such a position will be at variance with the consistency principle that the theory must satisfy.

The theory of perfectly competitive markets in microlevels and macrolevels was constructed to answer specific questions about economic operations arising from given political and legal arrangements in a particular state. The orientation of the theory has been on the phenomenon of the allocation of given resources under assumed institutional arrangements and to examine how well the economic participants, individually and collectively, do in periods of rest. The theoretical construct is questionable as to the adequacy of its ideas, and its main propositions serve as a useful knowledge base for prescriptions that would provide an evolution of kind and, hence, lead to a transformation from economic underdevelopment to development. The theory has not established an empirical base for supporting the prescriptions of the ideologues, and this is complicated by an unsettled state of knowledge with sharply disputed points where socioeconomic choice is studied in a fixed institutional environment. Here, the theory leaves us in complete darkness as to how arrangements of markets and private ownership of production provide the dynamics of change that encompass the qualitative and quantitative characteristics of the socioeconomic system.

The whole prescription of privatization as a facilitator of economic improvements has no foundation in the theory of perfectly competitive markets. The conception of private and public sectors is basically a convenience of classification and a tool of analysis. The analytical power of these concepts is lost when one fails to hold them in the unity of analysis. The government and individual activities in the fields of human endeavors are intersupportive in a society. The role that the individual assumes in relation to the collective is relative to the cultural norms of the society, which tend to define and establish the appropriate and proportionate roles of government and private sectors in all activities of life. That relationship between the individual and the collective, between private sector and the public sector, and among social currents is dynamic, and its direction depends on social exigencies. The private and public sectors are in unity within the society.

Even the economists who confide in the basic and main propositions of the market mechanism as conceived by the theory of perfectly competitive markets concede that some sort of government interference with the market is not only generally inevitable but also specifically necessary in economies of developing countries who opt to go the path of markets in the sense of the capitalist (11). However, they suggest that governmental interference should be confined to actions that can improve the functioning of the market mechanism. Thus, the market is accorded the characteristic of the essential vehicle for fostering economic development, with a limited role assigned to the government. In this way, the material progress and destiny of the members of the society are trusted to the controls of the market forces, while the members of the society and the state apparatus react and respond to the signals of the markets.

Prescriptions constructed on the basis of the theory of competitive markets to promote economic development fail on several counts and reveal a number of theoretical difficulties.

The prescriptions lack any coherent system or logical unity directed to provide the required dynamics of economic transformation even if institutions of private property of the means of production are accepted.

The prescriptive construct from the theory of perfectly competitive markets has a number of logical inconsistencies where the government's activities in the market institutions are viewed as constraining the mechanism for market creation and efficiency while, at the same time, urging that the government's assistance and leadership are necessary for creating the required market mechanism by which societal economic destiny and progress are to be shaped.

The chain of transformation and the law of motion that governs it are not provided to indicate how the market mechanism must be created and how such mechanism is linked to the economic development process. Furthermore, all other complementary institutions necessary for the proper functioning of the markets are completely neglected. The empirical foundation and predictive power of the theory on which the prescriptive construct is derived are weak and ontologically fictional. The following are some of the reasons:

The focus of the theory is on the explanation of phenomenon of efficient allocation of given resources in a fixed environment. As such, it has little to offer for our understanding and prescription of a complex and difficult problem of quantitative and qualitative transformation of the socioeconomic system.

The claim that there is an inherent mechanism in the institutions of perfectly competitive market systems by which the economic forces and agents can allocate resources efficiently if undisturbed is not empirically borne. The needed transmission mechanism for coordinating institutions of various sectors and stages of change is lacking in the theory as well as in the prescriptions that are offered. The failure of the markets to provide desirable social progress has compelled the supporters of the theory of perfectly competitive markets (like McKinnon) to admit the need for government intervention in the market: "This pressure [of undesirable solution] for public intervention is the result of severe fragmentation in the underdeveloped economy" (140, p. 5). It is also instructive to examine a statement by the Research and Policy Committee of the Committee for Economic Development "Redefining Government's Role in the Market System," published in July 1979, New York.

The precedents in history, as our database, do not provide indisputable support of the proposition that economic development was achieved through free markets. History seems to suggest that undisturbed free play of market forces does not even explain developed economies. Free play of market forces has always been ideological fiction for deceptive practices (the trade tension between the United States and the newly industrialized countries is a recent example of this ideological fiction).

A question also arises as to whether development leads to efficiency in the markets or vice versa. History seems to support the position that competitive markets, as we know them in advanced capitalist economies, are produced through a long process of economic development with heavy doses of internal and external government intervention and restructuring, including social institutions and values that encapsule the institutions of markets. In this respect, the set of prescriptions based on explanatory theory of perfectly competitive markets assumes away the problem for which it claims to provide a solution. It may also be pointed out that a properly functional private sector requires an efficient institutional framework of the public sector that provides a comprehensive network of social infrastructure. In this direction, the role of the public sector or the government is completely assumed away by the proponents.

The system of prescriptions provided on the basis of the theory of perfectly competitive markets is plagued not only with logical flaws regarding dynamics but also with confusion and inconsistencies in the basic propositions of its approach in such a way that empirical verification or falsifiability becomes a nightmare of the user.

These criticisms merely suggest that, so far, those who confide in the theory of perfectly competitive markets have failed to advance a prescriptive construct that is logically consistent. The criticisms do not suggest that a logically consistent set of prescriptions cannot be constructed from the theory; it suggests that success has not been epistemologically achieved in this direction.

Interventionist Prescriptive Theories

Most of what is claimed in contemporary literature as theories of economic development can be comfortably placed under the class of interventionist prescriptive theories. The research agenda of development economics as seen by the interventionists is developed on the notion that a process of economic development can be triggered and/or accelerated by taking certain rational steps. Implied in this research agenda is a belief that the economic systems of developing countries cannot internally accomplish a high rate of development on their own except through rationally constructed shocks. This belief is expressed in the works of R. G. Green as, "Regardless of their attitudes towards enterprise, income distribution or socialism, states starting development late and at a comparative disadvantage have found massive social and economic intervention essential" (63, p. 1).

The technique and method of the interventionists are directed to probe into the system of acts that hopefully would effect development in the less-developed countries that select the capitalist path. The interventionists accept the market institution as a vehicle for bringing about development. However, they admit the inability of the market to efficiently allocate economic resources at the present stage in developing countries (212). In respect of this belief of market failure, the interventionists' prescriptions are directed to involve the government or other agencies in helping the markets to function properly. The prescriptions of the interventionists are basically the same as those of the free market advocates except that interventionists believe that the market system will become an efficient vehicle for allocating resources and will promote economic development if the government can manipulate certain economic variables, the levels of which are not market determined. In this respect, economic institutions of the society are assumed to automatically adjust accordingly, while other social institutions are assumed to be correct.

Given the acceptance of the government's role to intervene for increased market efficiency, the interventionists' prescriptive construct is based on the selection of certain key economic variables that are assumed to be constant in a similar way as those in the static theory of perfectly competitive markets, such as physical capital, human capital, or technology for policy manipulations to effect evolution of a kind of economic states. In the process of transformation of kind, it is believed that higher quantity and quality of the selected economic factors will influence the market and, hence, widen the production possibility sphere for an increased growth rate of development that will be sustained by the established institutions of the market.

The Methodology of Interventionist Prescriptive Construct

The methodological approach of the interventionists is similar in many respects to that of those whose prescriptive construct is based on the theory of perfectly competitive markets. The epistemological technique is to accept a known or some aspects of a known but not necessarily an empirically valid explanatory theory of economic development on the basis of which a set of prescriptions is constructed for practice. Essentially, the interventionists accept one or more of capital-based theory, technology-based theory, and human-capital-based theory of economic development as valid in explaining the phenomenon of the economic development process. Additionally, institutions of market and private ownership of the means of production are assumed to constitute the right environment for organizing resources to bring about development.

There are many subsections of the interventionist school. They range over a wide spectrum from Marxist leanings to classical and neoclassical tendencies. The prescriptions for improving the market are based on the classical and neoclassical economic knowledge. On the other hand, the prescriptions to affect the levels of the key variables are abstracted on the basis of Marxist theory of economic evolution (154, p. 91).

The epistemological basis of the approach of interventionists is closer to the Marxist school, which projects that internally generated infusion of certain physical capital in both width and depth with the intent of influencing income distribution stimulates significant changes in economic production along with changes in social institutions and factors, thus propelling the economy through stages. The predictive aspects of Marxist theory regarding movements within economic stages in the sense of Marx but not of Rostow are taken and operationalized into prescriptive rules for affecting quantitative changes within the neoclassical framework and markets under the assumed conditions of institutions of ownership.

In sum, the procedure for prescriptive construct of the interventionist may be outlined as:

1. Strip the Marxist theory of its revolutionary dynamics of changes in the fundamental social institutions.
2. Accept aspects of Marxist theory of the dynamics of key economic factors that affect intrastage changes, defined in the sense of Marx.
3. Accept the stage classification by Rostow and his idea of externally impressed interstage changes.
4. Neglect Schumpeter's entrepreneurial dynamics.
5. Artificially graft the accepted aspects of factor dynamics of the Marxist theory onto the neoclassical theory of allocation, production, and distribution.
6. Design prescriptive rules on the basis of 1 to 5 and recommended for policy practice.

The constructed prescriptions take as given the institutions of private ownership and markets. The abstracted prescriptions may be summarized as:

Governments should intervene to improve the functioning of the markets and related institutions whenever it is necessary to produce desired outcomes.

Physical capital must be infused into the economy through external sources.

Human capital must be upgraded to improve the productivity of labor.

Technology must be acquired and improved through transfers from external sources.

Within the interventionists' school of economic development, some emphasize physical capital at the expense of human capital and technology and vice versa. Irrespective of what key economic factor is emphasized, the basic objective is to abstract a law of motion for category conversion or interstage transformation in the sense of Rostow within the framework of capitalist order.

The prescriptive construct of the interventionists seems to conceive a policy environment where economic activities can be understood and changed in isolation from contemporary institutions. The prescriptive construct does not conceive a need to intervene in the noneconomic institutions of the society of interest to expedite the needed development. As perceived by the interventionists, economic development is achievable in any institutional framework if the institutions of market can be made to function properly. The driving force of change is perceived to be external to the system in the framework of Rostow, thus, denying the dynamics of internal self-motion or corrective self-adjustments of the social organism.

Given the efficient functioning of the market and the prescriptions for government intervention, a question arises as to how much capital should be infused into the economy. To answer this question, input-output projections are made under the assumption of the existence of well-established and integrated markets equivalent to those of economically advanced countries (212). An empirical correlation is shown to exist between the isolatedly selected factors of production and future output. Generally, the correlation is abstracted from the experience of the developed economies without logical regard for the sociopolitical background of the countries in which these economies are anchored (153). The simple correlation is not only considered sufficient but also taken as establishing conditions of causality.

Evaluation of Interventionist Prescriptions

The interventionist prescriptive construct has a number of theoretical and practical difficulties. There is a problem of logical consistency of the mode through which prescriptions are derived and operationalized for policy practice. The problem of the logical inconsistency results from attempts to project the frameworks of Marx onto the neoclassical system of thinking in the context of perfectly competitive markets. Additionally, the interventionists' prescriptions are not derived from any logically self-contained theory of explanation. The set of prescriptions is neither logically self-contained and complete nor is it developed as a theory that can stand independently.

The contradictions are amplified by implicitly held premises that economic development can be achieved by controlled interventions in an unplanned economy. Furthermore, the logical tools of the prescriptive construct are abstracted from aspects of theories that are designed for noncapitalist economic type. Additionally, the sociopolitical conditions of advanced capitalist systems are assumed to hold in economic systems for which the prescriptions are designed. This implicit or even explicit assumption does not meet the ontological conditions of factual correctness and, hence, provides no realistic basis of prescriptive construct for convertibility of categories of economic development. The analytical approach of selecting one factor of production, such as capital (see 200), and establishing sufficient conditions for causality with growth to the neglect of important institutions and other necessary factors of development transmission falls short of the requirements of science.

Economic development is not viewed as a process governed by a law of transformation with multidimensionality where sociocultural and political factors are essential determinants (153, p. 85). However, many leading development economists have identified political processes and social institutions as major determining factors for the transmission of economic development. On this point, Lloyd G. Reynolds concluded his survey article on economic growth of developing countries between 1850 and 1980 with the following statement: "My hypothesis is that the single most important explanatory variable is political organization and the administrative competence of government" (173, p. 976). Arthur Lewis puts it this way: "The economics of development is not very complicated; the secret of successful planning lies more in sensible politics and good public administration" (124).

In addition to institutions of politics and good public administration, legal and ideological institutions are equally important in providing the transmission mechanism through which economic development can occur. These important factors are almost always neglected by the interventionists, and when they are mentioned, it is only in passing. Essentially, the concept of social intervention is Marxist in nature. Its application compels simultaneous interventions in institutions of economics, politics, and law in order to create the conditions required for convertibility of economic categories. The prescriptive construct of interventionists ignores all relevant institutions except narrowly defined institutions of economics.

The prescriptive construct of the interventionists fails to integrate various essential aspects of economic development. Furthermore, it neglects certain vital economic factors, such as the increasing cost of resisting low-intensity warfare and destabilization activities carried on by some major powers and superpowers as well as disproportionate resource allocation to unproductive ventures such as military establishment and security apparatus. These factors, as important as they are, are hardly acknowledged in the prescriptive construct.

In principle, the testability and falsification of the hypothesis contained in the prescriptive construct are easy. By the very nature of the constructs, the prescriptions are intended to tackle practical and concrete problems. The actual outcomes and results of policy practice of these prescriptions will constitute the test and validity of the construct in empirical realms.

Essentially, the epistemological position of those who support prescriptions based on the theory of perfectly competitive markets is the same as that of interventionists. Both groups subscribe to the central idea that, in the ultimate analysis, economic development can be achieved through a properly functioning market mechanism.

Theory of Development Planning

In examining the epistemics of what has come to be known as the theory of development planning, it is useful to observe that prescriptions from perfectly competitive markets and the interventionists' approach suggest that, ultimately, economic development can be achieved through a proper functioning of the market mechanism. The important difference between the two approaches is how to make the market efficient. The approach of perfectly competitive markets holds the fundamental proposition that the market mechanism is self-correcting and, hence, requires no government intervention to function properly. Contrarily, the interventionists hold a fundamental proposition that the market mechanism is not self-corrective and that undesirable solutions result from the untampered market mechanism in the allocation of resources and distribution of goods and services.

The implicit stance of the interventionist is that the market system (but not the socioeconomic system) can and must be controlled by an agent of the government in accord with the social will. On the other hand, the advocates of prescriptions based on the theory of perfectly competitive market think that the market mechanism is automatically self-controllable; as such, the government's external interference not only is unnecessary but will distort the process of self-correctibility. Epistemologically, both positions do agree on the presence of a process of controllability, with a major difference being the source of the control process. Their similarity lies in the conception that the market mechanism, but not the social system, must be the object of control.

Epistemologically, the theory of development planning separates itself from all others in its approach to effect socioeconomic development. Fundamentally, the theory of development planning offers the following conceptual propositions: development is an historic map of successful decisions, such successful decisions can be duplicated through a scientifically designed decision-making process where a rational plan is constructed, and the rational plan is then totally and strategically implemented toward the goal of development. The basic conceptual propositions require erecting an edifice of self-contained theory of development planning whose propositions are not derived from an explicit explanatory theory of an economic phenomenon.

The required theory must be a construct derived from combined theories of change and organization. The theory of development planning is about organization of productive use of resources and the changes in their uses in accord with a defined rationality toward the goal of development. It is a theory of social engineering that specifies the targets and rationally and scientifically designs the means and methods that are the mechanism for achieving them.

According to this approach, the socioeconomic organism is viewed as a living entity whose growth and development take place through internal differentiation and elaboration. The process of differentiation and elaboration is law-governed through self-regulation. The self-regulatory instrument is a human *decision-information-interactive process* based on perceptions and interpretations of the output relative to the inputs and targets. The approach recognizes the knowledge base of the theories of information, cybernetics, and systemicity and then constructs an action program that constitutes the set of prescriptions where the market is seen as part of the outcome of decision-information-interactive process and, hence, is subject to the laws of prescriptions.

If the market institutions are part of the set of outcomes of evolution of human decisions, then it may be held, within the thinking system of the theory of planning, that the prescriptions for achieving economic development derived from the propositions of the market mechanism are inadequate, because the market mechanism can generate wrong signals and derail the required process of the track of the economic development. Furthermore, the conflict between private and social values does not permit a rational use of socioeconomic resources, and such a conflict cannot be resolved by the market mechanism, no matter how efficiently it functions.

The theory of development planning conceives the problem of socioeconomic development as a problem of optimal decision making (124). Development, like democracy, dictatorship, poverty, or any social outcome, is a potential that can be actualized. As a potential, development competes with all other potential elements in the decision-information-interactive process for actualization. The actual outcome depends on the nature of the decision process and the use of information. The chances of bringing economic development into being can be raised substantially above all other potential elements by a scientifically designed chain of decisions and information utilization. The task of the theory of development planning is to establish structured rules of good decision-choice behavior with efficient utilization of information and management of the organism.

The reasoning basis of constructing a theory of planning is the notion that economic development is a victory over odds when it occurs. As a victory, economic development does not appear by itself. Its occurrence cannot be ensured by a simple passage of time, nor can it be guaranteed by following the dictates of the market datum. To bring about development, society must organize resources and utilize them to combat the environment, subdue adverse circumstances, and recast relevant institutional configuration on rational thought and action. The rational thought and action may be derived from the theory of development planning whose task is to logically assemble a set of prescriptive rules to be followed to increase the chances of development outcome. These rules of rational behavior must encompass the major sectors of the socioeconomic organism for balance, fairness, and equity. The cognitive basis is that governments or planning agencies have greater chances of effecting socioeconomic development if there is a decision plan to follow and if such a decision plan is based on scientifically structured rules of good decision behavior, management, and organization (2, 41, 93).

In order for a development plan to constitute a set of prescriptive rules, its construct must be based on the theories of optimal dynamic decision and organization, which, together, must constitute the theory of development planning. The theory of development is dynamic and, yet, reflective of static characteristics of the socioeconomic system in motion. Its theoretical structure must contain laws of motion that must indicate directions of change, magnitudes of change wherever possible, and transformation of structure and form.

The principal objective of the theory of development planning is to assemble a set of prescriptive rules of rational decision by exploiting the mechanism of change that can serve as an effective basis for scientific management of a society. These prescriptive rules must include the following:

optimal rules for creating required institutions through which socioeconomic transformation and convertibility of kind are made possible for stages of development;

a set of rules for interstage and intrastage transformations in an optimally managed process of quality and quantity changes, including goal-target setting and ranking of alternative socioeconomic states;

a set of rules for optimal allocation of inputs of resources and optimal distribution of the outputs among sectors and members;

a set of rules for monitoring the functioning and progress of the socioeconomic system, including the recording of the outcomes and deviations from targets, goals, and optimal values;

a set of rules for collecting, processing, storing, retrieving, distributing, and using information by units and personnel within the management body of the socioeconomic system in accord with the function, control, and task; and

a set of rules for optimal decisions and choices among various interstages and intrastages.

These prescriptive rules must be constructed on the basis of social preferences or increasing order of development rates in accord with either individual or collective self-interests or both.

Methodology of the Theory of Development Planning

The methodology of development planning is based on the concept of the autonomy of the science of decision making, which is conceived to be independent of any explanatory theory that is directed toward the understanding of a single phenomenon in the decision space. According to this approach, a desired (undesired) condition can be created (destroyed) through rules of optimal behavior, which are derived from a scientifically structured theory of decision making.

As epistemologically conceived, the theory of decision making is an important part of prescriptive science, which may be referred to as *nonclassical science.* Unlike the classical view of science, prescriptive science holds the position that the primary aim of science is to improve reality, not just explain it. Furthermore, an improvement of reality does not necessarily need a theory of explanation about the phenomenon to be improved. Its methodological approach is problem solving by prescribing rules for actualizing the potential in nature that will lead to improvement in reality.

The theory of development planning as an integral part of prescriptive science shares the methodological approach of this science. Scientific activity and research in this regard have the primary objective and goal of influencing the object of epistemological inquiry where the influences are derived from prescriptive rules of the theory. The utility of this approach and the subject area of science are not the discovery of truth but the cognitive power that the approach and the specific area of science bring to actualizing a potential through problem solving.

Development plan is a model of the potential required for actualization. Its construct is based on perceptions of the desired reality. Such perceptions are influenced, to a greater extent, by the patterns of normative values, cultural environment, and accumulated social knowledge. The cognitive framework for constructing a theory of development plan or the research program of prescriptive science adheres not to the principle of value neutrality but to the principle of value nonneutrality.

Like the theory of Marx (132, 133) or Nkrumah (161), the value premises of the scientific statements about the model of the plan are stated explicitly as part of the scientific investigations and theoretical constructs. These value premises include judgments about relative desirabilities of perceptions of current and future realities. The theory of development planning is not directed toward better description and explanation of observed behavior; rather, it is directed toward changing reality through positive actions guided by optimal decision rules that will lead to the disappearance of the old and the emergence of the new in accord with a social will. Alternatively stated, the theory of development planning is a theory of how to effect socioeconomic transformation.

As a theory of social transformation, the theory of development planning seeks to change social states by moving from a socially least preferred state to a more preferred state. The construct requires a certain minimal fundamental ideal of methods of analysis. Central to the methods of construct are that reality is independent of cognition, every social system is a social arrangement that belongs to a category, and in a social transformation, there is always a primary category of reality from which all other categories are derived.

The important objective of methodological approach of the theory of planning is to provide the means for transforming one category to another. In other words, it must provide the process or mechanism of categorial convertibility. In this process, philosophy is called upon to analyze and assert the ontological conditions of factual correctness of the primary category and to show that other categories of development can arise from the primary category through a process. Logic and science then are called upon to establish the process of convertibility of categories of development states within the principles of transformation. Again, philosophy is called upon to assist in the analysis and understanding of the value and cultural basis for judging the relative desirabilities of different categories and social states before transformation.

In order to satisfy the conditions of categorial convertibility or transformation of kind, the theory of development planning must depict the world not simply as states and things but as processes and facts where *perception is not reality but a model of it*. In this analytical approach, states are conceptual and perceptual entities, and processes are the lifeblood of realities. In this respect, the theory of development planning becomes scientific. It also becomes dialectical so as to ensure and engender the decision basis for the conversion of categories of development and social states where the socioeconomic system or state loses old properties and acquires new ones that are judged to be better.

In the theory of development planning, social arrangements in their most complex forms are seen as categories that are convertible under the right conditions. The right conditions require the establishment of institutional configuration that can support a particular conversion process. The creation of such an appropriate institutional configuration through which a dialectical moment can be introduced into the social process to effect the required quantitative and qualitative motion requires a conscious effort to ascertain the prescriptive decision rules that are an integral part of the theory of development planning.

The fundamental ethical position in constructing a theory of development planning is that a social organism and its institutional arrangements can be rationally produced and directed toward a set of desired goals. The set of desired goals defines the collective and individual welfare and happiness in the social organism. On the basis of values and preferences, the set of desired goals can be rationally constructed. Human beings are their own organizers. They are the creators of their organization. They are the inputs and the beneficiaries of the outputs. They are also the controllers of the system in time and over time. They seek changes when the social system is unable to generate the required output for survival, comfort, and happiness.

The guiding principles of such changes must be the collective welfare and the rationality of the theoretical construct of development planning crafted on the basis of the science of decision making. Here, prescriptive rules are constructed to assist the planners of socioeconomic development to take stock of the economy and assess its relative categories for transformation; identify weaknesses in institutions and values that must be corrected; identify the sectors of the economy where allocation of productive resources can yield the maximum gains in terms of output and social welfare; design an incentive structure that will support maximum gains in terms of output and social development; and design a management and administrative structure to monitor and oversee the transformation of social arrangements that are complex interrelated subsystems with partially autonomous parts of the socioeconomic system.

Methodologically, the theory of development planning is general to particular in its decision construct and in its distribution of decision-making power. It is, however, particular to general in its information construct where every decision unit is seen in an organic sense and viewed as part of a larger decision whole. Changes of states and convertibility of categories are conceived in terms of processes and systems. The objective is to find the fundamental principles of good decisions and synthesize them into prescriptive rules to create a dialectical moment for dissolving unsatisfactory social states as well as bringing into being desired forms.

Evaluation of the Theory of Development Planning

We may now evaluate the theory of development planning in terms of presence of transformation process, logical consistency, and nature of empirical content. Epistemologically, the theory of development planning is a dynamic theory of organization of the totality of societal resources for change of state and transformation of kind. The objective of transformation is to replace one social arrangement of organization, allocation, production, and distribution by another when the previous one is socially judged to have failed to support societal survival, comfort, and happiness. The judgment of the desirability of a social arrangement is an aggregate of conflicting values of individuals and groups, based on social currents.

The desired social arrangement to replace an existing one is always one of many potentials that can be actualized. The value of the theory of development in accord with the science of decision, informatics, cybernetics, and systemicity is to develop prescriptive rules to identify the potential for actualization. In this framework, two epistemological approaches may be identified: historical and voluntarist epistemics. The voluntarist approach subscribes to a condition of infinite potential for actualizing socioeconomic development. The desired systems of production can be created anywhere if only the process of decision making is correct. In this respect, the decision-making structure is viewed as the most essential transforming factor to bring about development.

The historical approach also accepts the decision-making structure as essential to the transforming process. It, however, limits the potentials that can qualify as a possible outcome. First, the primary category or the state must be established and shown to meet the ontological conditions of factual correctness. The next step is to show that the desired potential is derivable from the category or state held as primary. For the primary category to meet the conditions of factual correctness, it must be in congruence with the social history of the societies.

The theory of development planning satisfies the conditions of empirical content. Empirically, one can verify the factual correctness of the primary category. The empirical validity of the main propositions that constitute the prescriptive rules are verified at ex post decision practice. The outcomes of the decision practice of the prescriptive rules constitute the empirical test of the main propositions of the theory. As a thinking system for problem solving, the theory of development planning satisfies the conditions of logical consistency, not only in its organic approach but also in its category formation. The degree to which the potential is actualized stands to inform us about the empirical relationship between the potential and the primary category, given the correct practice of the prescriptive rules. The equations of motion for transformation through transients are generated by the dialectical moment as engendered by the prescriptive rules. Such a dialectical moment is derived with the help of the principles of constructionism, production, systemicity, contradiction, and praxis.

Socioeconomic development is viewed as a rational construct based on the accumulated knowledge of the science of nature and society. As a model of decision, the theory of development planning shares some of the epistemological problems of the theory of rational decision construct:

How rational are the prescriptive rules from the theory of development planning?

Can the deliberative prescriptive rules implied by a decision-choice rationality that is derived by logical processes from valid premises of theory of development planning be unintelligible to agents who must practice and follow the prescriptive rules?

Is rationality an attribute of decisions and choices involving socioeconomic development or is it an attribute of the process of socioeconomic development itself?

Is it conceivable that the prescriptive procedures for rational behavior implied in the theory of development planning might, in fact, make socioeconomic development worse rather than better if such rigid rules of prescription are followed?

Finally, is it possible to conceive of a socioeconomic system that can be rationally controlled in the sense of being engineered and directed to a preferred destination according to human calculated intelligence, reason, and will? Can such a rational socioeconomic system improve the conditions of humans as focused by prescriptive science if the prescriptive rules implied in the rationality of the construct of the theory of development planning are followed?

It may be pointed out that these questions are not intended to raise doubts about the virtues of the human intellect and application that may be required of it. They are intended to raise some epistemological concerns about the intelligibility of the prescriptive rules implied by the rational construct of the theory of development planning. Similar epistemological questions and discussions have been advanced and discussed by Dompere (41).

7

Conclusions and Suggestions

CONCLUSIONS

The purpose of this book has been to epistemologically evaluate the theories of economic development on the basis of a criterion of scientific theory. The criterion of evaluation is constructed from the generally acceptable requirements of scientific theory in addition to the methodological debates of classical and modern economists. Special consideration is given to the epistemological positions of Karl Popper, Thomas Kuhn, and Imre Lakatos. Additionally, the methodological debates among the positivist, instrumentalist, and operationalist schools of economists are given special attention.

After taking into consideration different aspects of the problem of an appropriate criterion for evaluating scientific theory, a rational-historical criterion of evaluation is constructed. It is argued that the criterion of evaluation should simultaneously encompass normative rules of rationality and historical perspectives. In addition to the general rules of the criterion of evaluation, specific conditions of the evaluative criterion are established. The general and specific conditions of the criterion of evaluation are designed in such a way that they could be applied to explanatory theories as well as prescriptive theories of economic development. The specific conditions include logical consistency, problem specification, explanatory condition, predictive condition, prescriptive condition, and the structure of the main propositions of the theory.

To scrutinize the theories of economic development on the basis of the criterion of evaluation, it seems necessary to categorize them. Theories of economic development are placed in two general categories, such as explanatory and prescriptive. Explanatory theories are further subdivided into stage-based and factor-based theories. The factor-based theories are further divided into capital-based, human-capital-based, and technology-based theories. In examining the prescriptive theory, it is necessary to distinguish prescriptions based on explanatory theories from prescriptive theories. Given this distinction, the structure and properties of prescriptive theory as applied to development are advanced and analyzed. The analysis includes interventions and development planning as rational constructs.

Our investigation of the theories of economic development shows that economists working in this field have contributed substantially toward the understanding of the problems of economic development. They have successfully probed different aspects of economic development. Furthermore, they have established valid correlations between different variables of economic development. However, most of the approaches fall short of qualifying as development theories. The main deficiencies of these theories are summarized in tables 7.1 and 7.2 and discussed below.

TABLE 7.1
Main Deficiencies of Explanatory Theories of Economic Development

Stage-based Theories

Marxist version	It fulfills most of the conditions of scientific explanation. Process of change is induced by internal conflicts among classes. The main propositions are not fully operationalized and tested in the empirical realms of dynamics of development.
Rostow's version	It fails to provide the rules and mechanism for change and, hence, does not explain the development process in a self-contained logical manner. The force of change is artificially grafted on through the act of an external mover, while the institutions through which changes must occur are taken as given and static.
Schumpeter's version	It fulfills most of the required conditions of the rational-historical criterion for scientific theory. The mechanism for change is indicated to be driven by internal social forces. The main propositions are partially operationalized. Some of them are tested against experience as we observe history. The role of entrepreneurs' innovations and competition among capitalists are central to the dynamics of economic development.

Capital-based Theories

Marxist version	It is part of Marxist stage-based theory and fulfills most of the explanatory conditions where capital is an important dynamic variable of transformation.
Non-Marxist version	It fails to provide a mechanism by which savings can be transformed into capital creation and, hence, accumulation. The process through which capital gets created and plays the transforming role is not advanced. The explanation of development is simply not available.

Table 7.1, continued

Human-capital-based Theories

Marxist version	It is a subtheory of the general Marxist theory of socioeconomic development. It enters as mental labor as distinct from physical labor. It plays a particular explanatory role in the dynamics of a sociotechnical system in the organic theory of Marxist explanation of social dynamics.
Non-Marxist version	The problem is ill-posed, while the theory lacks an explanation as to how the user of capital can become the creator of capital in the production process. Physical capital is taken for granted without establishing a precise relation between physical and human capital components. It fails to advance the laws of motion and intervening mechanism within the framework of the main propositions that explain the transient process. Human capital is established as a sufficient condition for economic development; however, it is not proven to be a necessary condition.

Technology-based Theories

Marxist version	It is presented as a subtheory of the organic theory of the Marxist explanatory construct of socioeconomic transformation process where physical and human capital are connected through the technological process and institutional changes that support it.
Non-Marxist version	The subject and problem of explanation are not well-defined. It fails to explain how and why different societies have different rates of, as well as capacities for, creation and absorption of technology. It has a limited explanatory power regarding interstage and intrastage changes. The predictive power is also limited.

It is found that, epistemologically, the Marxist theory of development process has most of the components of an explanatory theory. Rostow's theory of stages of economic growth fulfills some conditions but does not explain the rules and mechanism of change; in other words, it does not provide a law of motion by which the transformation from one stage to another stage can be explained within his stage classification. The Schumpeter theory is logically complete but partial in its assessment of the mechanism of development.

Evaluating the factor-based theories, we conclude that most of the claimed theories in this category are prescriptions rather than explanatory theories. Furthermore, they do not qualify as explanatory theories, nor do they qualify as prescriptive theories. The Marxist theory of capital is a part of the general Marxist theory of stages of economic development that satisfies all the requirements of an explanatory theory. The non-Marxist theory of capital as applied to the development process seems to be derived from the Marxist theory except in its assumption of automatic transformation of savings into

TABLE 7.2
The Main Deficiencies of Prescriptive Theories of Economic Development

Theory of Purely Competitive Markets
   It assumes away the problem of institutional changes.
   It does not specify the chain of events that will lead to its specified goal of
      development.

Interventionist Theory
   It has a logical inconsistency in its mode of derivation of prescriptions where the
      underlying explanatory theory is not revealed. The discussion of the factual
      correctness of the primary category or stage is neglected.
   It specifies the basic sufficient conditions but ignores the necessary conditions for
      transformation.
   It is based on inappropriate assumptions about initial conditions and
      institutional framework.

Theory of Development Planning
   The voluntarist approach to development planning leads to an unrealistic
      decision-making process.
   The historical approach to development planning fulfills most of the conditions
      required for prescriptive theory where capital and labor processes are
      logically linked.

capital. In this way, the problem of saving-investment transformation in
development process is assumed away. Its failure to present a mechanism of the saving-investment process deprives it of any legitimate
claim to either explanatory or prescriptive theory of development. It is,
therefore, argued that the non-Marxist approach degenerates into a
mere set of prescriptions derived from some theory. Such a theory often
is not made explicit.

The theory of human capital tries to solve a fundamental problem
faced in the process of economic development, namely, the lack of appropriate quality and quantity of manpower. The theory successfully
establishes a correlation between economic development and human
capital but fails to provide a causal relationship. Furthermore, most of
the time, it wrongly assumes the existence of appropriate quantity and
quality of physical capital. Moreover, it does not establish a precise
relationship between physical capital and human capital. Our assessment is that, as it stands, the human-capital approach constitutes a
prescription to an aspect of the process of economic development. The
basis of such a prescription is not offered. In its bare essentials, it seems
to be derived from Marx's identification of the variable of mental labor
as distinct from physical labor. It fails, however, to explain the mechanism of economic development on the basis of human capital. Technology-based theories of economic development also share most of the
characteristics of human-capital theory. This theory also appears to be a
prescription for raising the level of economic development rather than

explaining the process. For the technology-based approach to constitute a theory, it must establish a theory of technological creation and progress and link them to explain how technology propels the socioeconomic system to bring about intrastage changes as well as interstage changes and, hence, development.

To properly evaluate the prescriptive theory, we have tried to stress the important differences between prescriptions and prescriptive theory and, hence, between the classical and nonclassical sciences. Furthermore, we have emphasized that there are fundamental differences among prescriptions based on predictions of explanatory theories (or intuitive predictions), prescriptions as single instrumental propositions, and scientifically structured prescriptive theory on the basis of the logic of prescriptive science. We have argued that a prescriptive theory of economic development is a theory of decision making about the future course of the economic process where a logical system of behavior that allows the potential to be actualized is constructed. Given the goal of economic development, the prescriptive theory should define the rules of good decision-choice behavior by means of which the goal can be achieved. The system of rules must include a set of instruments where one stage is transformed to the other so as to ensure category convertibility.

The characteristics of a prescriptive theory seem to reveal that the prescriptions for economic development through perfectly competitive markets do not qualify as a prescriptive theory. The set of prescriptions based on perfectly competitive markets defines a situation where optimal welfare can be achieved if perfectly competitive markets are permitted to allocate the scarce economic resources. It, however, does not prescribe the means by which the competitive markets can be created. Furthermore, it does not clearly establish whether the free markets are the product of economic development or vice versa. Missing in the argument is the most important element that propels development, which is the creation of an institutional support system through which a transformation process can be introduced and sustained.

The essence of the interventionists' prescriptions of economic development is very close to that of the theory of competitive markets. This approach also suggests that economic development can be brought about through the competitive market system, although the required market system cannot come into being without government intervention. The logical failure of this approach is that it does not specify the nature of intervention except by giving some general ideas for manipulating the selected economic variables. As a matter of fact, it wrongly assumes that the government is a rational actor willing and capable of manipulating the economic variables toward the desired end. Furthermore, it has been argued in its prescriptive construct that a meaningful intervention cannot be limited to economic variables. It should include intervention in the other institutions of the society. It, however, fails to define the rules of behavior by means of which the institutional framework can be changed to bring about the desired transformation. One may conclude that the system of the interventionist prescriptions does not constitute a structured prescriptive theory of economic development.

Finally, we scrutinized the theory of development planning. The approach advances the notion that the economic potential of a country can be actualized by simultaneous rational interventions in all the institutions of the society. In its basic construct, it holds that economic development is purposeful, and the purpose is to improve the reality of human conditions. The improvement implied in socioeconomic development takes place through appropriate human institutional organization of resources and decisions. The required institutions can be effected by a rational construct based on the accumulated history of success-failure decisions. We differentiated between the voluntarist and historical versions of the theory of development planning. It then was argued that the voluntarist approach of development planning is idealistic and impractical. Its prescriptive construct fails to account for factual correctness of the primary category from which transformation must occur. Thus, the prescriptions may not support the transformation of existing currents. The historical approach of the development process provides a more appropriate epistemological basis for the prescriptive theory of economic development. It defines the rules of good decision in all areas of human endeavor in the fields of organization, allocation, and management so as to actualize the desired potential of the society. This approach of the theory of development planning takes into account the historical limitations of different societies, as well as stages and categories of socioeconomic development. By historical methods, it first establishes the actual correctness of the primary category and examines the potential stages and categories that are desirable. Prescriptive rules for selecting the desired potential and its actualization are then constructed. Similarly, prescriptive rules for establishing correct institutional configuration, accounting for sectors and subsectors, conflict of interests, interactions, and relationships among sectors, are constructed for praxis. The main goal is to construct a dialectical moment to effect the transformation of kind either in stage or category.

Finally, if we admit the legitimacy of raising some fundamental questions about human beings in the choice-decision-information field, as well as in human social organizations and institutional arrangements regarding problem solving, resolutions to conflicting interests of different groups, the efforts of people to transcend the natural and social limitations so as to make progress by constructing and reconstructing their social and institutional arrangements and by defining and redefining their decisions and choices over time, then the approach of the theory of development planning has some important claims of scientific superiority of rival universal systems of thought of how to expedite transformation of societies, social categories, and stages so as to bring about socioeconomic development. On the side of the theory of explanation, the Marxist theory stands on scientific grounds superior to those of any of the rival universal systems of thought on explanation of dynamic process of the socioeconomic system. These claims, we think, should command our attention and respect.

SUGGESTIONS FOR FURTHER RESEARCH AND DEBATE

The scrutiny of the theories of economic development reveals a need for substantial improvement of research in this field. Specifically, the following aspects require special attention.

The process of economic development should be treated in a historical context where the ontological conditions of factual correctness regarding the primary category or stage must be established on the basis of accumulated experiences. The process of economic development must be seen as a multidimensional process that encompasses multitudes of socioeconomic factors. On the other hand, the state of economic underdevelopment is an outcome of interactions among various institutions of social creation that have failed to respond to social advances on all levels of human activities.

Generally, one can take comfort in the statement that economic, sociopolitical, and legal institutions with corresponding ideologies are responsible for the outcome of economic development and underdevelopment. One should keep in mind that just as the state of underdevelopment is transformable to a state of development, the reverse is also possible by means of a dialectical moment generated by the institutional configuration. In this connection, the works of Marx and Schumpeter are importantly instructive. To explain the phenomenon of either underdevelopment or development, one needs a theory that can fully account for the essential dynamic interactions of key institutions and how they have solved structural problems of transformation, how they have emerged and disappeared, and how they transmit change. Additionally, the theory should identify the laws of motion or transformation that explain how the socioeconomic system moves from one stage to another over its trajectory. The required theory of explanation must be directed to provide an understanding of how society organizes itself to manage the complex, multiinstitutional, dynamic, living, and constantly changing economic system in which human beings play active roles in deciding, choosing, and implementing decisions and choices.

To construct such a theory, general laws should be abstracted from the experiences of different societies in the present and the past. In this way, the economic situation of presently underdeveloped societies will not be considered unique. The history of human societies should be taken as the embodiment of a common essence by which the general laws of economic transformation can be discovered. From the general laws of economic transformation, particular laws should be inferred. This process will enable us to place the economic development of different societies into proper perspectives, and, hence, the possibility of constructing an explanatory theory of economic development becomes more feasible and reachable. In addition, the explanatory theories should be put to the test of the scientific criteria of evaluation as outlined and discussed in previous chapters.

Most of the suggestions presented for the improvement of explanatory theories also apply to the prescriptive theories. For the construction of a prescriptive theory, the goals should be clearly defined. More importantly, the identification of these goals should be based on the existing potentials of the economic as well as legal and sociopolitical institutions. Usually, the potential for economic development varies from one society to the other because the natural endowment and the configuration of institutions are different in each case.

Once the goals of economic development based on the existing social currents and attainable potential are well-defined and ranked, the rules of rational behavior should be constructed according to the science of decision making, informatics, and systemicity. These rules of behavior also should specify the dynamics of transformation between transient points. Additionally, the rules should identify the value system as well as the chain of events that must occur in the course of transformation and the properties of the potential trajectory on which the system will move in accordance with the prescribed rules if practiced. The allocation of resources, the production of goods and services, the distribution of these goods for consumption, and the socioeconomic relations that they engender must be viewed as composed of numerous segments of industry, agriculture, transportation, circulation of goods, and so on. In other words, the development process must be seen as organic, where the subsystems must be rationally balanced to produce a desired end by the constructed prescriptive rules for indicating the mechanism of change and the key factors that must be manipulated through the mechanism. Here, information, objectives, rationality, and computability of rationality and its implementability are important inputs into the final outcome of the constructed prescriptive rules with indicated cognitive limitations.

Finally, the powerful role played by institutions and their arrangements in defining the mechanism for change must be understood and acquire cognitive significance. Institutions are products of development and human social struggles. They also are determinants of the quality and quantity of development, as well as conflicts that arise. By defining negative and positive relationships among individuals and groups in the society, between the society and the natural environment that it has inherited, and between the internal social arrangements and external social world, institutions create the dialectical moment for socioeconomic transformation as well as exert preponderating influence on the path and direction of development. Given the natural environment and the society that occupies it, the available institutions define the social capacity to create progress, and this capacity is enhanced by the people's foresight to craft new and relevant institutions that relate to their social exigencies and resolve conflicts in the decision-choice space through positive actions.

The emphasis placed on the important explanatory role of institutions through which the defined key aggregate variables are manipulated to explain the development process by Marx and Schumpeter is derived from the above recognition. It is this logical landmark that separates Marx and Schumpeter from others. This landmark also enhances the explanatory force of their theories. We may add that any theory of economic development that assumes within its exposition a given institutional configuration becomes mere rhetoric in the sense of McCloskey ("The Rhetoric of Economics," *Journal of Economic Literature* 21 (1983): 481–517). The theory strips itself of the explanatory dynamics, and deprives the development process of its living logic — the logic that helps to explain why certain institutions disappear and new ones emerge in the social decision space whose outcomes define the path of development.

References

1   Ackoff, R. L., et al., *Scientific Methods*. New York: John Wiley, 1962.
2   Afanasyev, V. G., *The Scientific Management of Society*. Moscow: Progress Pub., 1971.
3   Anikin, A., *A Science in Its Youth*. Moscow: Progress Pub., 1975.
4   Archibald, G. C., "The State of Economic Science," *British Journal of Philosophy of Science* 10 (1959): 58–69.
5   Arrow, K., *The Limits of Organization*. New York: Norton, 1974.
6   Aubin, J. P., et al., *Mathematical Techniques of Organization, Control and Decision*. Boston: Birkhauser, 1981.
7a Ayer, A. J., *Language, Truth and Logic*. London: Victor Gollancz Pub., 1936.
7b ___, "Philosophy and Science," *Soviet Studies in Philosophy of Science* 1 (1962): 14–19.
8   ___, *Logical Positivism*. New York: Macmillan, 1959.
9   Ayres, R. U., "Social Technology and Economic Development," *Technological Forecasting and Social Change*, 28 (September 1985): 141–57.
10 Bahn, A., *Polarity, Dialectic and Organicity*. Springfield, Ill.: Charles C. Thomas Pub., 1970.
11 Baran, P. A., *The Political Economy of Growth*. New York: Monthly Review Press, 1957.
12 Bauer, P. T., "Economics as a Form of Technical Assistance," in *Leading Issues in Economic Development*, edited by G. M. Meier, p. 77. New York: Oxford University Press, 1976.
13 Baurwald, F., *History and Structure of Economic Development*. Scranton, Pa.: International Textbook Co., 1969.
14 Benson, J. K., "Organizations: A Dialectical View," *Administrative Science Quarterly* 22 (March 1977): 1–21.
15 Beranek, W., et al. (Eds.), *Science, Technology and Development: A Historical and Comparative Study*. New York: Praeger, 1978.
16 Bergmann, G., "Outline of an Empiricist Philosophy of Physics," *American Journal of Physics* 11 (1943): 248–58.
17 Berry, L. Ya., *Planning a Socialist Economy*, Vols. 1 and 2. Moscow: Progress Pub., 1977.
18 Blaug, M., *The Methodology of Economics*. New York: Cambridge University Press, 1980.
19 ___, *Economic Theory in Retrospect*. New York: Cambridge University Press, 1985.

20 Blitzer, C. R., et al. (Eds.), *Economy-wide Models and Development Planning*. New York: Oxford University Press, 1977.

21 Bognar, J., *Economic Policy and Planning in Developing Countries*. Budapest: Akademiai, Kiado, 1975.

22 Boland, L. A., *The Foundations of Economic Method*. New York: Allen and Unwin, 1982.

23a Bowley, M., *Nassau Senior and Classical Economics*. New York: A. M. Kelly, 1979.

23b Bridgeman, P. W., *The Nature of Physical Theory*. New York: Dover, 1936.

24a ___, "Operational Analysis," *Philosophy of Science* 5 (1938): 114–31.

24b Brody, B. A., *Readings in the Philosophy of Science*. Englewood Cliffs: Prentice-Hall, 1970.

25 Cairnes, J. E., *Character and Logical Method of Political Economy*. London: Frank Press, 1965.

26 Caldwell, B. (Ed.), *Appraisal and Criticism in Economics*. Boston: Allen and Unwin, 1984.

27 Carson, R. B., et al. (Eds.), *Government in the American Economy*. Lexington, Mass.: D. C. Heath and Co., 1973.

28 Chakravasty, S., *Capital and Development Planning*. Cambridge, Mass.: MIT Press, 1969.

29 Checkland, S. G., "Theories of Economic and Social Evolution: The Rostow Challenge," *Scottish Journal of Political Economy* 7 (November 1960): 169–93.

30 Chesnokov, D. I., "Hypothesis, Analogy and Typication as Methodological Techniques for Societal Knowledge," *Soviet Studies in Philosophy* 5 (1967): 21–32.

31 Cohen, S. I., et al. (Eds.), *The Modeling of Socio-Economic Planning Processes*. Bookfield, Vt.: Gower, 1984.

32 Collingridge, D., *The Social Control of Technology*. New York: St. Martin's Press, 1980.

33 Cornforth, M. *The Open Philosophy and the Open Society*. New York: International Publishers, 1968.

34 Copernicus, as discussed in T. S. Kuhn, *The Copernicus Revolution: Planetary Astronomy in the Development of Western Thought*. Cambridge, Mass.: Cambridge Press, 1957.

35 Crawshay-Williams, R., *Methods and Criteria of Reason*. London: Routledge and Kegan Paul, 1957.

36 Crosson, F. J., et al. (Eds.), *Philosophy and Cybernetics*. New York: Simon and Schuster, 1959.

37 Degler, C. N., *The Age of the Economic Revolution, 1876–1900*. New York: Scott Foresman and Co., n.d.

38 Dobb, M., *Socialist Planning: Some Problems*. London: Lawrence and Wishart, 1970.

39 ___, *Studies in the Development of Capitalism*. New York: International Publishers, 1970.

40 ___, *An Essay on Economic Growth and Planning*. New York: Modern Reader, 1969.

41 Dompere, K. K., "On Epistemology and Decision-Choice Rationality," in *Cybernetics and System Research*, edited by R. Trappl, pp. 82, 219–28. New York: North Holland, 1982.

42 Dray, W., *Philosophical Analysis and History*. New York: Harper & Row, 1966.

43 Dretske, F. I., *Knowledge and the Flow of Information*. Cambridge, Mass.: MIT Press, 1981.

44   Duesenberry, J. S., "The Methodological Basis of Economic Theory," *Review of Economics and Statistics* 36 (November 1954): 361–63.

45   Easterlin, R. A., "Is There a Need for Historical Research on Underdevelopment?" *American Economic Review* 55 (May 1965): 104–8.

46   Einstein, A., quoted in L. A. Boland, *Foundations of Economic Method*. Boston: Allen and Unwin, 1982, p. 1.

47   Enke, S., "Economists and Development: Rediscovering Old Truths, *Journal of Economic Literature* 7 (December 1969): 1125–39.

48   Farber, M., *Phenomenology and Existence*. New York: Harper & Row, 1967.

49   Ferguson, C. E., *The Neoclassical Theory of Production and Distribution*. Cambridge: Cambridge University Press, 1971.

50   Feyerabend, P. K., *Against Method: Outline of an Anarchist Theory of Knowledge*. London: NLB Press, 1975.

51   Fishlow, A., "Empty Economic Stages," *Economic Journal* 75 (March 1965): 112–25.

52   Friedman, M., *Essays in Positive Economics*. Chicago: University of Chicago Press, 1953.

53   Frisch, H. (Ed.), *Schumpeterian Economics*. New York: Praeger, 1982.

54   Ganovski, S., "Interrelations of Science, Technology and Man in Social Philosophical Perspective," *Soviet Studies in Philosophy* 13 (Summer 1974): 24–36.

55   George, F. H., *Philosophical Foundations of Cybernetics*. Tunbridge Wells: Abacus Press, 1979.

56   Georgescu-Roegen, N., *Analytical Economics*. Cambridge, Mass.: Harvard University Press, 1967.

57   ___, "Economic Theory and Agrarian Economics," *Oxford Economic Papers* 12 (February 1960): 1–40.

58   ___, "Mathematical Proofs of the Breakdown of Capitalism," *Econometrica* 28 (1960): 225–43.

59   Gerschenkron, A., *Economic Backwardness in Historical Perspective*. Cambridge, Mass.: Harvard University Press, 1976.

60   Ghislin, M. T., *The Triumph of the Darwinian Methods*. Berkeley: University of California Press, 1976.

61   Ginzberg, A., *Technology and Social Change*. New York: Columbia University Press, 1964.

62   Gordon, D. F., "Operational Propositions in Economic Theory," *Journal of Political Economy* 63 (1955): 150–62.

63   Green, R. G., "The Role of the State as an Agent of Economic and Social Development in the Least Developed Countries," *Journal of Development Planning* 6 (1974): 1–39.

64   Grunbaum, A., "Causality Science of Human Behavior," *American Scientist* 40 (1952): 665–76.

65   Hall, R. H., *Organizations*. Englewood Cliffs: Prentice-Hall, 1972.

66   Hanson, N. R., *Patterns of Discovery*. Cambridge: Cambridge University Press, 1965.

67   Harding, S. G. (Ed.), *Can Theories Be Refuted? Essays on the Duhem-Quine Thesis*. Dordrechet: D. Reidel, 1976.

68   Harrison, R. (Ed.), *Rational Action*. New York: Cambridge University Press, 1979.

69   Hartwell, R. M., "The Causes of Industrial Revolution: An Essay in Methodology," *Economic History Review* 18 (1965): 164–82.

70   Hazlewood, A. (Ed.), *Planning Development*. Reading, Mass.: Addison-Wesley, 1970.

184   References

71   Heertje, A., *Economics of Technical Change*. London: Weidenfield and Necolson,
      1973.
72   ____ (Ed.), *Schumpeter's Vision: Capitalism, Socialism and Democracy after 40
      Years*. New York: Praeger, 1981.
73   Hempel, C. G., et al., "Studies in the Logic of Explanation," *Philosophy of
      Science* 15 (1948): 135–75.
74   ____, "A Definition of Degree of Confirmation," *Philosophy of Science* 12 (1945):
      98–115.
75   Hershlag, Z. Y., *The Philosophy of Development Revisited*. Leiden: E. J. Brill,
      1984.
76   Hetzler, S. A., *Applied Measure for Promoting Technological Growth*. London:
      Routledge and Kegan Paul, 1973.
77   Hick, J., *Capital and Growth*. New York: Oxford University Press, 1972.
78   Higgins, B., *Economic Development*. New York, W. W. Norton, 1972.
79   Hogarth, R. M., et al. (Eds.), *Rational Choice*. Chicago: University of Chicago
      Press, 1987.
80   Holland, S. (Ed.), *Beyond Capitalist Planning*. New York: St. Martin's Press,
      1978.
81   Hollis, M., et al., *Rational Economic Man: A Philosophical Critique of Neo-
      Classical Economics*. Cambridge: Cambridge University Press, 1975.
82a   Hoselitz, B. F. (Ed.), *The Progress of Underdeveloped Areas*. Chicago: University
      of Chicago Press, 1971.
82b   Husain, M., *Methodology of Development Economics*. Ph.D dissertation, Howard
      University, 1987.
83   Hutchison, T. W., *The Significance and Basic Postulates of Economic Theory*.
      London: A. M. Kelley Press, 1965.
84   ____, *Knowledge and Ignorance in Economics*. Chicago: University of Chicago
      Press, 1979.
85   Ilyenkov, E. N., *Dialectical Logic: Essays on Its History and Theory*. Moscow:
      Progress Pub., 1977.
86   Janssen, J.M.L., et al. (Eds.), *Models and Decision-Making in National
      Economy*. New York: North Holland, 1979.
87   Johnson, H. G., *Money, Trade and Economic Growth*. London: George Allen and
      Unwin Ltd., 1962.
88   Jones, G., *The Role of Science and Technology in Developing Countries*. New
      York: Oxford University Press, 1971.
89   Kantordvich, L. V., *Essays in Optimal Planning*. White Plains, N.Y.:
      International Arts and Sciences Press, 1976.
90   Kapitsa, P. L., "The Inference of Scientific Ideal on Society," *Soviet Studies in
      Philosophy* 18 (Fall 1979): 52–71.
91   Kaplan, A., and Harre, R., *The Conduct of Inquiry: Methodology for Behavioral
      Sciences*. New York: Thomas Y. Crowell, 1964.
92   Kedrov, B. M., "Philosophy as a General Science," *Soviet Studies in Philosophy*
      1 (1962): 3–24
93   ____, "The Road to Truth," *Soviet Studies in Philosophy* 4 (1965): 3–24.
94   ____, "On Determinism (1)," *Soviet Studies in Philosophy* 7 (1968): 46–53.
95   ____, "Toward the Methodological Analysis of Scientific Discoveries," *Soviet
      Studies in Philosophy* 1 (1962): 45–65.
96   ____, "On the Dialectics of Scientific Discovery," *Soviet Studies in Philosophy*, 6
      (1967): 16–27.
97   Keynes, N., *The Scope and Method of Political Economy*. New York: Kelley and
      Millman Press, 1955.

98 Khachaturov, T. S. (Ed.), *Methods of Long Term Planning and Forecasting*. New York: Macmillan Press, 1976.

99 Kickert, W.J.M., *Organization of Decision-making: A Systems Theoretical Approach*. New York: North Holland, 1980.

100 Kiker, B. F. (Ed.), *Investment in Human Capital*. Columbia: University of South Carolina Press, 1971.

101 Killick, T., "The Possibility of Development Planning," *Oxford Papers* 28 (October 19, 1976): 161–84.

102 Klix, F. (Ed.), *Human and Artificial Intelligence*. New York: North Holland, 1979.

103 Kmita, J., "The Methodology of Science as a Theoretical Discipline," *Soviet Studies in Philosophy* 12 (Spring 1974): 38–49.

104 Knight, F. H., *On the History and Method of Economics*. Chicago: University of Chicago Press, 1966.

105 ___, "The Significance and Basic Postulates of Economic Theory: A Rejoinder," *Journal of Political Economy* 49 (1941): 750–53.

106 ___, "Institutionalism and Empiricism in Economics," *American Economic Review* 42 (May 1952): 45–55.

107 ___, "Methodology in Economics," *Southern Economic Journal* 27 (January 1961): 185–93; (April 1961): 273–82.

108 ___, "What Is Truth in Economics?" *Journal of Political Economy* 48 (February 1940): 1–32.

109 Kornai, J., *Mathematical Planning of Structural Decisions*. New York: North Holland, 1975.

110 Krupp, S. (Ed.), *The Structure of Economic Science*. Englewood Cliffs, N.J.: Prentice-Hall, 1966.

111 Kubat, L., et al., *Entropy and Information in Science and Information*. New York: Elsevier, 1975.

112 Kuhn, T., *The Structure of Scientific Revolution*. Chicago: University of Chicago Press, 1970.

113 Kuyvenhoven, A., *Planning with the Semi-Input-Output Methods*. Boston: Martinus Nijhoff, 1978.

114 Kuznets, S., *Towards a Theory of Economic Growth*. New York: W. W. Norton, 1968.

115 ___, "Modern Economic Growth: Findings and Reflections," *American Economic Review* 63 (June 1973): 247–58.

116 ___, "Notes on Stage of Economic Growth as a System Determinant," in *Comparison of Economic Systems*, edited by A. Eckstein, pp. 243–67. Berkeley: University of California Press, 1971.

117 ___, *Six Lectures on Economic Growth*. Glencoe, Ill.: The Free Press, 1959.

118 ___, *Economic Growth of Nations*. Cambridge, Mass.: Harvard University Press, 1976.

119 Kuznetsov, I. V., "But Philosophy Is a Science," *Soviet Studies in Philosophy* 1 (1962): 20–36.

120 Lakatos, I., *Mathematics, Science and Epistemology: Philosophical Papers*, Vol. 2, edited by J. Worrall and G. Currie. Cambridge: Cambridge University Press, 1978.

121 ___, *The Methodology of Scientific Research Programmes*, Vol. 1. New York: Cambridge University Press, 1978.

122 Lakatos, I., et al., *Criticism and the Growth of Knowledge*. New York: Cambridge University Press, 1979.

123 Lewis, A., "The State of Development Theory," *American Economic Review* 74 (March 1984): 1–10.

124   ___, "On Assessing a Development Plan," *Economic Bulletin of the Economic Society of Ghana* 3 (May–June 1959): 2–16.

125   Loose, J., *A Historical Introduction to Philosophy of Science*. New York: Oxford University Press, 1972.

126   Machlup, F., *Methodology of Economics and Other Social Sciences*. New York: Academic Press, 1978.

127   Mandle, J. R., "Marxism and the Delayed Onset of Economic Development: A Reinterpretation," *Journal of Economic Issues* 14 (September 1980): 735–49.

128   Manescu, M., *Economic Cybernetics*. Tunbridge Wells: Abacus Press, 1980.

129   Mansfield, E., et al., *Technology Transfer, Productivity and Economic Policy*. New York: W. W. Norton, 1982.

130   March, J. C., and H. A. Simon, *Organizations*. New York: Wiley, 1958.

131   Marx, K., *The Marx-Engels Reader*. New York: W. W. Norton, 1978.

132   ___, *Contribution to the Critique of Political Economy*. Chicago: Charles H. Kerr and Co., 1904.

133   ___, *Capital*, Vols. 1, 2, and 3. Moscow: Progress Pub., 1887.

134   ___, *Theories of Surplus-Value*. Moscow: Progress Pub., 1963, Part I; 1968, Part II; 1971, Part III.

135   ___, *Economic and Philosophic Manuscripts of 1844*. Moscow: Progress Pub., 1967.

136   ___, *Pre-Capitalist Economic Formations*. New York: International Publishers, 1965.

137   ___, *The Poverty of Philosophy*. New York: International Publishers, 1971

138   Marx, K., and F. Engels, *Selected Works*, Vol. 1. Moscow: Progress Pub., 1969.

139   ___, *Correspondence 1846–1895*. New York: International Publishers, 1975.

140   McKinnon, R. I., *Money and Capital in Economic Development*. Washington, D.C.: The Brookings Institution, 1973.

141   Meadow, D. H., et al., *The Limits of Growth*. New York: Universe Books, 1972.

142   Meir, G. M., *Leading Issues in Economic Development*. New York: Oxford University Press, 1976.

143   Menges, G. (Ed.), *Information, Inference and Decision*. Boston: D. Reidel, 1974.

144   Miliband, R., *The State in Capitalist Society*. New York: Basic Books, 1969.

145   Mill, J. S., *Collected Works: A System of Logic, Ratiocinative and Inductive*, Vols. 7 and 8, edited by J. M. Robson. London: Routledge and Kegan Paul, 1973.

146   Mises, L. Von, *Human Action, a Treatise on Economics*. London: William Hodge, 1949.

147   ___, *The Ultimate Foundation of Economic Science*. Kansas City: Sheed Andrews and McMeel, Inc., 1978.

148   Mishan, E. J., *Technology of Growth*. New York: Praeger, 1969.

149   Morgenstern, O., et al., *Mathematical Theory of Expanding and Contracting Economics*. Lexington, Mass.: Lexington Books, 1976.

150   Morris, C. T., et al., *Comparative Patterns of Economic Development, 1850–1914*. Baltimore: Johns Hopkins University Press, 1988.

151   Musgrave, R. A., "Notes on Educational Investment in Developing Nations." In *Financing of Education for Economic Growth*. Paris: OECD, 1966.

152   Myint, H., "Education and Economic Development," *Social and Economic Studies* 14 (March 1965): 8–20.

153   ___, *Economic Theory and Underdeveloped Countries*. New York: Oxford University Press, 1971.

154   Myrdal, G., *An Approach to the Asian Drama*. New York: Vintage Books, 1970.

155   ___, *Beyond the Welfare State*. New Haven, Conn.: Yale University Press, 1960.

156 Nader, C., et al. (Eds.), *Science and Technology in Developing Countries*. New York: Cambridge University Press, 1969.

157 Naletov, I., *Alternatives to Positivism*. Moscow: Progress Pub., 1984.

158 Nelson, R. R., "A Theory of Low-Level Equilibrium Trap," *American Economic Review* 46 (December 1956): 894–908.

159 Neurath, O., et al. (Eds.), *International Encyclopedia of Unified Science*. Chicago: University of Chicago Press, 1962.

160 Nikolayev, A., *R and D in Social Reproduction*. Moscow: Progress Pub., 1975.

161 Nkrumah, K., *Consciencism*. New York: Modern Reader, 1970.

162 Novack, D. E., et al. (Eds.), *Development and Society: The Dynamics of Economic Change*. New York: St. Martin's Press, 1964.

163 Novik, I. B., "Some Aspects of the Interrelation of Philosophy and Natural Science," *Soviet Studies in Philosophy* 8 (Winter 1969–70): 295–310.

164 Nozick, R., *Philosophical Explanations*. Cambridge, Mass.: Harvard University Press, 1981.

165 Nurkse, R., *Problem of Capital Formation in Underdeveloped Countries and Patterns of Trade and Development*. New York: Oxford University Press, 1970.

166 Papandreou, A. G., *Economics as a Science*. Chicago: Lippincott, 1958.

167 Phelps, E. S. (Ed.), *the Goal of Economic Growth*. New York: W. W. Norton, 1962.

168 Poats, R. N., *Technology for Developing Nations*. Washington, D.C.: The Brookings Institution, 1972.

169 Polanyi, M., *Personal Knowledge*. London: Routledge and Kegan Paul, 1958.

170 Popper, K., *The Logic of Scientific Discovery*. New York: Harper Torch Book, 1965.

171 Redford, E. S., et al., *American Government and the Economy*. New York: Macmillan, 1965.

172 Redman, D. A., *Economics and the Philosophy of Science*. New York: Oxford University Press, 1991.

173 Reynold, L. G., "The Spread of Economic Growth to the Third World: 1850–1980," *Journal of Economic Literature* 22 (September 1983): 941–80.

174 ___, *Image and Reality in Economic Development*. New Haven, Conn.: Yale University Press, 1977.

175 Robbins, L., *An Essay on the Nature and Significance of Economic Science*. London: Macmillan, 1935.

176 Robinson, J., *Economic Philosophy*. New York: Anchor Books, 1962.

177 ___, *Freedom and Necessity*. New York: Vintage Books, 1971.

178 ___, *Aspects of Development and Underdevelopment*. New York: Cambridge University Press, 1979.

179 Rosenstein-Rodan, P. N., *Programming in Theory and Italian Practice in Investment Criteria and Economic Growth*. Cambridge: Cambridge University Press, 1955.

180 ___, "Problems of Industrialization of Eastern and Southeastern Europe," *The Economic Journal* 53 (1943): 202–11.

181 ___, "Notes on the Theory of the 'Big Push'," in *Economic Development for Latin America*, edited by H. S. Ellis et al. New York: Macmillan, 1961.

182 Rostow, W. W., *The Stages of Economic Growth*. Cambridge: Cambridge University Press, 1960.

183 ___, *Theory of Economic Growth from David Hume to the Present*. New York: Oxford University Press, 1990.

184 Rozen, M. E. (Ed.), *Comparative Economic Planning*. Boston: Heath and Co., 1967.

185   Russell, B., *Logic and Knowledge*. New York: Capricorn Books, 1971.

186   ___, *Human Knowledge, Its Scope and Limits*. New York: Allen and Unwin, 1948.

187   ___, *Our Knowledge of the External World*. New York: W. W. Norton, 1929.

188   Sachkov, Iu. Y., "The Evaluation of the Style of Thought in Science," *Soviet Studies in Philosophy* 7 (1968): 30–40.

189   Salter, W.E.G., *Productivity and Technical Change*. New York: Cambridge University Press, 1969.

190   Samuelson, P. A., *Foundations of Economic Analysis*. Cambridge, Mass.: Harvard University Press, 1948.

191   ___, "Economic Theory and Mathematics: An Appraisal," *American Economic Review* 42 (May 1952): 56–66.

192   ___, "Maximum Principles in Analytical Economics," *American Economic Review* 62 (June 1972): 249–62.

193   ___, "Operationalism in Economic Theory: Comment," *Quarterly Journal of Economics* 69 (May 1955): 310–14.

194   ___, "Problems of Methodology: Discussion," *American Economic Review* 53 (May 1963): 231–36.

195   ___, "Professor Samuelson on Theory and Realism: Reply," *American Economic Review* 55 (December 1965): 1164–72.

196   ___, "Some Notions on Causality and Teleology in Economics," in *Cause and Effect*, edited by Daniel Lerner, pp. 99–143. New York: Free Press, 1965.

197   ___, "Theory and Realism: A Reply," *American Economic Review*. 54 (September 1964): 736–39.

198   Santos, T. D., "The Structure and Dependence," *American Economic Review* 60 (May 1970): 231–36.

199   Sato, R., *Theory of Technical Change and Economic Invariance: Application of Lie Groups*. New York: Academic Press, 1971.

200   Schatz, S., "The Role of Capital Accumulation in Economic Development," *Journal of Development Studies* 5 (October 1968): 39–43.

201   Schlegel, J. P. (Ed.), *Toward a Redefinition of Development*. New York: Pergamon Press, 1977.

202   Schoeffler, S., *The Failure of Economics*. Cambridge, Mass.: Harvard University Press, 1955.

203   Schultz, T. W., *Investment in Human Capital*. New York: Collier-Macmillan, 1971.

204   Schumpeter, J. A., *Essays*. New Brunswick, N.J.: Transaction Publishers, 1989.

205   ___, *The Theory of Economic Development*. New York: Oxford University Press, 1980.

206   ___, *History of Economic Analysis*. New York: Oxford University Press, 1954.

207   ___, *Capitalism, Socialism and Democracy*. New York: Harper and Brothers, 1950.

208   ___, "John Maynard Keynes, 1884–1946," in *The New Economics: Keynes' Influence on Theory and Public Policy*, edited by S. E. Harris, pp. 73–103. New York: A. A. Knopf Pub., 1947.

209   ___, "March into Socialism," *American Economic Review* 40 (May 1950): 446–56.

210   ___, "Theoretical Problems of Economic Growth," *Journal of Economic History* (Supplement) 8 (1947): 1–9.

211   ___, "The Analysis of Economic Change," *Review of Economic Statistics* 17 (1935): 2–10.

212   Seers, D., "The Limitation of the Special Case," *Bulletin of the Oxford Institute of Economics and Statistics* 25 (May 1963): 77–79.

213 Shell, K. (Ed.), *Essays in the Theory of Optimal Economic Growth*. Cambridge, Mass.: MIT Press, 1967.

214 Shishkin, A. F., "On the Ethics of the Scientist," *Soviet Studies in Philosophy* 5 (1966): 3–13.

215 Shvyrev, V. S., "The Neopositivist Conception of Empirical Significance and Logical Analysis of Scientific Knowledge," *Soviet Studies in Philosophy of Science* 2 (1963): 10–29.

216 Simmons, J., "Education for Development Reconsidered," *World Development* 7 (November/December 1979): 1005–16.

217 Singer, H. W., *The Strategy of International Development*. London: Macmillan, 1975.

218 Skinner, A. S., "Adam Smith, Science and the Role of the Imagination," in *Hume and the Enlightenment*, edited by W. B. Todd, pp. 164–88. Edinburgh: Edinburgh University Press, 1974.

219a Smith, A., *Wealth of Nations*. London: Penguin Series, 1937.

219b Smith, A., *The Early Writings of Adam Smith*, edited by J. R. Lindgren. New York: Augustus M. Kelley, 1967.

220 Sterman, J. D., "The Growth of Knowledge, Testing a Theory of Scientific Revolutions with a Formal Model," *Technological Forecasting and Social Change* 28 (September 1985): 93–122.

221 Sukhotin, A. K., "The Problem of Assimilation of Scientific Information," *Soviet Studies in Philosophy* 12 (Summer 1973): 54–72.

222 Suppe, F., *Structure of Scientific Theories*. Urbana: University of Illinois Press, 1977.

223 Tavanets, P. V., et al., "Some Problems in the Logic of Scientific Knowledge," *Soviet Studies in Philosophy* 1 (1962): 33–49.

224 Thomas, D., *Naturalism and Social Science*. New York: Cambridge University Press, 1979.

225 Tinbergen, J., *Development Planning*. New York: McGraw-Hill, 1967.

226 Toye, J., *Dilemmas of Development*. Oxford: Basil Blackwell, 1987.

227 Watkins, J.W.N., "Ideal Types and Historical Explanation," in *Readings in Philosophy of Science*, edited by H. Feigl, et al. New York: Appleton-Century-Crofts, 1952.

228 Wykstra, R. A. (Ed.), *Human Capital Formation and Manpower Development*. New York: Free Press, 1971.

229 ___ (Ed.), *Education and the Economics of Human Capital*. New York: Free Press, 1971.

230 Ziman, J., *Public Knowledge: The Social Dimension of Knowledge*. Cambridge: Cambridge University Press, 1967.

231 Zinovev, A. A., "On Classical and Non-Classical Situation in Science," *Soviet Studies in Philosophy* 7 (1968): 24–34.

Name Index

Subject Index

About the Authors

KOFI KISSI DOMPERE is Associate Professor of Economics at Howard University. The author of several articles and monographs, he is interested especially in economic theory and operations research and cost-benefit analysis as it relates to policy and is a contributor to the theory of fuzzy decision, mathematics, and intelligent fuzzy control systems. He also researches epistemic problems of scientific methods, especially those in economics and decision theory. He is also a consultant to a number of international development organizations.

MANZUR EJAZ is a health economist with the government of the District of Columbia and works with the World Bank on various development projects. He is also a newspaper columnist and a literary critic. He has taught philosophy in a university in Pakistan.

ISBN 0-313-29513-1

HARDCOVER BAR CODE